Leadership in *Star Trek*

Leadership in *Star Trek*

Lessons from the Captain's Chair

Jason A. Kaufman *and*
Aaron M. Peterson

Foreword by Aaron J. Waltke

McFarland & Company, Inc., Publishers
Jefferson, North Carolina

This book has undergone peer review.

Library of Congress Cataloguing-in-Publication Data

Names: Kaufman, Jason A., 1974– author. | Peterson, Aaron M., 1983– author.
Title: Leadership in Star Trek : lessons from the captain's chair / Jason A. Kaufman and Aaron M. Peterson.
Description: Jefferson, North Carolina : McFarland & Company, Inc., Publishers, 2023 | Includes bibliographical references and index.
Identifiers: LCCN 2023035531 | ISBN 9781476690445 (paperback : acid free paper) ∞
ISBN 9781476650968 (ebook)
Subjects: LCSH: Leadership—Case studies. | Star Trek television programs—Social aspects.
Classification: LCC HM1261 .K38 2023 | DDC 303.3/4—dc23/eng/20230802
LC record available at https://lccn.loc.gov/2023035531

British Library cataloguing data are available
ISBN (print) 978-1-4766-9044-5
ISBN (ebook) 978-1-4766-5096-8

© 2023 Jason A. Kaufman and Aaron M. Peterson. All rights reserved

No part of this book may be reproduced or transmitted in any form or by any means, electronic or mechanical, including photocopying or recording, or by any information storage and retrieval system, without permission in writing from the publisher.

Front cover images © 2023 Shutterstock

Printed in the United States of America

*McFarland & Company, Inc., Publishers
Box 611, Jefferson, North Carolina 28640
www.mcfarlandpub.com*

To Dina and Mira, may you come to live in a world of reason and compassion.—*J.A.K.*

To William and Henry, may you have the faith, courage, and heart to make this world brighter for those around you.—*A.M.P.*

Table of Contents

Acknowledgments   ix

Foreword by Aaron J. Waltke   1

Prologue   5

CHAPTER 1
Basic Leadership Skills   19

CHAPTER 2
Archer: Adolescent Explorer   33

CHAPTER 3
Burnham: Rapid Adapter   52

CHAPTER 4
Pike: Reluctant Warrior   73

CHAPTER 5
Kirk: Charismatic Cowboy   89

CHAPTER 6
Picard: Diplomatic Scholar   107

CHAPTER 7
Sisko: Ethical Realist   127

CHAPTER 8
Janeway: Tireless Thinker   146

Epilogue   165

References   175

Index   187

Acknowledgments

None of us achieves much of anything without the benefit of others. I could thank innumerable individuals for what they have taught me or done for me over the years, all of which has somehow led to the writing of this book. However, my deepest gratitude is to my parents, Harvey and Glenda Kaufman. My father taught me how to think for myself. My mother taught me to never think only of myself. Whatever modest success I have encountered has been unquestionably due to the unconditional love and unwavering support of my parents. Thanks Mom and Dad for more than I will ever be able to express. I also thank my wife, Amy, for continuing to put up with my intellectual peregrinations and frequent absentmindedness while together we have built a home of love and meaning.

Finally, I am grateful to Aaron Peterson for his willingness to entertain one odd idea after another and always be willing to give it a shot. Who knew that first night of class that we would become active collaborators and good friends?

—Jason A. Kaufman

I never would have imagined that I would have the opportunity to undertake an endeavor like this. To say that I am thankful would be an incredible understatement. I would first have to give thanks to the Lord, who reminds us that through Him, all things are possible. Next, I am thankful to my family. I thank my wife, Heather, for being my best friend and for the prodding to keep going even when I don't feel like it. I also thank my boys, William and Henry. You both keep me young and inspire me to take on new challenges.

I want to acknowledge both of my parents, Orlyn and Lisa Peterson. Your unwavering support throughout my life has made projects like this a reality. I especially want to thank my mom in that she brought me to *Star Trek* by first showing me *The Original Series* and then later bonding over *The Next Generation*.

Acknowledgments

Finally, I want to give a shout out to my partner on this trek, Jason Kaufman. I am forever grateful for your mentoring, but more importantly, your friendship.
—Aaron M. Peterson

We extend our thanks to the entire team at McFarland for making the process of bringing this book to reality such a pleasure. However, special thanks go to our editor, Layla Milholen. As an editor, she has been everything for which a writer could ask.
—From Us Both

Foreword

by AARON J. WALTKE

"There are three things to remember about being a starship captain: keep your shirt tucked in, go down with the ship … and never abandon a member of your crew."
—Captain Kathryn Janeway, *Star Trek: Voyager*

Difficult decisions are not only part and parcel with sitting in a Starfleet command chair—they are the primary job description. As a captain, you've been entrusted with the lives of hundreds of scientists, engineers, tacticians, explorers; their well-being and daily purpose are guided by you and you alone as you venture into the cosmic unknown, in search of questions you may not know to ask yet. Your actions reflect on your crew, to be sure, but also on the greater Federation you represent—you are an emissary to the stars, and your choices become theirs by default.

It can be scary, yes. But it can also be exhilarating, enlightening. And profoundly rewarding.

Star Trek has always been a guiding star in my own life, especially when navigating the rigors of shared responsibility, employment, or even seeking out that next horizon in my career that one might consider ambition or aspiration. I found comfort in Gene Roddenberry's assertively optimistic view of the future, one where uncertainty and weirdness are part of the job—and are always met with empathy and curiosity, rather than fear.

The world made a little more sense to me when I viewed it through the lens of Starfleet's eager accommodation of a wide spectrum of humanity—and other lifeforms—into a fold where cooperation and discovery are paramount. It showed a society where leaning on another

Foreword by Aaron J. Waltke

was not a weakness, but the means by which the tapestry was always stronger than the thread.

Together, a Starfleet crew was capable of solving any problem, correcting any course, and through their tireless efforts revealing more about the universe ... and themselves.

When I got the call from the Hageman brothers to work on *Star Trek* myself, as a writer and later co-executive producer and co-head writer of *Star Trek: Prodigy*, I considered it a tremendous honor to play in a galactic sandbox that had so profoundly shaped my own creative and philosophical sensibilities. It had brought so much joy to me, it is a harrowing thought that our incredible crew was bringing the wonders of the franchise to the next generation.

Star Trek taught me that kindness and compromise are fundamental to building something greater than the sum of both of us. That understanding your rivals is the key to negotiation, mutual respect, and may even lead to an alliance. And when commanding your own crew, you cannot expect everything from everyone—instead, identify their specialties and play to the abilities they possess that you do not. In short, surround yourself by brilliant and intelligent people, and challenge one another to create something none of you could do on your own.

The crew of *Star Trek: Prodigy* reflect that journey of self-actualization. In the stories of Dal, and Rok, and Zero, and Gwyn, we see a desire for belonging and purpose that is only found in each other. Once misfits aboard a derelict Starfleet ship, they come to embody the ideals it represents and set a course for Starfleet, hoping for a brighter tomorrow for all of them. They learn this through the gentle guidance of a holographic Captain Kathryn Janeway, who sees past their insecurities and shortcomings to the possibilities they hold within. Like unmolded clay, our young *Protostar* crew are slowly shaped into their better selves—who in turn aspire to help others on that same journey.

When I wrote the episode "Kobayashi," I couldn't help but reflect on all the other Starfleet hopefuls who would have taken that same test over the centuries. Kirk, Spock, Picard, Sisko, Janeway herself—they all were greenhorn cadets once, before they became the leaders that future history required of them. They all faced the no-win scenario, only to realize its purpose lies in how you react to failure. The best know the answer—you learn from it.

Foreword by Aaron J. Waltke

It is my sincere hope that these case studies of leadership throughout *Leadership in Star Trek* provide some of the same inspiration they did for me, watching them time and again over the years as a fan and as a creative myself.

We could all stand to be a little more Starfleet today. And even when the decisions are difficult, know that with the right perspective, you'll always have a crew who will help you ride through the storm—at least until you find that next horizon.

Aaron J. Waltke *is an Emmy-winning and Annie-nominated screenwriter, executive producer, and showrunner. His credits include work on* Trollhunters, Wizards: Tales of Arcadia, Unkitty!, *and* Star Trek: Prodigy.

Prologue

Imagine, if you will, the view from the cockpit as your shuttlecraft descends toward San Francisco. Before you is a sprawling city, with the historic Transamerica building dwarfed by the surrounding ultramodern towers reaching toward the sky. Greenery is visible amidst the plazas and paths far below. The view of the metropolis rapidly approaching from below instills a sense of awe. As your gaze drifts away from the city center, you note to the east across the bay the rings of hamlets spreading over the rolling hills. To the north, you can see the Golden Gate Bridge, bedecked with solar panels, connecting the city center with Marin and the familiar peak of Mount Tam. Contrary to the urban sprawl of centuries past, the scene as you descend is one of technological sophistication in harmony with the natural environment.

Upon arrival at the spaceport and its constant hum of activity, you hail an automated cab and head toward your favorite tea shop in Chinatown. Although its food might be replicated, the tea is still sourced (by robots, of course) from small farms across the globe. You notice during the ride across town that traffic on the streets is brisk this morning. Countless people are out and about while the overhead streams of hovercars zip this way and that, making little noise and leaving no pollution.

As your cab courses over the Tenderloin, your mind drifts to history. No longer is the world afflicted with poverty, strife, and greed. The Earth has recovered from the ecological and martial follies of the early Anthropocene. With the advent of replicator technology, humanity evolved from a barely organized set of independent states to a global postscarcity society that fostered the rise of an increasingly humanist and Galaxy-spanning society (Saadia, 2016).

As you exit the automated cab and walk through the Dragon Gate on Grant Avenue (one of your kitschy but favorite habits when you visit), the myriad of peoples, languages, scents, and wares serves as a reminder

Prologue

of how a return to Enlightenment thinking brought forth a flourishing of human potential through the discovery and transmission of knowledge (Pinker, 2018).

What is this wonderful world in which we imagine ourselves? In 1966, the debut of Gene Roddenberry's *Star Trek* marked what would blossom into a fictional canon spanning more than 55 years of television and film. It would become a "unique pop-culture phenomena [*sic*] that is unlikely to ever be repeated" (Gross & Altman, 2016, p. 31). As Roddenberry (as cited in Daum, 2016) explained, *Star Trek* was intended as

> an attempt to say that humanity will reach maturity and wisdom on the day that it begins not just to tolerate, but take a special delight in differences in ideas and differences in life forms.... If [humanity] is to survive, [it] will have learned to take a delight in the essential differences between [peoples] and between cultures. [It] will learn that differences in ideas and attitudes are a delight, part of life's exciting variety, not something to fear.

Central to this future is the fictional society of the United Federation of Planets, an

> interstellar union of planetary governments that agreed to exist semi-autonomously under a single central government based on the principles of universal rights, liberty, equality, peace, justice, and progress, and to share their knowledge and resources in peaceful cooperation, scientific development, space exploration, and mutual defense (Memory Alpha, n.d. a).

The Federation, as it is commonly known, demonstrates how a society might exist in concert with diversely enlightened ideals. It offers a glimpse into the potential of humanity to actualize its potential in a manner that not merely honors but seeks out diversity in ideas, peoples, and practices as the crucible of a vibrant society. It leverages the mind and the heart "to discuss any problem that presents itself" (Committee on Freedom of Expression, 2014). In the Federation, competing perspectives are understood to be central to human flourishing. Importantly, with each new series written and released, we can observe how the ideas behind the Federation have evolved and kept pace with the changes in today's world as times change and human civilization becomes increasingly interconnected across cultures and countries. As in life, so in Trek.

Prologue

Although we will seek to make the argument that *Star Trek* has much to offer the aspiring leader, the reality is that the oeuvre has been near and dear to us both since our childhoods. We would even go so far as to say that it proved formative in our development. Moreover, the very fact that our respective youths were separated by nearly a decade yet were so equally impacted by *Star Trek* says something about the staying power of its vision for humanity's future. That the franchise is experiencing a second golden age after more than 55 years and well over 800 episodes is nothing short of remarkable.

Jason grew up with the original series of films, having just entered elementary school with the release of *Star Trek: The Motion Picture* (Foster & Wise, 1979). The films stoked his imagination of a possible future to come. Although the crew faced major challenges that invariably involved the fate of Earth, the Alpha Quadrant, and sometimes the entire Galaxy, the movies portrayed a future in which the heroes were not merely fast and strong but highly intelligent, deeply ethical, and buoyed by camaraderie. There was also the implicit message that the future was a positive one, reliant upon a diversity of peoples and ideas. All were welcomed and indeed encouraged to sit on the proverbial bridge. In middle school, he was introduced to the geekery of the *Star Fleet Technical Manual* (Joseph, 1986) and became forevermore immersed in its lore. However, this turned out to be but a prelude to the release of *Star Trek: The Next Generation* (Roddenberry et al., 1987–1994). Don't even get him started on the number of hours he dedicated to pouring over the "new" technical manual (Sternbach & Okuda, 1991). Fast forward more than 30 years and not a week has gone by that his thoughts on some point or other have not drifted to *Star Trek*. Those formative influences on his childhood have been rekindled by the release of the new streaming series. What could be better than to look toward strange new worlds of discovery and growth?

Aaron's passion is similar, but it followed a slightly different course to reach his present level of geekery. He began his trek while first watching *Star Trek: The Next Generation* (Roddenberry et al., 1987–1994) with his mother. She had grown up watching *Star Trek: The Original Series* (Roddenberry, 1966–1969) with her father, and *Star Trek* thus became a way for him and his mother to bond. Intrigued by *Star Trek: The Next Generation*, he became compelled to find copies of *The Original Series* as well as any VHS copy of the original films (none of our children understand what that means). He also began collecting various books that explored adventures of the *Star Trek* captains that never made it to the silver or home screens. With the new series that have come out and those that have yet to explore strange new worlds, it truly is a wonderful time to be a *Trek* fan.

Star Trek

What makes the Federation so special as a possible future is not merely the starships and phasers and Romulan ale that stoke the young (and not so young) imagination. It is more than that. What makes *Star Trek* visionary and so relevant to leadership today is that it portrays a society in which people's basic needs are met and they are freed by the very institutions of their society to work to better themselves. It is a future in which digital and social technologies offer a pathway to a bright green future (Steffen, 2009; Kaufman & McNay, 2017), one rooted by the mutual guideposts of reason and compassion. This notion is not mere science-fiction but the result of two major conceptual events separated by more than a century.

History is punctuated with good ideas that have profoundly impacted the course of human societies. Writing. Codes of law. Longitude. The scientific method. Representational democracy. Pizza delivery. The Prime Directive. However, most relevant to our trek into leadership is the development of Enlightenment thinking.

The Enlightenment of the 17th and 18th centuries was characterized by an "aspiration for intellectual progress, and the belief in the power of such progress to improve human society and individual lives" (Bristow, 2017, ¶2). It was an age of reason that arose partially in response to the major societal upheavals of national reorganization and revolution in response to events in Europe and beyond (Kissinger, 2014). Concurrently, natural philosophy was maturing into what we now know as science (a term attributed to William Whewell in 1833). Seminaries meanwhile were transitioning from institutions of belief to universities teaching the liberal arts and sciences. The two centuries that followed the Renaissance were a time in which much of humanity was considering the world and its place in it anew through the powers of the intellect.

Prologue

Of course, as the saying goes, not all was well on Risa. Pinker (2018) summarized it well as he reflected on our current times:

> The ideals of the Enlightenment are products of human reason, but they always struggle with other strands of human nature: loyalty to tribe, deference to authority, magical thinking, the blaming of misfortune on evildoers. The second decade of the 21st century [saw] the rise of political movements that depict their countries as being pulled into hellish dystopia by malign factions that can be resisted only by a strong leader.... These movements [were] abetted by a narrative shared by many of their fiercest opponents, in which the institutions of modernity have failed and every aspect of life is in deepening crisis—the two sides in macabre agreement that wrecking those institutions will make the world a better place. Harder to find is a positive vision that sees the world's problems against a background of progress that it seeks to build upon by solving those problems in their turn [p. 5].

Not all was replicators and respite during the Enlightenment. Bigotry in its various manifestations was still very much evident within even the most progressive of nations. Racism remained resistant to extinction, misogyny was alive and well, and antisemitism remained globally pervasive. But as Immauel Kant (1784, as cited in Bristow, 2017, ¶4) wrote, Enlightenment thinking demonstrated the ability of humanity to transcend its self-imposed immaturity. Amidst its foibles, the Enlightenment was a time in which a growing proportion of humanity began to recognize that no questions were off limits. It was a time in which basic education became compulsory in many nations of the world. One in which it was simply assumed that we, as a species, would rise above our present challenges and achieve our full potential.

By the close of the nineteenth century, many individuals were beginning to apply the new tools of science to ask questions of the human condition. What makes people act the way they do? Early attempts to understand human behavior focused on disorder and how to treat it. Along the way, the world witnessed the major upheavals of two world wars and genocide of unimaginable scale. One outcome was that the world saw major shifts in migration patterns as refugees sought the promise of safety. Another result was that many scientists working to understand human behavior began to ask a different set of questions. Instead of focusing on why people do bad things, they began to question how people might be nurtured toward the good. Two thinkers stand out among the mix as especially relevant to our discussion of leadership.

Prologue

Abraham Maslow was born in 1908 as the first of seven children to Jewish parents who had emigrated from Russia. A lonely young man who found solace in his books, Maslow initially studied law to appease his immigrant parents' desire for him to become a successful American. However, he soon became enamored with the study of psychology and would eventually help to pioneer the field of humanistic psychology (Boeree, 2006a). Maslow recognized through his research that people must meet their basic needs before they can meaningfully seek to fulfill their personal aspirations. Although widely misused by corporate trainers and educational pundits, his theory of self-actualization can serve us as a tool in leadership. A leader must remain cognizant that, at any given time, the individuals in an organization likely need different things to help them succeed. Indeed, Maslow (1968) recognized that people must meet their basic needs (e.g., food, safety, a good Wi-Fi signal) in order to pursue a meaningful life:

> I should then say simply that a healthy [person] is primarily motivated by [their] needs to develop and actualize [their] fullest potentialities and capacities. If a [person] has any other basic needs in any active, chronic sense, then [they are] simply an unhealthy [person].... If this statement seems unusual or paradoxical the reader may be assured that this is only one among many such paradoxes that will appear as we revise our ways of looking at [people's] deeper motivations. When we ask what [a person] wants of life, we deal with [their] very essence [Maslow, 1943, p. 394].

Compare this perspective to our current world in which personal development is often stymied by the social and financial limits around us. It is difficult to reach one's full potential in the face of fragile egos and one-upmanship, to say nothing of bigotry and poverty. As Scott Barry Kaufman (2020) has argued, when "society can create the conditions to satisfy one's basic needs ... what naturally and organically emerges tends to be the characteristics that resemble the *best* in humanity" (p. xxiii, italics in original).

Carl Rogers was born in 1902 (the early twentieth century was a heady time for the "third wave" of psychology). The fourth of seven children in a devoutly Christian home, Rogers became a solitary young man who initially studied at seminary. After traveling to China and later being exposed to more liberal religious ideas, Rogers left his religious background to study psychology. His pioneering clinical work would affect standards of psychotherapy to the present day. Rogers' ideas also

Prologue

find purchase in the practice of leadership. Contrary to the management style of the 1950s, Rogers came to understand that people can be motivated to grow when provided with a few basic conditions.

Rogers (1965) found that three conditions are optimal, if not necessary, to facilitate self-actualization in others. Empathy is the ability to recognize the emotional state of others and reflect that recognition in your own actions. Genuineness is simply being honest with others. Tell the truth, and if you cannot, refrain from lying. Unconditional positive regard is a bit more challenging. It requires always treating everyone with respect. Always. Imagine how the world might look today if we each exercised these three conditions in our daily interactions with others. How might leadership look?

Carl Rogers described such individuals as being self-actualized. In other words, having met their basic needs, such individuals would be able to progress through their higher-level needs and seek their full potential. Such individuals, he wrote, are

> able to live fully in and with each and all of his feelings and reactions. [One who] is making use of all [their] organic equipment to sense, as accurately as possible, the existential situation within and without. [One who] is using all of the data [their] nervous system can thus supply, using it in awareness, but recognizing that [their] total organism may be, and often is, wiser than [their] awareness. [One who] is able to permit [their] total organism to function in all its complexity in selecting, from the multitude of possibilities, that behavior which in this moment of time will be most generally and genuinely satisfying. [One who] is able to trust [their] organism in this functioning, not because it is infallible, but because [they] can be fully open to the consequences of each of [their] actions and correct them if they prove to be less than satisfying [Rogers, 1963, pp. 21–22].

When we consider the idea of self-actualization (i.e., compassion) together with the worldview of the Enlightenment (i.e., reason), what results is a potential future that begins to look very much like the Federation of *Star Trek*. In the Federation, humanity largely has internalized Enlightenment thinking in a self-actualized way and made it manifest across a vast starfaring civilization. People think of themselves as part of a diverse whole, an attitude congruent with what research makes clear.

It had been during the Enlightenment that humanity began to part ways from echoes of ancient myth (Armstrong, 2005) and looked

Prologue

toward the potential of rational thought informed by exposure to diverse ideas to liberate humanity from the shackles of bigotry and narrow-mindedness. A new consciousness eventually swept across the Earth with the promise of respect and democracy for all. In the Federation of the future, the belief that "there are no others" (thought to have been coined by Ramana Maharshi) was recognized as not a goal but as self-evident. Seeing one another as individuals of worth is more important than limiting one to membership in a group identity (Kitayama, 2021).

Captain Picard once observed in the twenty-fourth century that "the acquisition of wealth is no longer the driving force in our lives. We work to better ourselves and the rest of humanity" (*Star Trek: First Contact*; Berman et al., 1996). This future version of Enlightenment thinking presents not some rigid or reductionistic enterprise as applied only to some, nor some wonky postmodern critique of truth, but as an earnest attempt to create a society that can feed the soul, extend our reach beyond the stars, and nurture the Earth. In this vein, *Star Trek* presents a society in which intellectually enlightened individuals actively work toward self-actualization and are driven by leadership to thereby function at their best. It can therefore serve as a source of lessons to instruct our own attempts to lead.

The Trek Ahead

There are any number of sources from which one might draw relevant cases for the study of leadership. For example, it is a truism that there never seems to be a lack of news. This is especially true in the current information age which has become characterized not merely by a surfeit of available information but as well a seemingly growing wealth of misinformation and disinformation. How is a professor or trainer of leadership, much less an aspiring student, to wade through so much stuff? Indeed, Johnson (2012) argued for the importance of the conscious consumption of information:

> What if we started managing our information consumption like we managed our food consumption? ... Coping with the problem isn't a matter of getting things done anymore; it's a matter of health and survival. Information and power are inherently related.... Like any good diet, the information

Prologue

diet works best ... as consuming more of the *right stuff and developing health habits* [italics in original] [pp. 5–7].

This logic can be extended to a consideration of sensitivity and inclusivity. We both know from teaching that what might seem innocuous to one individual can prove off-putting to another. That word you used for emphasis might resonate with personally or historically uncomfortable associations for someone else. It is important that the cases one uses to teach leadership are not merely understood but can be safely internalized by anyone as exemplars to model.

We thus utilize examples in the classroom from popular culture to demonstrate the fictional embodiment of the basic leadership skills of *communication*, *patience*, and *relationship* through a curated yet ever-shifting collection of case studies. We chose this approach because of the fictional nature of the captains. Fiction allows us to consider self and others from a psychological distance. We think this distance is important. Over our combined years of teaching, we have noticed a trend. Students of leadership are human. Go figure. Because we are all human, we bring to our studies biases of thought and experience. We have observed how these biases in the classroom can cloud the capacities of quite competent people to solve problems. If issues close to home can make it difficult for people to solve leadership dilemmas among a table of friendly classmates, how much more dire must the situation be in practice when one must lead without the support and forgiveness of a learning environment.

Identifying myriad leadership examples from popular culture can be an antidote to such cognitive roadblocks. The series and films of *Star Trek* offer a depth of writing coupled with a sizable volume of storytelling across decades of the franchise. While we might be a little bit biased in our adoration of the canon, our utilization of *Star Trek* is not done naively. Each of the captains, as fictional characters, manifests a unique mix of strengths and weaknesses. Indeed, across this pantheon of leaders we will see a wide range of abilities. For example, Captain Picard was already an established leader when we first encountered him on the way to Farpoint Station. Alternatively, it required four seasons to demonstrate the growth of Captain Burnham into a leader of nuance. This is exactly why we have chosen to utilize these fictional yet so real captains as exemplars to be studied and potentially emulated.

Be it in the classroom or the boardroom, we have found major value

Prologue

in utilizing the lens of *Star Trek* to inform our own practice. The captains demonstrate across hundreds of episodes and more than a dozen films the ability to successfully lead in situations from the mundane to the emergent. *Star Trek* also reminds us along the way that the challenges we face today will not be inherently different from those that arise in a distant postscarcity future. People have been people for tens of thousands of years. We thus feel comfortable predicting that people will continue to be people far into the future. As Mithen (2003) reflected,

> Although the history of any region was conditioned by the type of wild resources it possessed and the specific character of its environmental change, neither of these determined the historical events that occurred. People always had choices and made decisions from day to day, albeit with little thought or knowledge of what consequences might follow [p. 505].

Complete with their dreams as well as their follies, people are driven to meet their needs (Maslow, 1943) and to find meaning in their lives (Frankl, 1966). The technologies might differ across the ages, but the fundamental issues facing leadership do not.

Over the ensuing chapters, we shall explore how each of the captains of *Star Trek* embodied their own unique balance of reason (Enlightenment thinking) and compassion (self-actualized functioning) in the service of leadership. The captains will show us how leadership can be a force for good from the local to the galactic. Along the way, we will not shy from recognizing when a captain was limited by their own biases or weaknesses. Failure is part of life, and it is most certainly part of leadership. The captains of *Star Trek* are "real" people who have much to teach us about how to lead in spite of being imperfect on even their best days (see Table 1). Is this not true of us all?

What will be important along the way is not to question whether you possess an innate ability to lead. We have written this book with a broad readership in mind. Perhaps you were born with certain traits that confer some relevant advantages (e.g., intelligence, good looks, facility at anbo-jyutsu). Regardless, one of the lessons inherent to *Star Trek* is that each of us can grow into leadership. At least a couple of the captains seem to have matured into their skill set through trial and error. Instead, we will focus on the ability to learn how to lead in an enlightened manner that is responsive to the necessities of the situation.

In Chapter 1, we introduce the basic leadership skills of *communication*, *patience*, and *relationship*. These basic leadership skills do not

Prologue

Table 1. Basic Leadership Skills

Captain	Communication Relationship	Patience
Archer: Adolescent Explorer	Expresses concerns about the situation. Solicits input from others.	Listens to alternative perspectives.
Burnham: Rapid Adapter	Ensures others are heard. Reveals own thought process.	Gives others a chance to lead.
Pike: Reluctant Warrior	Presents with formality and flexibility. Uses muted humor to comfort others.	Requests competing opinions.
Kirk: Charismatic Cowboy	Shares perspective with honesty. Explains rationale of decision.	Asks for clarification of options.
Picard: Diplomatic Scholar	Solicits diverse options and information. Trusts others to perform well.	Weighs options in search of solutions.
Sisko: Ethical Realist	Shares emotions in a transparent manner. Treats those around them as friends.	Channels passion into seeking solutions.
Janeway: Tireless Thinker	Clarifies importance of mission. Works to build a sense of family.	Weighs options before acting.

provide a panacea for problem-solving. Instead, they can form the foundation of an enlightened and actualized approach to leadership that is agnostic to personal style and adaptable to organizational constraints.

In Chapter 2, we begin our enterprise by considering how Captain Jonathan Archer led as an *adolescent explorer* during the early days of humanity's entrance upon the galactic stage. Although beset by a hotness of temper, Archer demonstrated an ability to express concerns during difficult situations, listen to alternative perspectives from those he led, and actively solicit input from others.

In Chapter 3, we continue our journey of discovery by evaluating how Captain Michael Burnham led as a *rapid adapter* through repeated crises. Although she assumed the captain's chair with much to learn, Burnham demonstrated how revealing one's own thought process and creating space for others to lead can result in the best of outcomes.

In Chapter 4, we turn our focus to the strange new worlds of Captain Christopher Pike. A *reluctant warrior*, Pike demonstrated a balance

Prologue

of formality and flexibility. Even when on the receiving end of truly terrible news, he sought out competing opinions from others and used a muted sense of humor to allay anxieties.

In Chapter 5, we spend time with the original treks of Captain James T. Kirk, *charismatic cowboy* and perhaps the most infamous of Starfleet captains. Although he often demonstrated a gregarious attitude in his leadership, Kirk always spoke with honesty, asked for options from those he served, and ultimately shared the rationale for his decision-making.

In Chapter 6, we ponder the somewhat unique opportunity to consider leadership and its next generation with the *diplomatic scholar* of Captain Jean-Luc Picard. Present for some of the most important events of history, Picard sought diverse opinions and information from those he served, weighed his options with care and forethought in search of solutions, and importantly trusted those he served to perform well. Later in life, he manifested these same leadership notes with a heightened maturity.

In Chapter 7, we go deep as we move from starship to space station to explore the leadership of the *ethical realist* Captain Benjamin Sisko. Beset with adversaries on all sides, Sisko nonetheless shared his emotions in a transparent manner while channeling the resultant passion into the seeking of solutions. Notably, he balanced this intensity with an ability to treat those he served as friends.

In Chapter 8, we take a voyage with Captain Kathryn Janeway. A *tireless thinker*, Janeway demonstrated the rare ability to lead effectively in near total isolation from support. She emphasized the importance of mission, weighed her options carefully before acting, and from the start, worked to build a sense of family among those she served. These decisions were especially notable given the dire straits through which she led.

In the epilogue, we close our discussion with a nod toward the future. Captain Saru presents a transition into a future characterized by ever greater diversity of thought and experience. As we shall see, the perspective of his leadership is so prescient and urgently needed in our modern time. We will elaborate on this point by considering how even on the proverbial lower decks, leadership is important. At the same time, leaders must take care not to let their own egos get the better of them. We will then consider what these various threads have to teach us

Prologue

about what our world today requires of its leaders to foster a society that is good for all. The result might be the best of what an enlightened society can offer.

Although we have written the chapters to provide a broad overview of the basic leadership skills through the captain's chair, we encourage you to focus on the chapters that most strongly resonate with you. Feel free to warp past those captains you find less compelling. Spend time on the bridge with your favorites, and don't be surprised at what you might encounter should you choose to boldly go and explore the other leaders in *Star Trek* canon. Leadership should be an enjoyable enterprise. However, it is also one that requires study and the benefit of experience.

Becoming a leader is not something that happens overnight. As we are about to explore, it sometimes requires going through some truly harrowing experiences to earn the right to sit in the captain's chair. Per aspera ad astra. Captain Picard may have summed it up best when he said, "It is possible to commit no mistakes and still lose. That is not a weakness. That is life" (*Star Trek: The Next Generation* S02E21; Kemper & Scheere, 1989). We think that leaders who maintain the ability to enact the basic leadership skills regardless of the situation are the ones who have a chance to succeed out there. So, let us begin our journey as we navigate the potential for *Star Trek* to inform leadership today.

GUIDANCE FROM GUINAN

Imagine yourself sitting at a small table under the arching windows of Ten Forward, the frontmost point and social hub of the U.S.S. *Enterprise*. The view out the windows is one of stark blackness punctuated by countless points of light, stars of every imaginable color. You have come to this gathering spot before to reflect as you gaze out at the wonders of the universe. Now, as you again become aware of your surroundings, you are suddenly greeted at your table by Guinan, the unofficial sage of the starship. You've heard stories about her from other crew members, and you have always been intrigued. Now she gently speaks to you.

"Welcome to Ten Forward" Guinan says with a knowing smile. "What can I get you?"

Having taken your order and wandered off, your attention drifts back to those seemingly countless stars shining beyond the tall glasteel windows arching over your little nook of the room. Word

Prologue

among the crew is that Guinan has seen it all, and that she can be trusted to keep a patron's woes in confidence.

"Here you are" Guinan says as she sets down on the gently glowing table top a sleek little glass. How did you not hear her approach, and why is she sitting down across the little table from you? You wonder if she does this with all of her customers or only those who seem to have something on their mind.

Guinan looks at you expectantly and says, "You don't look like you came here only for a drink. It seems like there may be something else you wanted to talk about."

Your mind racing at Warp 9 with so many questions to ask this transcendent figure, you don't even know where to begin. Guinan just looks back at you with her knowing smile. You realize that this is a special opportunity.

And with that, you find yourself sharing with Guinan the leadership situation on your mind.

Chapter 1

Basic Leadership Skills

With thoughts of the captains in mind, you ponder how their stories can inform your own practice of leadership as you gaze upon the scene before you from the window of your favorite tea shop in Chinatown. You are struck by the beautiful diversity of people coming and going, the myriad cooperative and competing languages amidst the signs and store fronts, the sheer openness to ideas new and old.

As you watch the passersby and ponder the Federation's actualization of enlightenment ideals, a soft chiming brings you out of your reverie. Looking down at your tablet resting on the little table next to your small bowl of partially eaten tea crackers, you notice a reminder for your upcoming meeting. It crosses your mind to head to the transporter station on Montgomery Street, but why use your transporter credits on such a short trip? Besides, the weather is perfect for a walk in this wonderful city.

Heading out into the brisk morning air, you head south to Market Street and then southwest through the thrumming heart of San Francisco. Skyscrapers built of transparent aluminum and wrapped with plant life reach to the wisps of clouds above. As you walk among their shadows, conversations in a multitude of languages fall upon your ears. Today is a good day in the city.

Yet, even this period in history has its challenges. People are still people, and that means there are always going to be disagreements to be solved. This was one of the things that attracted you to your current position. Some days have been easier, some days more difficult. Most days have been meaningful.

As you wait at a pedestrian intersection for an ancient cable car to trundle past, its bell ding-dinging, you find yourself wondering: How would the captains of Star Trek lead?

The canon of *Star Trek* offers a seemingly inexhaustible source of case studies through which to explore the potential of Enlightenment thinking and the development of self-actualization in the service of leadership. This is because *Star Trek* offers a worldview that capitalizes upon the potential of people while recognizing the social and political realities in which they operate. It also allows us to have some fun along the way. Of course, it is one thing to model ideals in the classroom or in front of the bathroom mirror, but it is another to utilize them in practice. How we, as leaders, can learn to internalize the necessary skills for effective execution in times of crisis is even more of a challenge. Toward this end, perhaps some background is in order before we head off to explore the strange new worlds of leadership.

Born of the Classroom

It has been our good fortune across our combined experience to teach leadership to a motivated and diverse range of students. We have worked with students from all walks of life and across an exceptionally broad patina of interests. Almost to the student, we have observed a desire to use leadership as a force for good in the world. And because we both teach leadership at the graduate level, our students invariably read whatever we assign and come to class ready to engage with the material. Yet, over the past several years we found ourselves noticing that even the most adept students often struggled to incorporate the content of leadership research and theory into the context of everyday leadership. It is one thing to excel at critiquing a leadership approach in a course paper or debating potential outcomes of a decision in small-group discussion. On these matters our students tended to do just fine. It is another thing to apply what one has learned within the crucible of practice. Students routinely would approach us before or after classes, in one-to-one meetings, or simply via email, with questions about how to handle their own very real issues at work. They were discovering that learning to lead is hard. Like so many things worth learning, what it takes to be an effective leader requires not just study, but its application in practice.

In response, we developed an approach to teach a set of *basic leadership skills*, habits of thought and practice which we perceive to be fundamentally crucial for effective leadership and learnable by anyone. The identification of these skills was an outcome of our observations of

Chapter 1. Basic Leadership Skills

where students struggle in leadership, what the research in and beyond leadership says about human functioning, and our own experiences in leadership positions formal and informal. It was important to us along the way that these basic leadership skills be agnostic to orientation. For example, when teaching the introductory leadership course in his department, Jason often asks the class to identify and explain which model of leadership most resonates with each of the students. The goal is to help aspiring leaders recognize their own beliefs around leadership and critically evaluate the strengths and weaknesses of any single model. Let's face it, the research on most of the models is scant at best and more a matter of author inclination than of empirical support.

The basic leadership skills we propose here eschew specific or popular solipsisms of fashionable leadership trends and instead focus on the importance of intrapersonal regulation coupled with interpersonal awareness to effective leadership. Both of which exist in everyone to one extent or another, and importantly, both can be improved through reflection and practice. We also made it a point to teach the basic leadership skills through numerous and often unrelated case studies. This is in keeping with a scientifically informed approach to teaching (Miller et al., 2008) to emphasize the higher-order thinking associated with better learning outcomes (Bransford, 2000) and necessary for effective leadership. Of course, even case studies can prove boring to the most motivated student. What is required is a suite of case studies that can motivate engagement to better ensure learning around leadership.

Importantly, leadership through the lens of *Star Trek* demands that we act with reason and compassion to help people grow as individuals as they help their organizations better function. But how might we leverage *Star Trek* to lead for a meaningful future while being grounded in the present? And how can the captains of *Star Trek* serve as exemplars of such leadership? As we recently wrote (Kaufman & Peterson, 2021):

> From *Star Trek: The Original Series* to *Star Trek: Picard*, the grand captains of *Star Trek* each portray an ability to lead during the direst of situations in a storyline that spans nearly three centuries across the breadth of our own Milky Way galaxy and beyond. Therein resides a plethora of opportunity to engage with entertaining case studies that demonstrate a curated set of leaders at their best (and worst) as they seek to navigate a broad range of challenges to save planets from annihilation, seek peace among disparate

Leadership in *Star Trek*

spacefaring cultures, and promote the advancement of diverse peoples. Importantly, *Star Trek* has always been transparent about revealing the captains' weaknesses as well as their successes.

The *Star Trek* perspective on leadership recognizes our shared humanity. The people we lead have needs and it is our responsibility at the minimum to recognize those needs. It is all the better if through our decisions we can help those we lead to actualize their own potential.

Of course, before we get into the specific skills, it is important to acknowledge the traits-versus-skills debate. How often have you heard someone comment that a given leader was made to lead? It is our impression that there is a common assumption that effective leaders are "born with it," that leadership is more of a suite of traits than a skill set. A trait is an ability with which one is born or develops in the first years of life. Zaccaro (2007) defined leadership traits as "relatively coherent and integrated patterns of personal characteristics, reflecting a range of individual differences, that foster consistent leadership effectiveness across a variety of group and organizational situations" (p. 7). Such traits are essentially wired into our wetware. They undoubtedly are important to the effectiveness of leadership, with some traits (e.g., intelligence, need to achieve) being more relevant than others (e.g., charisma; Kirkpatrick & Locke, 1991).

Michael Jordan was not born an exemplary basketball player. He was born with the potential to grow to a notable physical height, develop an extraordinary ability to coordinate his technique, and within an environment that nurtured his love of the game. Steve Jobs was not born with the ability to design wickedly beautiful computers. He was born with a keen intellect, into a social environment of mentors, and with a chip on his shoulder that would motivate much of his striving.

As distinct from an inborn trait, a skill is a learned ability. No one is born with the ability to program a computer (no, not even that kid at the genius bar wearing the modish t-shirt). Instead, people from different walks of life and with distinct interests can learn to become competent programmers across a wide range of applications. The situation is the same with the development of leaders. Leadership skills must be learned through experience as one's responsibilities increase (Mumford et al., 2000a). As Mumford et al. (2000b) observed,

Chapter 1. Basic Leadership Skills

> Without appropriate developmental experience, even the most intelligent and motivated individual is unlikely to be an effective leader in organizational settings. Along similar lines, people who lack the abilities needed to develop these skills in a timely fashion are unlikely ever to become effective leaders. Thus, leaders are not born, nor are they made; instead, their inherent potentials are shaped by experiences enabling them to develop the capabilities needed to solve significant social problems [p. 24].

It's nice to have the traits that predispose one to leadership, whatever those might be, but it's crucial to develop the necessary skills.

At the same time, the development of a skill set is not sufficient on its own to ensure effective leadership. No less important is the applicability of those skills to the situation in which one leads. As Mumford et al. (2000b) recognized,

> leadership skills and expertise are likely to be more closely bound and constrained by situational requirements. Individuals with particular kinds of skills and expertise can, indeed, be leaders in one situation but not in others that require very different knowledge and technical skill sets [p. 9].

Truly, leadership is often constrained by a skill-situation fit that overshadows the relevance of expertise (Zaccaro, 2007). Edgar Schein (1986) counseled decades ago that leadership occurs within an organizational culture.

Toward this end, we think that the captains of *Star Trek* routinely demonstrate three critical leadership skills that are agnostic to situation: *communication*, *patience*, and *relationship*. They represent a method of incorporating a mix of reason (Enlightenment thinking) and compassion (to promote self-actualization) in a manner that can be readily adapted to any situation in which a leader might find themself. Utilizing these basic yet potentially transformative skills in our leadership can allow us to better meet the needs of the individuals we serve while supporting broader organizational wellness. What is important is that proficiency in the basic leadership skills is not limited by innate abilities or personal quirks. It can be learned through practice and by example. So, what do these skills actually entail?

Communication

Communication is fundamental to effectively leading any group or organization. Modern organizations are complex entities (Boyatzis,

1982; Spencer & Spencer, 1993) that require leaders to effectively convey the relevant information to make informed decisions (Johansson & Bäck, 2017; Erjavec, Arsenijević, & Starc, 2018). How many stories have you read in the news of leaders catching ire for poorly worded memos or ill-conceived social media posts? Communication that is intentionally crafted toward the needs of those one serves can minimize the challenges presented by the responsibilities of leadership. As Captain Freeman (*Star Trek: Lower Decks* S01E04; Kim & Kelly, 2020) observed, "...being a captain is a lot like vocal jazz. It's all about the notes you don't scat." We are well served as leaders when we consider how our words will be received before sending them across subspace. But what does it mean to communicate for effective leadership? Communication in effective leadership requires the use of two closely related behaviors.

Honesty is crucial to communication in leadership. We invite you to consider your own experiences. How have you felt when you discovered that a leader in your sphere had been dishonest about something important? Conversely, have you ever worked with a leader who was honest to a fault? We suspect those two experiences were quite different from one another. It has been our observation that a reputation lives and dies largely upon people's perception of one's honesty. As leaders, we always have the option of speaking the truth. Always. We do not debate that there might be times when there are certain things better left unsaid. Sometimes discretion is the better part of valor. However, even amidst such situations one can still provide candor in their comments. A good reputation takes time to acquire, but it can be lost in a moment of poor decision-making.

Closely related to the necessity of honesty is the importance of *transparency* in effective leadership. These are similar but separate tools. It is entirely possible to be honest but not overly transparent with the people one serves or to whom one reports. We suspect most of us can recall an example of a leader who was honest but not forthcoming with information. There certainly are times when a leader must proverbially play their cards close to their chest. There are also times, such those that involve human resources procedures, in which one is legally prevented from sharing information. Hiring and firing are two broad categories about which leaders must ensure their familiarity with the relevant laws of the land and procedures of the organization. However, in essentially all other cases, it is incumbent upon leaders to be

Chapter 1. Basic Leadership Skills

transparent in their dealings with others. This is often one of the surest ways to decrease the anxieties of others, especially during times of uncertainty.

Jason has a habit of responding quickly yet thoughtfully to email queries (at least, he thinks he does). Most of the questions he fields are straightforward and have to do with fairly easy problems to solve. Plus, he dislikes having email waiting in his inbox. Nonetheless, when he served as an interim dean at a previous college, he regularly received questions for which he had no knowledgeable answer. This left him with two options. He could either reply quickly to his colleague, or he could seek out the answer and then reply with accuracy. Similarly, serving as a director at his current university, Jason again occasionally encounters questions from fellow faculty to which he has no informed reply. In such situations, he does the unthinkable (no, not really). He replies with honesty that he does not know the answer and transparently explains how he will find it.

There is power in being honest and transparent when we interact with others. Communication is much more than just an opening of hailing frequencies. Yet, it is often transactional in nature, as it requires a sender, a medium of transmission, and a receiver to hear and then interpret the message. Communication nonetheless can consist of so much more than just a transaction. Communication is multidimensional. It offers us opportunities to lead through what we say and how we say it. Quite often amidst problems, we perceive ourselves as being in conflict with others due to differing interests. In reality, in most cases the conflict is really about a perceived incongruency of interests (Mayer, 2000). As leaders, we must take the initiative to clearly communicate our interests while actively listening to the interests of others (Mayer, 2000). We must be aware of not only the message they seek to deliver but how it might be received. Being honest and transparent can help us get there.

As we noted above, understanding interests (ours and others') is critical in how we lead through communication. Aaron had a chance to work with this notion during his time as a student relations director at a university. The position was unique in that it encompassed advising students in order to help them be successful, but also acting as a liaison with the faculty of a given college. He would often be present at various events in order to speak to prospective students about the programs in which they could study. However, after some time, he noticed there were some programs that did not have any faculty representation at these events. Unsurprisingly, these tended to be the programs with low or decreasing enrollment. At college meetings, the chairs of these departments could not understand why their enrollment numbers were low. He decided to set up meetings with these departments to motivate better representation at recruitment events. He specifically encouraged these faculty members to be more open-minded in their approach to attracting students. As Gerzon (2006) noted, "Narrow-mindedness is subtle and everchanging; before we know it, we have exchanged one kind for another" (p. 76). By taking time to communicate transparently, he was able to help his faculty colleagues to recognize their shared interests and thus better recruit students to their programs.

Patience

The importance of *patience* should speak for itself but too often does not. Discord is endemic to leadership. Whenever two or more people are involved in a problem, there are going to be potential disagreements. People can achieve new possibilities if they allow themselves the opportunity to engage in the process of conflict with others. Many of us have been attracted to positions of leadership, large and small, because of the potential to solve problems that matter to us. However, problem-solving requires a proactive stance that often benefits more from listening and less from doing (Kouzes & Posner, 2017). As Commander Shax demonstrated on more than one occasion, too often we are pushed to act rashly and without careful consideration of the interpersonal consequences (e.g., "Please, please let me shoot their warp core. I have been very good this month" [Cochran & Suarez, 2020]). The ability to stop, think, and listen (Haque et al., 2017) allows us to better regulate our urge to instantly respond (Comer & Sekerka, 2014). When we are patient, especially in moments of urgency (yes, that's right), we have a greater potential to offer more considered solutions (Milkman, Chugh, & Bazerman, 2009). Additionally, leadership tempered by patience can demonstrate our respect for the needs of those we serve while allowing them space to make their own decisions. Leveraging patience in service of effective leadership involves the awareness of two key elements that are related but meaningfully distinct from one another.

Chapter 1. Basic Leadership Skills

At its core, leadership is the practice of using one's voice to guide, motivate, and solve problems. *Speech* is thus central to these tasks. We are likely all familiar with the idiom that says "don't tell me, show me." While we agree with the sentiment that actions speak louder than words, the reality is that what one says often results in a greater impact than what one does (politicians, anyone?). This seems especially true today when speech has been extended through technology in both time and space. Have you ever received a work email, only to have it quickly followed by a "so-and-so retracts the previous email" message? This is akin to a judge telling a jury to disregard that last remark (*CSI: Star Trek*?). It can't be done. Whether we are talking with someone on the phone, sending an email to those we lead, or even posting something we perceive as harmless on our personal social media feeds, effective leadership necessitates that we are patient in our speech. It requires that we think before opening our mouths, putting fingers to keyboard, or letting our thumbs wander across that little screen you keep in your pocket.

During a brief time serving in academic administration, Jason was treated very well by his faculty colleagues. They welcomed him to their department meetings when something was awry, greeted him in the hallways when he would engage in campus walkabouts, and sometimes sent him updates via email regarding their scholarship. On one such occasion, a fine arts professor sent him an image of a recently completed project that was to be displayed in a show. It is important here to provide a bit of context. He was serving at the time in the division of humanities and fine arts. But he was a scientist, one who very much admired the arts but lacked any real savvy about them. Perhaps unsurprisingly, when he received the email from his fine arts colleague, he responded with what he thought was a playful and even complementary observation that the piece reminded him of a certain part of a farm animal (sheesh, get your mind out of the holodeck). This response, which in retrospect was flippant but at the time seemed in good nature, caused hurt feelings on the part of the professor. To this day, he feels guilty about the interaction. Words often matter more than we realize. To lead well, we must be patient in our speech, especially when that speech is so readily mediated by technological tools.

Aaron often teaches a full load of courses during the academic year as well as throughout the summer. As one might imagine, this schedule leaves somewhat limited downtime. He enjoys being engaged in this way, but it has also forced him to become more adept at looking ahead in order to find time to work on his research. In addition to research, he also finds it necessary to have quality time with his family. The result is that he has learned to be intentional about finding opportunities to pause and plan how he will navigate not just the next day, but also multiple semesters in advance.

Such patience ought to be present beyond the mere moment. Think of the leaders you most admire, the ones who really had staying power. These are likely individuals who understood the advantage of playing the long game. *Planning* is crucial to effectively leading a group or organization beyond the short-term horizon. As Das (2011) observed, we peoples of the modern world have a tendency to get attentionally stuck in the here and now, but not in a good way. Das urged that we should learn how to ground ourselves in the present without distraction or dysfunction. We would argue that equally important for a leader is the ability to look forward and ask what is coming next. Now, we are not going to suggest there is an easy way to do this. To our knowledge, no crystal ball has passed the test. We would instead offer that patience in leadership is often best demonstrated through an unwillingness on the part of a leader to act for short-term gain. Instead, effective leadership tends toward making decisions that manifest long-term outcomes.

Relationship

As important as communication and patience are to the leadership enterprise (just ask Picard), we think that effective leadership is ultimately dependent upon *relationship*. How we interact with those we serve must be a central consideration of our choices (Popper, 2004). We are social animals (just ask Captain Kirk). Establishing positive relationships based upon transparency and an orientation to the work before us can promote human growth (Carter et al., 2013). It also can help form an organizational climate that better prepares all involved to rise to the challenges of the work (Tierney, 1999). This is not to say that one must like everyone with whom one works. What is important is that there is a show of respect for the individual and recognition of their needs. We lead and learn and love not by chance alone but through the interactions we have with others, especially when they help us along the

Chapter 1. Basic Leadership Skills

way (Aronson, 2010). In this regard, the often maligned and quite mislabeled "soft" skills of building and maintaining relationships are the most important in leadership. It is not the leaders who keep the proverbial trains running on time we remember most fondly but those who demonstrated themselves to be humane. It is through the ability to relate with others that we meet our interpersonal obligations (Goleman, 1998). Relationship in effective leadership thus requires the consideration of two points that reinforce one another.

Listening is key to effective leadership. Honestly, we could almost just leave it there. Leaders must be able to actively listen to what their stakeholders tell them. One of the risks inherent to leadership is that we can sometimes take ourselves too seriously. We can stop seeing the people we lead and only the problems that need to be solved. Yet, leadership is fundamentally about people. When we listen to what they have to share, we are better equipped to understand the challenges before us. Such listening is called "active" because

> ...the listener has a very definite responsibility. He does not passively absorb the words which are spoken to him. He actively tries to grasp the facts and feelings in what he hears, and he tries, by his listening, to help the speaker work out his own problems [Rogers & Farson, 1957, 2015, p. 1].

Leadership thus entails putting the concerns of those they lead ahead of their own worries. It likewise means recognizing that those in the group or organization one leads might have something very real to contribute. Those who lead must be able to instill confidence among those who follow, but there must be appropriate balance to take time to truly hear what the crew is telling them. When we receive this valuable input from others, we must also fight (with a proverbial inner bat'leth if necessary) the urge to immediately respond. Runde and Flanagan (2008) reinforced this point when they stated that "when listening for understanding, it's imperative that you listen with the intent to understand rather than with the intent to respond" (p. 96). Leveraging relationship in leadership also means being present with those around us. Being a competent leader means giving the space to those that follow to have the time to appropriately weigh in.

Aaron has had many opportunities to learn how to listen with the intent of understanding, but there was one time with a student that really stands out. He was in his first year as an actual professor at a university, and he was doing everything in his power to stave off the nebula of "imposter syndrome" that can cloud one's sensors. He tried to be extremely mindful of responding to his students and dispensing little crumbs of wisdom. Isn't that what a professor and mentor is supposed to do? He had one student in a course who reached out to him through email that she was thinking of dropping out of the program. She was a year into the graduate program but didn't feel like she was connecting to other fellow learners. She also was doubting whether she could complete the program. He responded by offering to meet the student with the student person to talk. Before the meeting, he prepared a number of possible suggestions he might be able to offer, based on the typical difficulties that many students face while in graduate school, to help support the student when they talked. When the student arrived, she was a bit quiet. He attempted to create space for her to engage by talking about how well the student was doing in her courses. Eventually, the student began to speak about things that were going on at home, and how she didn't feel as connected to her fellow learners because of her heritage. He thought about responding at various points, but the student continued and he simply listened. Every time he thought about interjecting with a comment, he restrained himself and kept listening. Finally, the student stated how great she felt to have a chance to be heard. She also decided to remain in the program and approached her studies with a new vigor. This example emphasizes how much can be accomplished when we combine patience and relationship by listening.

Attending those we lead with an open ear is also the most ready way to clearly demonstrate our recognition of their *dignity* as individuals. How many interpersonal (not to mention international) problems might be avoided were people to always demonstrate a fundamental respect for one another's rights as autonomous beings? It has been our observation that across arenas, especially at the higher echelons of positional power, those in positions of leadership risk treating those they serve with fundamental respect.

Jason recalls some years ago working as a child and adolescent therapist in a day treatment program. Once per year, the CEO of the facility would call an all-staff meeting for the sake of organizational planning, recognizing accomplishments, and sundry other topics common to such meetings. During this particular meeting, the cafeteria was packed with the entire company. Therapists, coordinators,

Chapter 1. Basic Leadership Skills

directors, secretaries, and even the janitorial staff were all present as the CEO made his remarks. It was a typically mundane "celebration" of the facility's accomplishments. However, what stands out to him some 20 years later is a specific moment during the meeting. Everyone was going around introducing themselves by name and role. When the introductions reached the CEO, he gave his name and then jovially stated he was the janitor. Brief laughter ensued from the crowd, and likely no harm had been meant. Yet, what did such sarcasm mean to the janitor who was standing nearby? It seems unlikely the words of the CEO sent a message that conveyed a recognition of dignity.

If one is to successfully sit in that chair on the bridge, a leader must effectively harness empathy and trust in the service of creating and maintaining relationships (MacInnis, 2012). When your tactical officer tells you that phaser banks are fully charged, it helps that they recognize your concerns about entering battle. When your chief engineer alerts you that the warp core has been breached, it is important that you trust them. When you speak with (or about) someone, it is fundamental that you treat them with dignity. People will notice your respect, and most especially your lack of it.

This dignity that we extend to others is not synonymous with simply agreeing with others all the time. It is quite the opposite. As leaders, we must recognize that not rocking the shuttlecraft might be preferable or easier at times, but it almost assures that nothing of substance will be accomplished if this is the course selected every time. Effective leaders understand that quality relationships are built and strengthened through the navigation of differences. Fisher et al. (1991) noted that "A good working relationship is one that can cope with differences. Such a relationship cannot be bought by making substantive concessions or by pretending that disagreements do not exist" (p. 157). Thinking in these terms while leading allows us to extend dignity to others when we create opportunities for the expression of differences in a constructive way.

At the proverbial end of the day, people want to perceive that they have been treated fairly and in a manner that is transparent (Kim & Mauborgne, 2003). In this way they can make the most informed decisions of their own. We want the people we lead to feel seen and valued so that they can actualize their full potential not merely as individuals but as agents of the organization. As Ensign Mariner ironically asserted in the twenty-fourth century, "What? You think I need therapy? No! It's the 80s, dude, we don't have psychiatric problems!" (*Star Trek: Lower Decks* S01E09; Rodgers & Suarez, 2020). We want our needs to be met without feeling belittled or ignored.

Hailing Frequencies Open

It is important to us that the case studies we use through the lens of the *basic leadership skills* demonstrate the rich diversity of human experience. The canon of *Star Trek* naturally lends itself to such a requirement and has continuously done so in a manner that improves with every new series. We invite you to read, question, debate, and most certainly enjoy your way through the following leadership lessons with the captains of *Star Trek*.

Chapter 2

Archer: Adolescent Explorer

The turbolift ride to the two-hundredth floor takes only a minute, giving you one last moment to think about the meeting to which you are headed. You became involved in the project last year. The topic piqued your interest, so you reached out and were invited to participate.

You quickly found yourself committed to the project and ready to take on the responsibilities of leadership because of the challenges inherent to the work. Problems were solved as they arose. Paperwork was submitted on time. Somehow, even in this age of technological wonder, one cannot escape the inevitability of paperwork. It seems to make little difference whether it was submitted on paper as in days of yore or via the touch of a holographic button. There seems never to be a shortage of the stuff.

The door to the turbolift wooshes open, calling you out of your musing. As you cross the elegantly monochromatic lobby to the desk framed by the floor-to-ceiling windows, you note the remarkable view of the city from this height. You also cannot help but notice the decor. But why is there so much lens flare?

The receptionist scans your identification and with a smile walks you back to the conference room scheduled for the meeting. This is the moment that has been so much on your mind as of late. You know the meeting has the potential to be difficult. You remind yourself that everyone present is committed to the project and likely means well. Of course, the road to Gre'thor is paved with good intentions.

As you enter the conference room you recall something from university. The nineteenth-century psychologist David McClelland (1987) said that people are motivated to achieve, to affiliate with others, and to secure a sense of power over their own lives. There is little doubt that the meeting about to begin is going to demonstrate in spades all three of these needs. Your colleagues each have their own opinions about the tasks at hand. Sure, everyone's basic needs have been met and society is all about enlightened living. But it seems people remain people when it comes to their egos. How would Captain Archer handle this situation? You make a mental note to clearly express your concerns in the meeting (basic leadership skill: **communication**), *listen carefully to alternative explanations (basic leadership skill:* **patience**), *and solicit input from others (basic leadership skill:* **relationship**).

Captain's Log

Jonathan Archer (played by Scott Bakula) was considered by many to be the most significant explorer of Earth's early interstellar history. Captain of the original U.S.S. *Enterprise*, he commanded the first Earth vessel capable of warp factor 5 and thus its first true starship (Memory Alpha, n.d. b). Under the leadership of Archer, *Enterprise* would serve the people of Earth as their first true emissary among the stars and their countless civilizations. However, human society still had much to learn about being an enlightened society in the twenty-second century. Canon suggests that it was a time of both progress and uncertainty. In this sense, the character of Archer and his time in (future) history provides for us a mirror of sorts with which to consider one's own leadership today.

Born in 2112 to a noted scientist, Archer was exposed from his earliest days to the possibilities of space exploration. As a child he even met Zefram Cochrane, the pioneer of warp drive technology (Memory Alpha, n.d. b). This exposure to achievement was coupled with a rigid model of expected accomplishment. For example, once when Archer shared with his father some anxieties about not succeeding in his studies, his father's advice was a succinct, "Don't fail" (LaZebnik et al., 2005). The young Archer unsurprisingly developed a major drive to succeed. He became an Eagle Scout as an adolescent before moving on to his undergraduate studies (there was not yet a Starfleet Academy) and ultimately flight training. Indeed, Archer would spend the next several years as a test pilot in the NX program, which was tasked with the development of experimental spacecraft.

In 2151, Archer was appointed captain of *Enterprise* after reluctantly agreeing to the stipulation that his bridge crew would include a Vulcan science officer. In their ensuing adventures over the next four years, Archer and his crew would make first contact with the Andorians

Chapter 2. Archer: Adolescent Explorer

(who would become founding members of the Federation), the Ferengi (who would not), and the Romulan Star Empire (who would definitely not). They would even encounter the Borg at one point in time. Needless to say, many of these interactions proceeded less than optimally. For example, on numerous occasions *Enterprise* would run into dispatches from the Klingon Empire or find themselves attempting to fight off marauding Suliban raiders. It was almost as if the history of the original *Enterprise* was one big retcon of the events of a next generation.

Throughout these many early adventures, Archer maintained the attitude of a brash pilot. This makes him one of the more difficult captains after which to model leadership. However, we think there is much to be learned, not so much from his actions, but from his growth as a leader. Archer stood in command of the most technologically advanced Earth starship of its time. Unlike the captains who would follow in his footsteps, Archer did not have the benefit of a guiding set of Federation principles to inform his problem-solving. The Federation would not exist until after the series finale. Nor did Archer have the fortune of being able to look back upon the examples of previous Starfleet captains. He was the first of his kind, a military officer serving more than 200 years before Earth became a postscarcity society. It is thus through a consideration of Archer's development as a leader during a time of major societal change (just like ours today) that there is much to be learned for our own leadership practice.

Instructive is how Archer matured as an *adolescent explorer* through those experiences as a leader by learning to wrestle with the ethical dilemmas inherent to leading a crew into the unknown. He learned to balance his gifts of reason and intestinal fortitude with an increasingly compassionate tone guided by experience. The result was that the once quick-tempered test-flight pilot would help save Earth from conquest and pave the way for the founding of a quadrant-spanning democracy. Indeed, Archer would ultimately serve as one of its earliest presidents (Sussman & Rush, 2005).

Canon Fodder

Captain of the very first *Enterprise*, Archer often shared his quandaries when presented by new situations and regularly welcomed the opinions of his bridge crew. True to his adaptability as a former test pilot, he proved his ability to quickly consider alternative perspectives in order to leverage the basic leadership skills of *communication*, *patience*, and *relationship*. Archer likewise demonstrated an ability to be authentic in his leadership. George (2003) defined authentic leaders as individuals who

> use their natural abilities, but ... also recognize their shortcomings and work hard to overcome them.... Others follow them because they know where they stand.... [They are] dedicated to developing themselves because they know that becoming a leader takes a lifetime of personal growth [p. 12].

Archer recognized that being among the first humans to explore the Galaxy necessitated an openness to experience and a willingness to learn in a manner reminiscent of Enlightenment ideals.

However, it is difficult to pursue enlightenment when the tasks of daily leadership are constantly confronted by the times. Much as our world today is wrestling with challenges political and historical, so too do we observe Earth society of the near future seeking to plot its course to better days for all. This is not to suggest that twenty-second-century Earth was a barbaric place. On the contrary, canon states that it was a time during which "Earth made the first steps toward a planetary government and prosperous society" (Memory Alpha, n.d. c). The fact nonetheless remains that the character of Archer grew up at a point in time when bravado was rewarded with greater praise rather than temperance. The *Star Trek* of later generations, when humanity reached for a greater understanding of the Galaxy and their place in it, was only just beginning.

Such irony always has likely existed during the start of major societal change, with the Enlightenment of the seventeenth and eighteenth centuries being no exception. For example, René Descartes was known to have been aristocratically proud (O'Connor & Robertson, 2014), Voltaire was socially ambitious (Cronk, n.d.), and Thomas Jefferson owned hundreds of enslaved people (Wikipedia, n.d. a). For better and worse, leaders are invariably reflections of their times. This excuses nothing, but it does help to provide us with some context with which to reflect upon the decisions of leaders whether looking forward or back. Archer provides an example not so much of Enlightenment thinking as of an individual who worked toward becoming increasingly dynamic in his thinking and open to growth during his tenure as a leader.

Chapter 2. Archer: Adolescent Explorer

In addition to an initial development toward more enlightened thinking, Archer demonstrated growth in leveraging compassion with his crew. The anger and abruptness we observe from Archer in the first episode of the series (*Star Trek: Enterprise* S01E01/2; "Broken Bow"; Berman et al., 2001) was not the same demonstration of the humbled uncertainty he evinced standing at the entrance to the Federation assembly in the final episode (*Star Trek: Enterprise* S04E22; "These Are the Voyages..."; Berman et al., 2005). The lesson to be gleaned from this interesting character is that we can (and must) grow as individual leaders through experience and interaction with others.

Broken

People new to positions of leadership sometimes risk losing the awareness that there are always bigger gormaganders in the Cosmic sea. It is easy to lose sight of the fact that positions of leadership almost invariably carry with them the requirement of reporting to others higher in the organizational hierarchy, whether it be to an administrator, officer, or board of directors. Not having the ultimate word in matters means that a leader sometimes must seek compromise when fulfilling their obligations to the people and organization they serve. In "Broken Bow" (*Star Trek: Enterprise* S01E01/2; Berman et al., 2001a), Archer was required to compromise his plans as captain of the first interstellar Earth ship by hosting a Vulcan science officer aboard in exchange for the use of her people's star charts (transactional leadership, anyone?). Although T'Pol eventually would become a trusted advisor and friend, her initial presence on the bridge was a constant reminder to Archer that he had not entirely gotten his way. This was no mere inconvenience. Archer had always manifested a quick wit coupled to an equally rapid temper. For example, he once responded to a seemingly snide comment made by a Vulcan ambassador amidst a diplomatic envoy by responding that "you have no idea how much I'm restraining myself from knocking you on your ass" (Berman et al., 2001a). The character of Archer undoubtedly felt stymied in his lifelong drive for achievement by the presence of a more experienced minder.

Indeed, in the episode we see Archer reluctantly learn the lesson through his interactions with Sub-Commander T'Pol that compromise is a necessary leadership skill when seeking to solve problems. As George (2003) cautioned, "being very competitive is not a bad thing ... but it needs to be channeled through purpose and discipline" (p. 25). "Broken Bow" (Berman et al., 2001a) ends with the bridge crew of the shiny new *Enterprise* having worked together to save the day and make friends (well, frenemies) along the way.

Leadership is more difficult when one is forced to seek results amidst a lack of control over the available options. Compromise requires an enlightened perspective that relies not just upon reason, but as well the ability to leverage compassion and thereby recognize differing perspectives. That's our point, really. More than any other captain, Archer demonstrated an evolution of personal maturity during his Galactic peregrinations. Each of us has undoubtedly been required, officially or politically, to be saddled with unwanted expectations. Instead of nursing a bruised ego, utilizing thoughtful compromise can help solve many problems. Sometimes we learn not in spite of adversity but because of it. The effective leader learns to recognize the affordances hiding among those limitations, and then makes clear their availability (basic leadership skill: *communication*) in a manner that results in an acceptable compromise (basic leadership skill: *patience*) among parties. The goal is not to get one's way, but to support the success of the organization and the people who comprise it (basic leadership skill: *relationship*).

Incident

One of the truisms of leadership is that we must sometimes collaborate with people with whom we truly don't get along. Another truism of leadership is that there will always be a need for computer maintenance. However, let's stick with the first issue. In "The Andorian Incident" (*Star Trek: Enterprise* S01E07; Berman et al., 2001b), Archer decided to visit an ancient Vulcan monastery whose adherents eschewed the use of technology and instead focused on inner spiritual development. His ostensible goal as an explorer was to encounter a new way of life. However, upon arrival, Archer and his officers discovered not a place of idyll but a monastery with a bashed-in door and a group of monks quite eager to see them back out through it. When the party were subsequently attacked by a squad of Andorian soldiers, Archer and his crew found

Chapter 2. Archer: Adolescent Explorer

themselves caught between two age-old rivals. What makes the episode instructive for our purpose is that we learn the Andorians attacked the Vulcan monastery because of their belief the site was actually a facade for a covert listening post with which the Vulcans could spy on the Andorians.

Archer was initially reluctant to accept such a seemingly unfounded assertion, especially since it was the Andorian commander shooting at him who claimed this to be true. Indeed, the very idea of it seemed preposterous to Archer and his officers. Tensions already were high and further bloodshed seemed inevitable with both the Vulcan monks and the Andorian soldiers doubling down on their truth claims. Nonetheless, Archer perceived a responsibility to help solve the problem in an equitable manner.

Fisher et al. (2011) observed that leadership is often a matter of negotiation between conflicting perspectives. They advised that "it is important to decide issues on their merits rather than through a haggling process focused on what on what each side says it will and won't do" (p. xviii). Such negotiation is based on interests and not positions. In the episode, the monks and soldiers both maintained strongly held and highly disparate positions. Archer and his officers similarly had their own initial assumptions about the situation. Everyone involved was certain of their certainty and unwilling to consider that there might be room for discussion. Have we not all been in such a situation? This is where Archer demonstrated his growing leadership. By listening to both the Andorian commander and the Vulcan elder monk, as well as consulting with his officers, Archer recognized the merit of the accusation and thus was able to consider new information. The result was a recognition of the competing needs of the two parties.

We think "The Andorian Incident" (Berman et al., 2001b) is one of the better episodes of the series because it demonstrated growth in Archer's character development as he moved past his impatience to consider competing perspectives. Perhaps more importantly, the episode ended on a rather dour note and thereby reflected the reality of principled negotiation (Fisher et al., 2011). Archer attempted to lead based not on position but on the principles over which he and the Andorian commander could agree had merit. Archer went out of his way, largely past his own initial assumptions, to listen to both sets of antagonists when at the monastery (basic leadership skill: *communication*). Although he still

Leadership in *Star Trek*

took steps to ensure the safety of his people and the unarmed monks, Archer did not stop paying attention to new information as the situation unfolded (basic leadership skill: *patience*). At the end of the episode, he recognized that progress can be made even when tensions remain high and feelings continue to be uneasy (basic leadership skill: *relationship*).

Flight

Archer had just received word that his old friend and fellow test pilot, Captain Robinson, had died in an accident on Earth. Thus began "First Flight" (*Star Trek: Enterprise* S02E24; Shiban et al., 2003), a flashback episode that followed a series of recollections through which Archer told the tale of Starfleet's initial attempts to achieve Warp 2. The A-story of the episode glorified the value of risk-taking in leadership as explored through Archer's relationship with his friend and their questionable decision-making skills along the way. Indeed, at one point Archer asserted that "the most important thing to me is that we succeed" (Shiban et al., 2003). Allow us to make clear we do not find this an overly compelling demonstration of effective leadership. As was often true in numerous episodes of the series, things did not go to plan in "First Flight" (Shiban et al., 2003). When Robinson attempted to push the *NX-Alpha* past Warp 2, Archer's old friend and fellow test-pilot encountered first-hand the truism that there is "no glory in being the first person to deploy an escape pod at warp" (Shiban et al., 2003). We learned through expository dialogue the result that Starfleet, upon the advice of the Vulcan advisors assigned to the *NX* program, had decided to ground all further attempts until problems could be worked out with the engine design.

Of interest to us is the B-story of the episode, which revealed the beginning of what would become a lifelong friendship between Archer and his eventual chief engineer, Charles "Trip" Tucker. The value for our consideration is that the formation of this friendship addressed the issue of loyalty in leadership. Our own observations concur with Reichheld's (2001) research that loyalty is not merely relevant to effective leadership but "the direct result of words and deeds ... decisions and practices" (p. 76) of leaders. In other words, loyalty in leadership is about more than paying lip service to people or programs. It was in the

Chapter 2. Archer: Adolescent Explorer

episode that we see the first time Archer met (then) Lieutenant Commander Tucker and essentially promised him the position on his ship someday (once he had a ship). The moment serves as one of many examples of the loyalty Archer repeatedly afforded to his crew.

To be clear, we are not suggesting that loyalty should be given carte blanche in leadership. Both of us have worked in environments where there was a preference to promote from within. This can be a positive organizational attribute when one is already a member of the organization and those within it are capable. Alternatively, such promotion from within can pose a barrier for those who seek to join from the outside or when the organization lacks the necessary human resources to achieve its goals. Who among us has not witnessed people promoted to positions because of their connections instead of their capabilities? There also is a very real risk of nepotism in leadership. We do think loyalty can be an effective tool when leveraged with care in the service of leadership. However, a leader needs to be wary of their biases.

In the episode, Archer recognized the potential of (now) Commander Tucker to acquit himself not only as a capable engineer but as a forthright individual by listening to what Tucker had to say (basic leadership skill: *communication*). Although it would be a decade until *Enterprise* flew under Archer's command, he eventually appointed Commander Tucker as chief engineer and second officer (basic leadership skill: *patience*). This loyalty was especially notable given Archer's tendency toward quick action. Finally, although the two officers became best of friends, Archer never lost his ability to separate his responsibilities of leadership from his loyalty to his officer. Much like the experimental precursors to *Enterprise*, all relationships eventually experience some fluctuations in the intermix. As Reichheld (2001) wrote, effective leaders "are forthright about telling employees where they stand" (p. 82). Loyalty has major value, but it must also have limits.

Prime

The conflict with the Xindi had not gone well. Things were said, weapons were deployed, and intel revealed that the Xindi Council were preparing to launch a weapon of such mass destruction that Earth would be utterly destroyed. Thus began "Azati Prime" (*Star Trek:*

Leadership in *Star Trek*

Enterprise S03E18; Berman et al., 2004), with *Enterprise* and its crew en route to prevent the launch of the planet-killing weapon. Shortly after arriving in the Azati Prime system, Archer revealed his intention to pilot a commandeered insectoid Xindi shuttle down to the planet so as to destroy the weapon. Unfortunately, the task necessarily would be a suicide mission. Not only did this prompt tears from Sub-commander T'Pol, but Archer was paid a visit by Temporal Agent Daniels. More accurately, Archer was inexplicably whisked 400 years to the future aboard the U.S.S. *Enterprise-J*, where he was strongly advised to sue for peace among the Xindi Council in his own time. True to form, Archer's inclination was to scoff at the very idea of brokering a treaty with a society set on the wholesale genocide of humanity.

The leadership lesson in this episode is that foresight is a difficult thing. Research increasingly demonstrates that the brain is a predictive organ (Hutchinson & Barrett, 2019), one that evolved to anticipate events, note the discrepancy between its expectations and what actually happens, and then refine its models to better prepare for what might happen the next time. Yet, although thoughtful planning is key to effective leadership, we humans are really bad at predicting the future with anything approaching accuracy. How many times have we thought we knew what was coming, only to be proved wrong? It has been our observation that some of the most adept leaders are those who are able to recognize that coming events might not proceed as they have foreseen and to plan for the expectation of surprise.

In "Azati Prime" (Berman et al., 2004), Archer was so committed to the mission of stopping the deployment of the weapon of mass destruction that he was unable to hear the guidance offered by a knowledgeable advisor (even if that advisor was from the future and wearing an exceptionally odd Starfleet uniform). This is an all-too-common error in leadership. We have both witnessed leaders large and small (especially small) take Farragut's attitude of forgoing the proverbial torpedoes and charging ahead without serious thought to the consequences of their decisions. A key example was Archer's decision to take the Xindi shuttle on the suicide mission. Although we respect his desire to not order anyone else to their death, the situation was more complicated than one of self-sacrifice.

Foresight might be one of the single most difficult responsibilities of leadership. Yet, it might also be one of the most valuable. The most

Chapter 2. Archer: Adolescent Explorer

adept leaders we have known have been those individuals able to meld a wealth of experience with an openness to new information. Such new information often comes by way of advising. We see in "Azati Prime" (Berman et al., 2004) how Archer was so entwined in his anxieties about the mission that he struggled to hear the guidance of his most trusted officers. It almost cost him his life. Most of us tend not to have the benefit of occasional visits by a temporal agent who has seen the future. However, we should all make it a point to surround ourselves with individuals who can offer thoughtful counsel. As the old Earth adage states, only Archer could go to Detroit.

Terra

One of the things that historically has set apart *Star Trek* from other science-fiction canons (aside from the transporters) is its intentional social commentary. In "Terra Prime" (*Star Trek: Enterprise* S04E21; Reeves-Stevens et al., 2005), we see the franchise at its best as it leverages the enlightened and compassionate lens of a fictional future through which to view the bigotry of our present day. A little context here is important. The episode, the penultimate in the series and we think easily one of its best, was released a little more than three years after the events of 9/11. The world was still responding to the import of those attacks, to include an increased incidence of expressed bigotry. As has been documented (Altman & Gross, 2016), the themes of the series had been reoriented to address the societal aftermath. Perhaps this is why the story of "Terra Prime" (Reeves-Stevens et al., 2005) continues to resonate today. One needs only turn to the news to read reports of bigotry near to home as well as in distant lands. Serving as a leader in no way removes us from this reality.

In spite of all of the misgivings among the various major civilizations of the Alpha Quadrant, the past four years had somehow witnessed a growing interstellar desire for collaboration. Embassies had opened on Earth and now representatives from the Andorian, Tellarite, and Vulcan governments had convened in San Francisco to consider the forming of a "federation" of star systems. Alas, to paraphrase the Bard, something was rotten in the state of Mars. "Terra Prime" (Reeves-Stevens et al., 2005) instead began with the efforts of Archer and his crew to stop the eponymously named terrorist group from utilizing a verteron array on Mars to vaporize Starfleet Command on Earth. The cabal's demand? The government of Earth was to immediately expel all non-human individuals from its proverbial shores. Held up as the poster child of the cause was a human-Vulcan infant labeled as "the most dangerous enemy humanity has ever faced" (Reeves-Stevens et al., 2005).

Leadership requires that we remain vigilant not to lapse into intolerance. If there is any lesson in *Star Trek*, it is that through infinite diversity comes beautiful opportunities for us to grow as individuals and as a species. Implicit is the understanding that such growth must include literally everyone. The difficulty is that we are human and thus "we rarely challenge our own preconceptions, privileges, and the standpoint from which we reason" (Delgado & Stefancic, 2017). Serving as a leader brings with it the responsibility to challenge bigotry, our own and that of others, when we encounter it within the purview of our leadership and to act in a meaningful way. Additionally, those of us who also benefit from greater societal privilege must shoulder more of the responsibility to make change and space for the voices who will benefit from that change.

Voyages

Leaders today are often portrayed in the popular press as charismatic individuals who enthusiastically wield their voices on the public stage. However, our observation over our combined years of teaching is that those individuals headed toward positions of leadership often are initially turned off by the notion of being in positions of power. They simply fail to see how they can use positional power in a comfortably ethical manner. Instead, it seems that many people are more typically drawn to leadership because of their dedication to the work than out of a desire to stand out in front of the crowd.

Archer was caught in just such a situation at the end of "These Are the Voyages" (*Star Trek: Enterprise* S04E22; Berman et al., 2005), the beautifully written yet creatively controversial final episode of the series. He was drawn from a young age to be an explorer. Never one to seek attention, Archer maintained a mindset focused firmly

Chapter 2. Archer: Adolescent Explorer

on the task at hand, whether it was testing an experimental craft or negotiating a first contact. As with some of the captains who would come after him, Archer desired to be out among the stars going boldly where humanity had not gone before. Yet, there he was in the episode, in full dress uniform and full of nerves, about to address the assembled delegates of multiple worlds. To give a speech. In public. Not on a starship.

Unbeknownst to the character at the time, Archer's speech would help set in motion the formation of the Federation, a union of societies that would eventually become the largest peaceful civilization of two Galactic quadrants. Yet, standing there in the moment with T'Pol present for support, all he could think about was turning back to the safety of his starship. Archer's character had always wanted to succeed, but he had never had much interest in notoriety. Now, he had been called upon to step well beyond his comfort zone. Part of being an effective leader is to recognize one's own limits. So, what was Archer doing there? Why did they want him of all people to give a speech? He was an explorer, not a politician.

Leadership sometimes brings with it situations that prove personally intimidating, and often those situations occur in the public sphere. In the episode, we watch Counselor Troi assure Commander Riker that Archer's speech to the delegates of many worlds would serve as an early pillar to the formation of the Federation. In other words, Archer had a responsibility as a leader to do it. It is all right to be afraid in leadership so long as that fear does not hold one back from action. This is the definition of courage. However, it never hurts to have a team at such times to who can be trusted to offer sound guidance. T'Pol guided Archer in his time of uncertainty; Troi assured Riker through his own vexation.

When Archer stepped onto the stage before the arena of delegates from around the Alpha Quadrant, he did so knowing he would have to trust in his ability to lend his voice to the cause of a better future (basic leadership skill: *communication*). Doing so further required that Archer allow himself to take a breath beforehand (basic leadership skill: *patience*) and accept the support proffered by his science officer (basic leadership skill: *relationship*). Archer thereby offers us all the lesson that the fear of going where one has not gone before is part of the leadership trek.

We Can't Be Afraid of the Wind

How can we take these lessons and apply them to our own leadership? It is one thing to respect a giant of leadership like Archer but another to implement his lessons into our daily choices. Let's take each of the examples above and see how they might fit with our own needs.

Compromise is a skill necessary for the effective leader. Leadership entails working with people, not merely fistfuls of data. This is not to suggest that research is not important to leadership. On the contrary, we live in a time unlike any previous when it is possible to measure the effects of our actions, and measure we must. However, data without context are insufficient. "Broken Bow" (*Star Trek: Enterprise* S01E01/2; Berman et al., 2001) demonstrates how even the most accomplished leader is sometimes forced to accept undesirable criteria in order to meet the responsibilities of their role. One antidote to such a situation is to understand the context of the evidence before us. In the episode, we learned that Archer had maintained a less than positive perception of Vulcans since childhood (bigotry was apparently still a problem in the twenty-second century on Earth). As captain of the first *Enterprise*, he chafed under the watchful eye of his Vulcan science officer and her damned logic. However, the actual problem was not T'Pol's behavior aboard ship. She proved useful if not indispensable in solving problems (and saving Archer's life) on countless occasions. The true leadership problem was Archer's attitude toward her presence on his starship. Ego is a powerful nemesis to effective leadership, and far too often the greatest obstacle to productive compromise. Leadership requires that we act not merely for those who support us but even for those we serve but who might see us in less than favorable light. We simply must be able to compromise with others in order to lead well.

Collaboration is crucial to effective leadership. Yet, sometimes circumstances conspire to require collaboration with suboptimal partners for the sake of success. In "The Andorian Incident" (*Star Trek: Enterprise* S01E07; Berman et al., 2001), Archer found himself between a monastery and a hard place. In the process of exploring a new opportunity, he and his crew quite literally landed amidst an ongoing conflict between two entrenched parties. This reminds us of one too many university department meetings. How often have we observed otherwise competent people double-down on their assertions instead of reaching

Chapter 2. Archer: Adolescent Explorer

across the table to work through an impasse? Compromise requires that leaders recognize the needs and listen to the language of both parties in conflict so as to negotiate a realistic solution. As Aaron has repeatedly taught, the goal of leading through conflict is neither its resolution nor its management. Rather, it is the intentional decision to engage in the process of conflict with others in order to discover outcomes previously thought improbable. Leadership does not occur in a social vacuum. Conflict will always be a possibility so long as two or more people are involved in the situation. In the episode, Archer demonstrated his awareness of the conflicting needs by listening to both the Vulcan monks and the Andorian soldiers. His goal was not to solve the age-old strife between their two peoples but to help broker some functional compromise in the moment. It was an example of how leadership is not merely the achievement of major goals but more often the stepwise progress brought about by compromise between stakeholders.

Sometimes, leadership provides us the opportunity to hire, retain, or promote individuals with whom we would very much like to work. For example, Jason has had the privilege to invite several of his former students into his research agenda as colleagues and even as friends. This has been one of the greatest joys of his career, not to mention that it has made his scholarship that much stronger. At the same time, one must take care not to allow *bonhomie* with those we value to cloud our judgment as leaders. In "First Flight" (*Star Trek: Enterprise* S02E24; Shiban et al., 2003), Archer was introduced to his future chief engineer when the latter demonstrated both his mechanical chops and his willingness to freely voice his opinion to Starfleet brass. Archer immediately recognized not merely a gifted officer but one with whom he could successfully collaborate. Although it would not happen for quite a few years, when the opportunity arose, Archer selected his friend and colleague for promotion to his crew.

Did Archer cross the line of professional propriety? Perhaps, perhaps not. Our goal here is neither to applaud nor condemn his decision but to offer it as a point of discussion. We would be remiss if we did not acknowledge the potential risk as well as reward of Archer's actions. How many times have we witnessed an individual in a leadership position leverage their positional (or political) power to oust someone else from either their role or the organization? Effective leadership demands we take care when favoring some for advancement. Are we being objective as leaders about their abilities to fulfill the role, or are we allowing a personal relationship to cloud our judgment? We must be even more vigilant when someone we lead falls into our disfavor. Do we promote the most competent individual even if we personally dislike them? There is no place for retaliation in enlightened and compassionate leadership.

"Azati Prime" (*Star Trek: Enterprise* S03E18; Berman et al., 2004) makes clear that the world would be a better place were all leaders to have *aides-de-camp* from the future. Of course, for better and worse, leaders are people. You might not have noticed, but people tend to be quite impoverished of imagination when attempting to accurately predict the long-term outcomes of their own decisions. Therein lies the irony. How many times have you been certain of an outcome, only to be proved wrong? Of those examples, how many times have you been able to convince yourself that you really knew it all along?

Leadership requires us to forecast the potential results of our actions with some semblance of accuracy. Archer revealed just how difficult this can be when one is trapped by their emotional reaction to events. The surest way to offer a clouded forecast is to lack the ability to step away from one's desires for the future. Yet, this is what must be done if we seek to meaningfully predict the consequences of our decisions. Having one or more trusted advisors during such dilemmas can be worth its weight in dilithium. Archer learned this lesson the hard way in "Azati Prime" (Berman et al., 2004). Instead of considering the information shared with him from the future, he let a sense of urgency born of remorse drive his behaviors.

It is important for a leader to trust in themselves, lest they regularly become bogged down in self-doubt and rendered unable to effectively lead. However, it simultaneously is crucial that one actively seeks the advice of others when seeking to solve problems of major import. We have both benefited from the counsel of others who are wiser (and probably more intelligent) than us. Even in times of urgency, the slight delay in response is likely to pale in comparison to the improvement in solution. And remember not to take yourself too seriously.

Star Trek has always provided a vision of the future that bent toward the utopian. This vision is one that has evolved over the decades in concert with the broader societal advances. For example, it is a long way between the chauvinism of "The Man Trap" (*Star Trek: The Original*

Chapter 2. Archer: Adolescent Explorer

Series S01E05; Johnson & Daniels, 1966) and the inclusivity of "Choose Your Pain" (*Star Trek: Discovery* S01E05; Berg et al., 2017). The series and films have increasingly demonstrated that everyone is welcome at the table in the ready room. It also is abundantly clear in our twenty-first century that we do not yet inhabit such a world. "Terra Prime" (*Star Trek: Enterprise* S04E21; Reeves-Stevens et al., 2005) thus remains as relevant to leadership today as it did when it premiered. Humanity (and apparently most species across the Galaxy) evolved with a number of cognitive biases that aid daily functioning. For example, neither of us has to think about protecting our children when we perceive something to be amiss. The response set is automatic. Yet, these same biases which can serve some can also hurt others directly or indirectly. It was fine to maintain a strong in-group bias when our species was limited to small bands roaming the savannah. Alternatively, in a multicultural and globalized world such as ours today, such thinking is more likely to promote bigotry than to ensure the health and welfare of others. Leadership carries with it the obligation to leverage whatever privilege one might have for the sake of all those one serves.

Indeed, "These Are the Voyages" (*Star Trek: Enterprise* S04E22; Berman et al., 2005) presented how our personal issues can limit our leadership. Instead of ego interfering with compromise, the episode touched upon the reality of fear. Serving as a leader is not always an easy voyage. It requires us to head into the unknown. Along the way, we are bound to worry that we lack the requisite skill set, that we will get lost, that we might even fail. Welcome to leadership! We recommend surrounding oneself with competent people who can provide honest feedback, guidance, and support. Contrary to popular belief, leadership is not a solo climb. You can bet that the truly exceptional leaders are belayed by really capable teams and that they most certainly had their moments of apprehension as they ascended in their positions.

Not long ago, Jason had the opportunity to direct the institutional review board (IRB) at his university, the committee charged to maintain ethical oversight of all human-subjects research. The work was a lot of fun for those who enjoy the finer points of research design and ethical geekery. However, the mechanics of directing the effort were sometimes cumbersome (Computer? Hello, Computer?). He transitioned into the role over a summer, mentored by the enigmatic and supportive outgoing director. The learning curve was steep but he made progress under her watchful eye. Nonetheless, as the summer neared its end and his position became official, he experienced some degree of trepidation as he was set free to lead. Such is a normal response to new responsibilities, especially those whose errors would very much be in the public sphere. The situation recalls the words of Archer's father. It is important not to be afraid of the wind.

Aaron experienced leadership when he wasn't necessarily seeking it out. During his last year of college, he joined the Civil Air Patrol, the auxiliary of the United States Air Force. One of its missions (among many others) is to lead cadets and perform flight and ground support missions for communities that people live in. He joined the Civilian Air Patrol because he was a pilot and desired another way to build flight time. He also wanted to experience a military setting with a purpose. He was primarily a pilot for his squadron and loved every minute of it. One day, his commander asked if he would consider becoming the deputy commander of the squadron. He thought about it for a while; he hadn't been looking for the responsibility of a leadership position. He just really enjoyed rocking the flight suit and aviator sunglasses! Nonetheless, he eventually accepted the offer, acclimated to the position, and actually thrived in it. When a few months later his squadron commander had to take an emergency leave of duty, he was moved into the commander position. It was truly a trial by fire, as it thrust him into all aspects of leadership. This temporary opportunity gave him a greater appreciation of the larger picture of leadership at a relatively young age, one he has incorporated to this day.

It is important in leadership that we do not allow our emotions to get the better of us while remaining true to ourselves. Archer demonstrated how an openness to experience (not to mention a prodigious wanderlust) prepared him for the discoveries that laid ahead for him and his crew. Indeed, his openness to the new seemed to mature during his first four years commanding *Enterprise*. We have seen the same trend in many of our students. They often arrive for their programs of study willing but not so much ready to take on the world. With study, experience, and intentional reflection under their belts, these students evolve into more enlightened leaders capable of balancing reason with compassion in their daily interactions with others. This does not mean they learn not to be afraid of the unknown. Instead, the best of our students develop the ability to navigate their anxieties as they become

Chapter 2. Archer: Adolescent Explorer

better educated and better experienced. This is certainly not an overnight process. After all, it takes a long time to get from there to here.

GUIDANCE FROM GUINAN

Imagine yourself sitting at a small table under the arching windows of Ten Forward, the frontmost point and social hub of the U.S.S. *Enterprise*. The view out the windows is one of stark blackness punctuated by countless points of light, stars of every imaginable color. Sitting across the table is Guinan, the unofficial sage of the starship. Wise beyond measure, Guinan has served for centuries as a guide to innumerable leaders. Now she is fully present in the moment with you.

"What's on your mind?" Guinan asks you with that knowingly subtle smile. "You mentioned you were thinking about Captain Archer. What about him stands out to you as a leader to model?"

Guinan continues to look at you expectantly. There is no hint of impatience, just that twinkle in her eye. "Think of Archer's approach to leadership," she suggests. "How does your behavior as a leader compare with his?"

Guinan looks out the windows to the stars for a moment, and then turns back to you. "How do you *communicate* with others in a manner that is intentional and transparent?"

After giving you a moment to think and respond, Guinan asks you, "How do you exercise *patience* by listening to what others have to say?"

Guinan listens to your response, momentarily closes her eyes and nods with a smile, and then poses one more question to you. "How do you develop *relationship* with others so that they feel seen and heard?"

After you respond, you and Guinan chat a bit longer before she has to return to her customers. You look back out at the stars, toward the seemingly endless potential of leadership, and think about how to lead more like Archer.

Chapter 3

Burnham: Rapid Adapter

As you step into the conference room and spot some familiar faces, your mind wanders for a moment to your own motivations. Why are you here? Certainly, the tasks of the project appealed to you. That truly was the primary impetus for your willingness to serve. However, if you are honest with yourself, you also knew that participation in the project would not reflect badly upon you. The project has become fairly significant, and though the names affiliated with it will be lost to the sands of time, the effects of its outcomes if successful could be felt far and wide.

You recall what a mentor once told you. The two most important statements in effective leadership are "I don't know" and "I don't know how." There is no shame in needing to learn something, but much to be lost when one seeks to lead without knowledge. In other words, it is important not to take oneself too seriously.

You are pulled from your thoughts, standing just inside the doorway, as a colleague brushes past you with a nearly inaudible "excuse me" emanating from your universal translator. Ah yes, there are so many languages spoken among the members of the project. And with language comes understanding, as well as misunderstanding. Even back in the twentieth century, scholars recognized the fundamental role of language to buoy as well as limit our thoughts. Lakoff and Johnson (1980) understood that

> *the concepts that govern our thought [sic] are not just matters of the intellect. They also govern our everyday functioning, down to the most mundane details ... the way we think, what we experience, and what we do every day is very much a matter of metaphor ... language is an important source of evidence for what that system is like* [p. 3].

In other words, it will be important during this meeting to note the words you and others use.

Chapter 3. Burnham: Rapid Adapter

*With a quick nod of confirmation, you make your way into the conference room. As you do so, you find yourself pondering how Captain Burnham addressed the power of language when speaking with others in service of leadership. You remind yourself to be clear and as free as possible of bias in the words you choose in the coming hours (basic leadership skill: **communication**), cognizant that what you first hear might not truly be what was meant or even said (basic leadership skill: **patience**). Finally, you remind yourself that here in the Federation, everyone is an equal with something to say (basic leadership skill: **relationship**).*

Captain's Log

Michael Burnham (played by Sonequa Martin-Green) was born in 2226 on Earth. As a young child, she and her parents relocated to the Doctari Alpha Research Outpost, a station in the Beta Quadrant staffed by a group of Vulcan and human scientists working together (Memory Alpha, n.d. d). It was there that Burnham's parents were ostensibly killed by members of a Klingon raiding party. Unbeknownst to Burnham at the time, her mother managed to escape, and eventually they would be reunited at a *much* later time. Thus, Burnham was subsequently raised by her adoptive parents, Amanda Grayson (who was human) and Sarek (who was a noted Vulcan ambassador). Although loved by her mother and instructed by her father, Burnham struggled to find her place within her mixed family and the less than tolerant Vulcan society of the time.

Burnham went on as a young adult to study quantum physics and graduated first in her class at the Vulcan Science Academy (Memory Alpha, n.d. d). Turned down by the Vulcan Expeditionary Group ostensibly due to racism, she was accepted as an officer in Starfleet and began her career as a xenoanthropologist aboard the U.S.S. *Shenzhou*. It was on *Shenzhou* that Burnham would rise to the rank of commander and serve as first officer. It was also aboard *Shenzhou* that she would lead a mutiny, be blamed for starting a war between the Federation and the Klingon Empire, and face court martial with a life sentence in a Federation prison (yes, they still had them in the twenty-third century). Burnham truly had a complex history as a character.

After spending six months in prison, Burnham was brought to the

Leadership in *Star Trek*

U.S.S. *Discovery*, a primarily scientific vessel, in order to help solve a vexing problem. It was there that she counterintuitively served the remainder of an extensive and illustrious career. However, first things first. Shortly after coming aboard *Discovery*, Burnham found herself working on an experimental spore drive. Before long, she also helped navigate an end to the Federation-Klingon War, a conflagration that had until its cessation gone very badly for the Federation and its allies. Burnham later found herself fighting for her life in the Mirror Universe where she took the place of her evil alter ego in an attempt to bring her prime crew home. For these and other efforts, Burnham was awarded the Federation medal of honor and reinstated to officially serve aboard *Discovery*.

However, the good feelings were temporary when it became apparent that there was an artificial intelligence attempting to eradicate all sentient life from the Galaxy. One thing led to another, and Discovery and crew ended up jumping far into the future. Leading up to this major event in her leadership, Burnham discovered that her mother was very much alive, living in that far future and trained as a Qowat Milat warrior nun (we would say one can't make this stuff up, but obviously one can). Oh yes, *Discovery* also had become self-aware and now went by the name "Zora." By this point in her career, Burnham had been assigned as captain of Discovery and would find herself in short order attempting to save the Galaxy twice more.

Throughout these experiences and many more, Burnham demonstrated her ability to be a *rapid adapter*. She was rarely caught by surprise and even demonstrated a particular facility for integrating new information into her problem-solving regardless of the seriousness of the crisis. Simultaneously, Burnham regularly sought the counsel of others to aid her in that ability to adapt to novel situations and one too many crises of epic proportions.

Canon Fodder

The newest captain to be introduced in the *Star Trek* franchise, Michael Burnham provides us with an example of a leader who grows before our eyes season after season. The series began with a character ridden with the emotional baggage of a few poor decisions. However,

Chapter 3. Burnham: Rapid Adapter

over the course of her adventures toward the captain's chair, Burnham demonstrated how even the most troubled soul has the potential to expand beyond their initial limitations. Indeed, Burnham increasingly modeled how the basic leadership skills of *communication*, *patience*, and *relationship* can help one overcome personal challenges in the service of leading others and organizations. Such growth was especially notable with the transition from the third to fourth seasons of the series. It was almost as if the character had been rewritten as a person. From this point forward, Burnham ensured that she heard others when making important decisions, to include regularly giving others a chance to lead. Finally, Burnham often revealed her own thought process when attempting to solve problems.

Such personal development offers us a model of Enlightenment thinking. A disciple of Vulcan logic, Burnham recognized the value of rational thinking to solve problems. However, the initial seasons of the series demonstrate her repeated struggles to overcome her rather emotional responses to events. This is not to suggest that Burnham lost sight of Federation ideals or otherwise failed to do what had to be done. Instead, the lesson to be learned is that, through experience, reflection, and consultation with trusted advisors, she was able (to paraphrase a certain android) to grow beyond her original programming.

Such growth offers us an example of how enlightened thinking can be coupled with an inherent drive toward self-actualization. It is fair to say that Burnham was in no way actualized prior to her captaincy. We instead witnessed time and again an exceptionally intelligent and motivated leader making the tough decisions in spite of her own insecurities. Alternatively, with the start of the fourth season of the series, we saw how the character manifested significantly greater psychological maturity. Relying heavily on logic, but informed by her experiences and the resultant gut feelings she could more clearly recognize, Burnham was able to find solutions through teamwork with others and in a manner that did not require unmitigated risks. Such growth was nicely summarized in more general terms by Sheehy (1976) regarding the developmental trajectory of adulthood:

> The work of adult life is not easy. As in childhood, each step presents not only new tasks of development but requires a letting go of the techniques that worked before. With each passage some magic must be given up, some cherished illusion of safety and comfortably familiar sense of self must be

cast off, to allow for the familiar expansion of our own distinctiveness.... What I'm saying is we must be willing to change chairs if we want to grow [p. 31].

And change chairs Burnham did, from a prison cell bench to the captain's seat. And while we most certainly did not observe Burnham achieve self-actualization over her many adventures, her character growth serves as a useful model of how we can each move toward reaching our fullest psychological potential as leaders.

Binary

It had been a difficult day. Burnham found herself in the brig of *Shenzhou* for her violation of orders and the resultant reinitiation of hostilities between the Federation and the Klingon Empire. Actually, this would be putting it mildly. *Shenzhou* was heavily damaged and the majority of Burnham's brig cell had been reduced to a three-dimensional force field separating her from the vastness of open space. Thus began "Battle at the Binary Stars" (*Star Trek: Discovery* S01E02; Berg et al., 2017) and perhaps one of the greatest demonstrations in *Star Trek* canon of how logic under fire can be utilized to find creative solutions to difficult problems. One of the challenges of leadership is that our powers of rationality often shut down amidst strong emotion, especially when that emotion involves worry. Such emotions interfere with decision-making (Soares et al., 2013) and reduce cognitive flexibility (Ionescu, 2012). The result is that our ability to effectively lead can be hobbled by our own very human nature.

In the episode, Burnham recognized that it was only a brief matter of time before the force field gave out and exposed her to the celestial vacuum. She first became upset, but relying on her Vulcan meditative training, Burnham was able to calm her mind and evaluate the situation. Having identified a potential solution to save her from an inevitable vacuum-induced death, she verbally engaged the ship's computer to assist her in a specific but risky course of action. Programmed to preserve the life of its crew, the ship's computer rejected Burnham's proposed solution. What followed was a rapid-fire demonstration of Burnham using an ethical calculus to justify her assertion that the maneuver would prove successful and indeed was the only viable

Chapter 3. Burnham: Rapid Adapter

solution to be had. Through the cool use of logic in an otherwise terrifying situation, Burnham was able to convince the ship's computer to give her a chance. If only real life were so ... logical.

Although beset with an ostensible tendency to respond with strong emotions to challenging events, in this case Burnham was able to leverage the affordances of logical thought to provide novel solutions to difficult problems. Therein resides the leadership lesson for the rest of us. Leadership will always require creative ideas in order to solve new problems as they arise. What is important is that one keeps their cool amidst the process. It is all too easy to be taken by surprise, especially early in one's leadership career. Yet, the use of logic coupled with an awareness of others' emotional needs can allow our best Enlightenment thinking to save the day. In the episode, Burnham demonstrated a keen ability to reason her way aloud through the problem (basic leadership skill: *communication*). Instead of allowing her frustration to grow unabated when the ship's computer initially rejected her solution, she kept her wits about her and persevered (basic leadership skill: *patience*). Although the ship's computer was neither sentient nor emotionally equipped, Burnham nonetheless recognized the limits of its programming and worked within those perceived boundaries (basic leadership skill: *relationship*).

Hope

It is important to surround oneself with capable and trusted advisors. However, the reality is that sometimes a leader finds themself alone, literally or socially. Perhaps this is due to logistics, or maybe it is the result of politics. Regardless, sometimes leaders find themselves truly flying solo. Perhaps you have recently been promoted to a new position and the position lacks staff or lateral colleagues. Alternatively, maybe you were sent to some far off location away from the mothership to a newly established office. In these and other very real situations, it is possible to feel quite stranded as a leader.

In "That Hope Is You, Part 1" (*Star Trek: Discovery* S03E01; Paradise et al., 2020), Burnham found herself all alone. When last we saw Burnham, she had been flying through space in a fancy EVA suit, surrounded by a small squadron of shuttles to protect her from enemy fire as she led *Discovery* into a wormhole. Now, she found herself far in the future on some random planet and with no *Discovery* in sight. As Burnham shared after being spit out by a giant space crustacean, "I really ... really didn't know how this day was gonna turn out" (Paradise et al., 2020). Is this not true so often in leadership? We never know how the day is going to proceed, whether our solutions to the problems at hand will prove effective. As Burnham experienced on the planet Hima of the far future, on occasion there will be no others with whom we can consult before making our choices.

Leading without the benefit of others naturally presents a number of problems. Most emphatically, and an issue commonly ignored in leadership training programs, is the emotional toll such isolating situations can take on an individual's state of mind. As Goleman (2003) wrote, destructive emotions are one of the greatest risks to effective functioning. These emotions can be triggered by external as well as internal events, but their effects are one and the same. We risk ruminating, getting bogged down in worry, and becoming cognitively stuck (Brosschot, Gerin, & Thayer, 2006) on the little things that distract us from the bigger picture. This was the situation in which Burnham found herself after being suddenly ejected into the future. Her ship was gone. Her crew was gone. She was alone, yet she had a mission to pursue. Her response was to gather her wits, take inventory of the situation and her options, and then proceed forth. We are not going to sugar coat the matter. Leading alone is hard.

Burnham expected *Discovery* to be right behind her through that wormhole. She had not planned for the possibility that she would spend the next year on her own. As effective leaders do, Burnham quickly sought out new colleagues with whom to interact (basic leadership skill: *communication*). She made it a point to adapt to her new environment and its expectations, ostensibly recognizing that doing so would take time (basic leadership skill: *patience*). Through it all, Burnham learned the parameters of her newfound role by learning from those around her (basic leadership skill: *relationship*). What matters for our purpose is that, while Burnham might have been alone, she actively explored ways to change that reality.

Maru

It had been more than a century since the nearly total cessation of warp travel due to a cataclysmic event wrought havoc across the Galaxy.

Chapter 3. Burnham: Rapid Adapter

Countless lives had been lost at the time, and fear lived on among the populations of a great many planets across known space. Now, with the threat over only months ago, the Federation began efforts to reach out to its former members with an invitation to rejoin its conclave of mutual interest. With that invitation came a freewill offering of dilithium, no strings attached. However, change can prove threatening, especially when that change purports to offer a better future after a history of strife. It is thus not entirely surprising that the attempt to renew diplomatic relations with a previously disenfranchised people at the start of "Kobayashi Maru" (*Star Trek: Discovery* S04E01; Paradise et al., 2021) was met with some doubt. The episode began with Burnham and Cleveland Booker, her compatriot in the far future, attempting to broker an alliance with the Alshain Empire. The discussion quickly escalated, there was some significant misunderstanding about a cat, and shots were fired. In this manner, the beginning of the episode offers an example of rather naive leadership and the importance of understanding both history and context.

Previously aligned with the Federation, the Alshainian people had become insular (like most worlds of the Galaxy) after the sudden end to safe warp travel. During the intervening century since their last contact with the Federation, the Alshainian people became isolationist. However, the Alshainian Empire possessed a range of exceptionally advanced technologies they knew to be superior to what the Federation maintained when last the two societies interacted. Thus, it should not have been entirely surprising that a Starfleet officer arriving on a powerful starship (by an unknown method of travel) bearing gifts and asking for nothing in return would be perceived with some degree of suspicion. Writing on the difficulties through the lens of organizational change, Fullan (2011) observed that

> You can't make people change, and rewards and punishment either don't work or are short-lived.... Grasping change involves giving people new experiences that they end up finding intrinsically fulfilling.... In other words, it is not inspiring visions, moral exhortation, or mounds of irrefutable evidence that convince people to change, it is the actual experience of being more effective that spurs them to repeat and build on behavior [pp. 51–52].

Unless they are Vulcan. As Fullan explained, practice drives theory in effective leadership. This is an observation we would do well to heed.

It can be very difficult to alter the direction of organizational momentum. Think, for a moment, of the times you have engaged in some task in a certain way because that's the way it has always been done. Consider how we are often reluctant to change our habits because of their familiarity, and even comfort, as opposed to the intention required to change our behaviors. This is as true of the smartphones we buy as it is of the way we lead. Once in an ecosystem, it is difficult to escape it without concerted effort.

In "Kobayashi Maru" (*Star Trek: Discovery* S04E01; Paradise et al., 2021), Burnham demonstrated her ability to speak clearly and honestly when attempting to negotiate with the Alshainian emperor (basic leadership skill: *communication*). Indeed, she remained steadfast in her commitment to assist then even they had shot at her and her compatriot, causing them to flee through the woods and rather dramatically utilize their personal transporters. Burnham recognized the importance of playing the long game to legitimately regain the trust of the Alshainian leadership (basic leadership skill: *patience*). Where she faltered was in overestimating the rapidity with which she could connect with their leaders on a personal level. Burnham did not read the room, as it were, by taking into account the fuller context and history of the situation. Nonetheless, she recognized the importance of communicating person to person (basic relationship skill: *relationship*). As Burnham replied with one of the most important statements of her character arc, it's what the Federation does.

Possible

There Burnham was, sitting at the table as the presidents and their counsel of the Federation and Ni'Var debated the terms of how the two powers might reform an alliance after months of difficult negotiation. Just as things appeared to be moving toward a resolution, the president of Ni'Var paused the process by requesting that her government maintain the option of unconditionally leaving the Federation should it appear unable to protect Ni'Varian interests at some point in the future. To support this request, she cited how her world perceived the Federation to have been unable over the previous decade to meet the needs of its member worlds. At this point, ostensibly sensing the potential

Chapter 3. Burnham: Rapid Adapter

collapse of negotiations, Burnham interjected that it would be a shame for the process to fall apart due to disagreement over a single issue. The Federation president took the opportunity to call a recess to the talks so that each side might consult among itself. "All Is Possible" (*Star Trek: Discovery* S04E04; McElroy et al., 2021) thereby provides us with an example of how an ability to "read the room" is often necessary for effective leadership.

It has been our observation that leaders too often come to meetings with a "git 'er done" attitude with the intention of achieving some seemingly simple agreement that will allow the team to move on to the work ahead. However, such an attitude is necessarily predicated upon a limited set of assumptions. First, what might seem simple or obvious to one individual might not be shared as such by others at the proverbial or literal table. In "All Is Possible" (McElroy et al., 2021), the Federation president opened the meeting unaware that the president of Ni'Var was going to propose a new and problematic addendum to their pending agreement. Second, the desire to keep moving forward toward a specific goal can actually prove its own obstacle along the way. When presented with the surprise of the Ni'Varian request, the Federation president was initially unable to change tacks and accommodate what was obviously a topic that required consideration. Third, recognizing the importance of group dynamics can be key toward leading a successful meeting, especially if that meeting is the locus of important decision-making. Fisher et al. (1991) summed up all three of these points well in their discussion of *inventing* versus *deciding* in a negotiation. They wrote that "since judgment hinders imagination, separate the creative act from the critical one; separate the process of thinking up possible decisions from the process of selecting among them. Invent first, decide later" (p. 60).

Tuckman (1965) relatedly recognized that groups of people, regardless of their mission (or presumably planetary citizenship), often progress through four stages of interpersonal dynamics. In other words, groups meeting together for the first or fifteenth time can typically be understood as existing in one of four stages of development, and that stage can tell us as leaders a lot regarding how much (or little) work they will be able to accomplish toward the tasks before them. According to Tuckman, newly formed groups initially experience a *forming* stage during which its members seek to test the boundaries of, and assert their independence within, the group dynamic. Groups often then demonstrate a *storming* stage of development during which members become sufficiently comfortable within the group dynamic to assert their own positions and/or anxieties. This tends to be the most emotionally tinted time in the process of group formation. Groups who successfully navigate the emotions of those interpersonal interactions often proceed to *norming*, the stage of group development during which group norms are established and thereby allow for initially meaningful work to commence. Finally, it is at this point that the group dynamic becomes one of *performing* the actual work necessitated by the purpose of the group first coming together.

Sitting there with the presidents and their counsel of those two great powers of Ni'Var and the Federation, Burnham recognized that the group dynamic at the table had not yet achieved the ability to perform without satisfying the encumbrances of some new norms. Instead of allowing the process to arrest, Burnham addressed the group in a manner that was responsive to the current stage of group dynamics (basic leadership skill: *communication*) by creating an opportunity for a functional pause in the discussion (basic leadership skill: *patience*). Importantly, she spoke with respectful strength, clearly recognizing that leading groups of people is always based upon interpersonal connections regardless of the stage of group development (basic leadership skill: *relationship*).

Rosetta

It seems these days that there is never a shortage of programs (or acronyms) in leadership. Bookstore shelves are filled with texts extolling the virtues of various methods to improve corporate productivity, student inclusion, learning in the college course room, and more. These programs often come with glittering recommendations from practitioners or pundits. Some are held close to the vest of a consulting firm, whereas others are more freely distributed for use. Perhaps you have a colleague who swears by Program X and cannot recommend it enough. You might even be tempted to implement that program where you lead. It couldn't hurt, right? Wrong. As Jason teaches in his courses, change for its own sake is as ignorant as insisting on maintaining the status quo for its own sake. Effective leadership requires that we not merely entertain novel solutions to ongoing problems, but that we base such decisions on evidence. You might say we need a fistful of data in order to effectively lead forward.

In "Rosetta" (*Star Trek: Discovery* S04E11; Burton et al., 2022), Burnham was tasked with communicating with the creators of the DMA busy wreaking havoc across the Alpha Quadrant. However, she was presented with an obstacle. Almost nothing was known about the species in question beyond the fact that they were extremely technologically advanced. Many of us have undoubtedly been caught in a similar situation, not with an extragalactic superpower, but caught in a situation beset with unknowns. Some leaders of lesser experience might have chosen to rush headlong into the confrontation. Instead, Burnham prudently insisted on spending precious time seeking clues to better understand the problem. Therein lies the rub for our purposes of leadership.

How often have you observed leaders implement some new policy or program with the intention of solving a problem? Given the field in which we teach, we have both repeatedly observed students (and too many faculty who should know better) insist on the viability of a specific program (typically a new program) to solve historically intractable organizational problems. Of course, as opposed to Burnham's recognition that evidence is key to effective leadership, these students and colleagues are often certain of the program's efficacy prior to its implementation. In other words, we think too many leaders are willing to make decisions that affect others without considering the necessary evidence. As Jason invariably replies in class when a student makes a truth claim: "What does the research say?"

Berliner and Glass (2015) offered a reasonable approach to such situations in which a leader is called upon to do something but has yet not the data to support a decision. They recommended that leaders "trust but verify," that they recognize the potential merit in programs that elsewhere have been successfully implemented and resulted in positive outcomes. However, Berliner and Glass also cautioned that such an attitude must be predicated upon a willingness to accept that what worked elsewhere and elsewhen might not work for you in your current organizational time and setting. In other words, an effective leader needs to do their research before making major decisions about program implementation (large or small). Part of such research must involve taking a boots-on-the-ground approach. Much as Burnham visited the ancient homeworld of the creators of the DMA, we must each come to understand the limits of a program's utility before and during the decision to implement it.

Burnham recognized the importance of better understanding Species 10-C before committing to a plan of action that may or may not prove successful (basic leadership skill: *communication*). She knew that looking for clues on their homeworld would cost precious time. Yet, Burnham comprehended that such time spent would be well worth the trade against the risk of moving ahead without knowledge (basic leadership skill: *patience*). She was able to rely on her team because they had come to trust her past behavior as being grounded in rationality and temperance (basic leadership skill: *relationship*).

Ten

"Species 10-C" (*Star Trek: Discovery* S04E12; Jarrow & Osunsanmi, 2022) is an episode with much to commend it and no little action both physical and cerebral. As Ensign Boimler observed, "first contact is a delicate, high-stakes operation of diplomacy" (*Star Trek: Lower Decks* S01E01; McMahan & Kelly, 2020). What the process lacks in paperwork it more than makes up for in high adventure (at least through the anodized lens of *Star Trek*). Relevant to leadership, Burnham, Saru, and other respected delegates of the Alpha Quadrant worlds found themselves standing in the shuttlebay looking out the backdoor of *Discovery* (don't overthink that one) in their first face-to-face meeting with representatives of Species 10-C. So different from expectations was the language of Species 10-C from anything previously known to the Federation or its former allies that even the universal translator could not make sense of it. It was a precarious situation that is all too familiar in leadership. Burnham had reached the limit of her understanding.

Ignorance in leadership is no less a reality than it is in science, and it is important to recognize that ignorance can be a driving force for effective leadership. As Firestein (2012) extolled, the purpose of the scientific method is to seek out and better understand what we do not already know. Similarly, the great joy and challenge of leadership is to effectively solve problems for the sake of the people and/or organizations we lead. Oftentimes, doing so necessarily takes us into new territory. There is no shame in not knowing, only in remaining ignorant by choice. We would all be well advised to recognize the most important statement in all of leadership, just as it is in scientific inquiry: "I don't know." Making such an admission, whether to ourselves in private or to others more publicly, requires that we recognize our own limits.

As she stood face to face with the wonderfully unexpected Species 10-C, Burnham came to realize that she did not possess the knowledge to solve the clear and present communication crisis. She recognized her ignorance and what she did not know. This, in itself, demonstrates the start of solid decision-making. However, what she did next reveals the power of her growing humility in the service of leadership. Burnham called for members of her bridge crew to beam down to the shuttlebay (because in the thirty-second century, you are never more than a tap of the communicator away) and upon their arrival set the task before them. Together, they sought to tackle the problem now before them all.

Each of us as leaders has limits. If we are honest with ourselves, and we must be honest with ourselves, it is not a question of whether but of when we will reach those limits in knowledge, experience, or fortitude. When that happens, we must decide how we will lead. Burnham understood after her initial attempts to speak with the representatives of Species 10-C that she was out of her league (basic leadership skill: *communication*). She recognized that this presented an opportunity not for frustration but one of potential consultation (basic leadership skill: *patience*). Because she had already cultivated a history of trust and respect with her bridge crew, Burnham was able to bring them directly into the situation to problem-solve and thereby compensate for her own limitations (basic leadership skill: *relationship*). Leadership is not a solitary mission.

Let's Fly

How can we take these lessons and apply them to our leadership? It is one thing to respect a leader like Burnham who ensured others were heard and had opportunities to lead while maintaining transparency regarding her own decision-making. It is another thing to walk such noble talk. Let's take the examples above and see how they might fit with our own practice.

Leadership in *Star Trek*

It is common during times of strife to become befuddled when a "fog of war" obscures elements of reality. Hailing back to the periods in human history when cannon and musket fire literally would cloud the battlefield, such situations remained as applicable during the twenty-third century they were during the eighteenth. In "Battle at the Binary Stars" (*Star Trek: Discovery* S01E02; Berg et al., 2017), Burnham made a series of questionable choices that precipitated all-out war between the Federation and the Klingon Empire. Her decisions were based, in part, on the availability of incomplete information at the time of decision-making. Things were said, people were killed, and things quickly got out of hand on a much larger scale. Today, we can observe a "fog of war" in the form of the disinformation and misinformation increasingly accepted by society as part of normative discourse.

Leadership does not grant us the luxury of being taken in by verbal perfidy no matter how moving the argument or how much we agree with the underlying sentiment. Burnham demonstrated how the use of logic, even (and especially) in the presence of high emotions, can and indeed must be leveraged for the sake of effective problem-solving. This is not to suggest that we ought to ignore the emotional needs of those we lead. On the contrary, the challenge before us during times of difficulty is to demonstrate an ability to empathize with others while keeping our own wits about us. Evasive maneuver 88 might sound good in the heat of debate, but we will be better served by first considering our options through a logical lens.

"That Hope Is You, Part 1" (*Star Trek: Discovery* S03E01; Paradise et al., 2020) serves as a related reminder that leadership sometimes requires us to act on our own, not because of a belief that we know best (one almost never does), but due to a lack of available counsel. Having time-traveled far into the future, Burnham unexpectedly found herself alone. Yet, she still had a mission to complete. The fact of her isolation was distressing but insufficient to prompt a sense of failure. Instead, Burnham did what all great captains do. She took the time to consider her options and then attempted to move forward to the best of her ability.

Leadership rarely allows for the opportunity of a commercial break to buy one some time to think (although the weekends can sometimes be leveraged as such). Instead, leaders are often expected to quickly solve problems regardless of the situation. What if that situation is novel to

Chapter 3. Burnham: Rapid Adapter

the leader? What if there is simply inadequate information upon which to base a sound decision? What if the leader is new to the organization and is "alone" amidst its culture? These are very real dilemmas that present themselves to many individuals in leadership. We would offer that the key in such moments is not to solve the problem but to keep calm and continue thinking. Solitude in leadership can breed uncertainty and its attendant destructive emotions. Burnham demonstrated how one can take solace by recognizing the minor victories along the way of the long game.

The *Kobayashi Maru* was not merely the name of a fictional wayward civilian transport ship popularized in so much of *Star Trek* canon, but a no-win scenario intended to test the psychological mettle of Starfleet cadets. It was also a scenario that has a great deal of relevance to leadership. As Commander Riker observed (*Star Trek: The Next Generation* S04E11; Apter et al., 1991), "some days you get the bear, some days the bear gets you." We are not talking about failure, but the reality that leadership regularly necessitates a broadening of perspective, or what might be called "pulling a Kirk." In "Kobayashi Maru" (*Star Trek: Discovery* S04E01; Paradise et al., 2021), Burnham sought to extend a proverbial olive (i.e., dilithium) branch between the Federation and an historically disenfranchised group. Although her intentions were sincere, the way she went about the process was not initially successful because she did not take into account how very different than intended her words and actions would be received.

This is an important lesson for leaders. What we think we are communicating is rarely the whole picture. Words carry context, both current and past, and that context cannot be controlled readily through the message itself. The practice of leadership requires just that, practice. We must work hard to recognize when our own perspective, our own understanding of the situation (or indeed, the world), limits our ability to meaningfully seek mutual understanding with others. In our current era of increasingly effective attempts to bring the beauty of human diversity to the leadership table, it is important for each of us, regardless of background, to note when our own biases present roadblocks to problem-solving.

Indeed, effective leadership necessitates an ability to not merely talk and listen, but to observe the others at the proverbial table. People are odd beings, be they human or any other species in the Galaxy. In an ideal world, we would all just get along after agreeing on a mutual course of action. Alas, that is not the world in which we live. Any situation in which there are two or more people will manifest the potential for discord. As Alanis Morsette (1995) reminded us, one plus one makes two. This truism is as valid in leadership as it is in personal relationships.

Recognizing where a group is in Tuckman's (1965) sequence of functionality is crucial for effectively leading that group toward meaningful work. "All Is Possible" (*Star Trek: Discovery* S04E04; McElroy et al., 2021) demonstrates how even a group of exceptionally intelligent, experienced, and well-intentioned individuals can become bogged down by group dynamics. This is where the major potential of leadership can be manifested. Leadership is often more about curation than creation. Burnham's role at the table with representatives from the Federation and Ni'Var was one of helping them to see commonality while feeling heard. It was not that she introduced anything new to the interpersonal equation so much as provided a blackboard upon which all could see it written.

Discovered in 1799, the Rosetta Stone includes copies of the same text inscribed in ancient Egyptian hieroglyphs, ancient but later Egyptian Demotic script, and ancient Greek written during the time of Ptolemaic Egypt (Wikipedia, n.d. b). It allowed for the deciphering of millennia of ancient Egyptian artifacts and an explosion of understanding between the modern world (more or less) and one of the great empires of human antiquity. Along the way, humanity came to know itself just a little better. Similarly, in "Rosetta" (*Star Trek: Discovery* S04E11; Burton et al., 2022) we observe Burnham recognize the value of research before action. Although such a practice might seem counterintuitive during our present and presently rushed times, being informed as a leader remains as important today as it was 2000 years ago and will be 1000 years hence.

Time spent doing one's research is never time wasted (a truism for leadership as well as tenure). Imagine how the world today might look if those in positions of power never acted without first studying the ground truth of their respective arenas and then asking what might realistically result from their decisions. Effective leadership must put data before decisions. This requires meaningfully understanding the specifics of a situation before implementing programs or policies to address it. One cannot put the proverbial genie back in the bottle. Leaders can read

Chapter 3. Burnham: Rapid Adapter

the research, ask for input from stakeholders, consult with trusted advisors, and even talk aloud to themselves. All of these tools can facilitate the gathering of research to guide decisions. Take-backs might work on the playground; they tend to be less effective in the boardroom. One need not find a Rosetta Stone of one's own, but we do need to do the research available to us before setting events in action.

It has been our observation that precious few individuals in leadership remain unaffected by their newfound roles. Whether through a loss of humility or an increased certainty in one's abilities, leadership can obfuscate the recognition of one's own limits. The irony is that such self-deception tends to cloud decision-making while opportunities for decision-making only grow as one becomes more successful in leadership. There consequently is real risk in failing to see what is before us when we become leaders. Burnham demonstrated a welcome alternative to such myopia in "Species 10-C" (*Star Trek: Discovery* S04E12; Jarrow & Osunsanmi, 2022) when she called for her bridge crew to help her navigate communicating with their newfound extragalactic friends.

However, as Burnham demonstrated through her more formative years (i.e., the earlier seasons of the series), it requires time and intentional effort to find one's footing while donning their EVA suit and walking amongst the stars. This was especially true for Aaron while he was still in college. He had the opportunity to become a resident advisor. For anyone who has worked in residential life (i.e., student housing), you can appreciate the significant step into a larger world such a position brings. You are in charge of a floor of college students while being a college student still yourself (take a moment to allow that irony to thoroughly sink in). He was merely in his sophomore year when he first became a resident advisor. Not only was he still adjusting to being a college student, he now had to be available to a whole floor of his peers to help them connect with other students and more broadly succeed in campus life. It certainly brought about some challenges and some unexpected situations for him (don't even get him started on the shenanigans he observed in the study lounge. Seriously, people?).

Yet, while many of his fellow resident advisors were dealing with obscene wall murals and literally being locked in their own rooms by their residents, Aaron looked for ways to connect with his own residents. He took the time to get to know them and understand what they needed. Consequently, his door was always open (even at 2:00 a.m.) to his residents. By year's end, he had some of the best attended programs and floor meetings in the dorms. While some of that success might have been due to the free pizza (oh, so much pizza), he would like to think that he was beginning to learn the importance of the basic leadership skills through interactions with his residents as they experienced the independence of being in college and away from home for the first time.

Returning to the episode, the remarkably intelligent Burnham tried again and again to crack the code of the Species 10-C language. Nothing she did resulted in much success. Recognizing that the problem was beyond her ability to solve, Burnham engaged in one of the most important of all leadership skills. She asked for help. Burnham put the problem ahead of the person, the outcome before the ego. How often have we each observed the opposite in action? We suspect too often. Instead, Burnham served as a model of how understanding one's limits is not a weakness but a strength when it comes to leading through difficult situations.

In the best of times, leadership can be a challenging vocation. In not so good times, it can require us to stretch beyond our preconceived notions in order to meet the needs of unexpected situations. Burnham demonstrated throughout her captaincy an ability to effectively meet the needs of the people she led and the organization in which she served time and again by thinking logically about the problems at hand while remaining connected to those around her. Perhaps even more instructive for our purpose is the demonstration over multiple seasons of how Burnham grew as a leader. Her character represents perhaps the single best example of professional development in the captain's chair in all of *Star Trek*. (Actually, that recognition ought to go to Saru, but his character didn't get his own show, so....) That growth included a recognition that she could not solve everything by herself, that we are each as leaders dependent upon others for guidance through counsel or example.

Jason utilized this lesson early in the days of serving as director of his university's institutional review board, the group charged with ensuring the ethical oversight of human-subjects at the university. One of his initial goals upon transitioning into the role was to change the campus perception of the board toward one of greater collegiality. Instead of the board being historically perceived as a gatekeeper, he

Chapter 3. Burnham: Rapid Adapter

worked to foster an expectation of the board as being a partner in ethical research. Toward that end, he found himself fielding many questions from faculty, staff, and students as word got around that the board was receptive to dialogue. Most questions he could answer in a straightforward manner. However, sometimes there were issues that were more complicated. Instead of offering a pat response, he shared his thought process with his colleagues during their discussions and made clear when the solution would require learning on the part of both parties. As he would assure his colleagues during such discussions, the goal was to find a procedure that would support those colleagues to successfully move forward. As Burnham similarly said at the end of "Coming Home" (*Star Trek: Discovery* S04E13; Paradise & Osunsanmi, 2022) to the oddly familiar looking president of United Earth when asked if she was ready to continue the work of leadership, "Let's get to it."

> ### GUIDANCE FROM GUINAN
>
> Imagine yourself sitting at a small table under the arching windows of Ten Forward, the frontmost point and social hub of the U.S.S. *Enterprise*. The view out the windows is one of stark blackness punctuated by countless points of light, stars of every imaginable color. Sitting across the table is Guinan, the unofficial sage of the starship. Wise beyond measure, Guinan has served for centuries as a guide to innumerable leaders. Now she is fully present in the moment with you.
>
> "What's on your mind?" Guinan asks you with that knowingly subtle smile. "You mentioned you were thinking about Captain Burnham. What about her stands out to you as a leader to model?"
>
> Guinan continues to look at you expectantly. There is no hint of impatience, just that twinkle in her eye. "Think of Burnham's approach to leadership," she suggests. "How does your behavior as a leader compare with hers?"
>
> Guinan looks out the windows to the stars for a moment, and then turns back to you. "How do you *communicate* with others in a manner that is intentional and transparent?"
>
> After giving you a moment to think and respond, Guinan asks you, "How do you exercise *patience* by listening to what others have to say?"
>
> Guinan listens to your response, momentarily closes her eyes

and nods with a smile, and then poses one more question to you. "How do you develop a relationship with others so that they feel seen and heard?"

After you respond, you and Guinan chat a bit longer before she has to return to her customers. You look back out at the stars, toward the seemingly endless potential of leadership, and think about how to lead more like Burnham.

Chapter 4

Pike: Reluctant Warrior

It seems that no matter how many centuries pass, the familiar trappings of a conference room remain invariant. Sure, the technology has changed with the times, but not the familiars. As the door whooshes shut behind you, you notice the lack of windows, the slightly irritating overhead lighting, and a table in the back laden with cookies and urns of coffee. The more things change, the more they stay the same.

You nod to a number of colleagues milling about the room, some standing in the corners and others at the table in the center of the room. Most of them are physically present but several are joining via holo. Automatically, you drift toward the snack table to select a cookie or two (or five) and a cup of coffee. There are so many cookies. Uh-oh, you think. The committee chair anticipates a long meeting.

Cookies and caffeine in hand, you find a seat at the conference table after exchanging the necessary pleasantries with a number of your colleagues. Some of them you regularly interact with by dint of your respective roles. Others you see only at these meetings.

As you settle into your chair and scan the room (how is it that we can travel amidst the stars on great interstellar ships but not engineer a comfortable conference chair?) you are reminded of what astrophysicist Avi Loeb (2021) once said about the importance of remaining rigorously curious about the Universe. Most of the people before you share this sentiment.

The chair calls the meeting to order and you pull up the agenda on your tablet. There is much to accomplish today and it will not be done without debate. Your attention is drawn toward the head of the table as you are asked to speak to the first item. You rack your brain for a leadership exemplar that might inform the moment and your thoughts settle upon how Captain Pike would begin his comments. As you pull up your notes, you remember the value of being formal yet flexible (basic

Leadership in *Star Trek*

leadership skill: **communication***) and making certain to ask for competing opinions when you make your strongest points. You also pepper your comments with a bit of humor (basic leadership skill:* **patience***), knowing that even a small degree of levity can facilitate the social dynamics often necessary in important work (basic leadership skill:* **relationship***)*.

Captain's Log

Christopher Pike (played initially by Jeffrey Hunter, more recently Anson Mount) was born circa 2205 in Mojave, California, on Earth, where he developed a fondness for horses at a young age. He was also exposed to science and comparative religion by his father, a teacher of both subjects. This would result in a decent amount of confusion on his part as he attempted to make sense of the world as an adolescent (Goldsman et al., 2019). Ultimately, Pike chose a future among the stars and applied to Starfleet Academy. While there, he earned top marks in all but one course and demonstrated a somewhat limited ability to process alcohol (Memory Alpha, n.d. e). Pike's first assignment subsequent to graduation was as a test pilot. He would later be stationed as an officer aboard the U.S.S. *Antares*, the U.S.S. *Chatelet*, and the U.S.S. *Aryabhatta*, and then as first officer under Captain Robert April on the U.S.S. *Enterprise* (Sullivan et al., 2019). Pike eventually would become captain of *Enterprise*, interrupted by a brief and ultra-top secret stint in command of the U.S.S. *Discovery*, and go on to explore many strange, new worlds.

Pike became recognized early in his career as a capable tactician. It thus came as a surprise to him that he and his crew were kept unaware and at a distance from the Federation during its war with the Klingon Empire. When Pike later asked why this had been so, he was told that *Enterprise* had been kept away so that the best of the Federation might survive should the Federation fall (*Star Trek: Discovery* S02E01; Sullivan et al., 2019). No pressure, right?

Indeed, Pike demonstrated a level of self-sacrifice few individuals would be able to make. In order to stop a malign sentient artificial intelligence from taking over the Galaxy (yes, it's a well-worn trope in *Star Trek*), he and the crew of the *Discovery* used their experimental drive to jump to the planet Boreth, the most sacred site in the Klingon Empire,

Chapter 4. Pike: Reluctant Warrior

to retrieve a time crystal from an ancient Klingon monastery. These time crystals revealed to the holder particular events in their future. Upon taking a crystal in hand, Pike saw his own future when in his mind's eye he was immediately transported to the engineering section of the U.S.S. *Republic*. There was chaos all around him. He saw himself (now adorned in the regalia of a fleet captain) rushing cadets out of that section of the ship. Warning sirens echoed through the corridors. Suddenly, a baffle plate ruptured in the ship's reactor, bathing Pike in deadly radiation and instantly disfiguring him.

After seeing his future-self so badly injured, Pike was then whisked to an empty hallway of what appeared to be a Starfleet corridor. Hearing an almost demonic beeping and hissing coming from something non-human, Pike turned around to see the hardly recognizable remnant of his former self confined to the neck in a life-sustaining wheelchair. At this point, he returned to the present moment back in the cave of time crystals. How does one move forward having literally seen one's end? As a *reluctant warrior*, when presented with the choice between walking away (literally and figuratively) from that future or setting the horrific destiny in stone, Pike recited the code of all Starfleet officers to himself and chose his fate in order to ensure the safety of those students he would eventually save (*Star Trek: Discovery* S02E12; Kim et al., 2019).

Canon Fodder

Pike demonstrated an exceptional ability to leverage both reason and compassion in his leadership. A leader with a formidable set of skills, he made it a point to actively solicit input from others in order to better make decisions. He also knew how to pepper even the most harrowing of situations with a subtle sense of humor that facilitated his ability to leverage the basic leadership skills of *communication*, *patience*, and *relationship*. Moreover, Pike was dedicated to serve those with whom he served, to "take the risks to initiate, to provide the ideology and the structure, to go ahead and show the way…." (Greenleaf, 1970, p. 41) to those who followed him. Pike understood that people working together meant there was more potential to solve difficult problems.

Pike also was clearly dedicated to the ideals of Enlightenment thinking. For example, we can observe his dedication to the use of logic in service of others amidst his decision-making when aboard *Enterprise*. In "Strange New Worlds" (*Star Trek: Strange New Worlds* S01E01; Goldsman et al., 2022), Pike found himself speaking to the leaders of two antagonistic factions on Kiley 279. Having been mired in centuries of war, the factions were ready to leverage unimaginable power to solve their disagreements once and for all. Instead, Pike cautioned against a reliance on power to solve problems. He instead argued for the utility of debate and negotiation to guide decision-making regardless of the stakes by explaining the ethos of the Federation. An enlightened society seeks not militaristic conquest but social growth through encounters with new peoples, experiences, and ideas. Long before replicators would help usher the Federation into a postscarcity society, Pike recognized the potential of logic to promote flourishing among those he led.

Pike similarly appears to have been well on his way toward self-actualization despite having only been in his 40s. We see this in the way he struggled with an acute awareness of his own mortality and how it helped him to lead with a sense of optimistic realism. While searching for time crystals in the Klingon monastery on Boreth (which we hear is lovely in the spring), Pike was made privy to a rather visceral glimpse of his future (*Star Trek: Discovery* S02E12; Kim et al., 2019). It was not bright, and its revelation forced him to seriously question the meaning of his decisions past and future. Rogers (1967) cited the importance of actively questioning not merely one's own identity, but of how such a consideration might allow for the creation of a more intentional personal future. With time and guidance, Pike was able to overcome what many would have perceived as an insurmountable psychological obstacle. As he said, "we can go forward together knowing that, whatever shadows we bring with us, they make the light all the brighter" (Goldsman et al., 2022).

Cage

Things are not always as they appear, and it is during such times that leading in an enlightened manner can be especially challenging. This proved abundantly true in "The Cage" (*Star Trek: The Original*

Chapter 4. Pike: Reluctant Warrior

Series S00E01; Roddenberry & Butler, 1988; but produced as a pilot episode in 1965) when Pike and his crew set course for Talos IV in response to a distress call. There, he was welcomed by a beautiful young woman amidst a seemingly idyllic setting. Unfortunately, it was revealed before long that Pike's experience on Talos IV was a telepathically induced illusion based on his memories and desires. The Talosians had actually summoned Pike to help provide breeding stock for their new society. Upon realizing what was going on, Pike refused to consent with the Talosians' plan, even rebuffing the offer of an Orion slave girl along the way (how very 1960s), and instead attempted to starve himself to death lest he be further manipulated. After some intercultural conflict and the use of Federation technology, the Talosians relented and allowed Pike and his crew to go free.

The episode certainly had some problematic issues. Yes, we understand it was written decades ago. No, that doesn't really excuse the blatant sexism and stereotypes. The episode nonetheless reminds us that there is always more than one way to look at a situation. Bolman and Deal (2017) advised that leadership benefits from a multi-frame perspective. This is akin to the notion that there are three sides to every story (e.g., Pike's, the Talosians,' and the truth). Leadership requires that we consider a broad possibility space around a problem and not be duped into believing that our initial insights are accurate. How do those involved understand the situation (basic leadership skill: *communication*)? What resources are available or absent (basic leadership skill: *patience*)? What does it all mean to everyone (basic leadership skill: *relationship*)? The answers we uncover may be complimentary, competing, or some combination of the two. What is important is that leaders consider a range of viewpoints before making major decisions. One person's trash is another person's gold-pressed latinum.

Brother

One of the most difficult tasks in leadership is to be asked to proverbially right the ship as its new captain. History is littered with the failed attempts of new presidents and chief executive officers, often backed with the blessing and stock options of their boards. The case of John Sculley at Apple is a prime example. Such transitions occur in many areas of leadership and are often difficult even in the best of times. People often fear the unknown, and change that is not well articulated in process can drive a resulting anxiety across an organization. The difficulties of leadership transition further can be compounded when the incoming leader is unfamiliar to those they serve and might be perceived, rightly or wrongly, as not having their best interests in mind.

In "Brother" (*Star Trek: Discovery* S02E01; Sullivan et al., 2019), Pike was given command of *Discovery* in order to determine the identity of a series of mysterious beacons discovered across the Galaxy. This sudden change of command came unannounced and during a time of crisis. Pike could not afford to lose time holding lots of meetings with his new crew to smooth things over. Instead, he sought to mitigate the anxiety (and anger) among the *Discovery* bridge crew by acknowledging the discomfort of the situation. He was there to serve, a stance that

> requires that the concerned individual accepts the problems [they see] in the world as [their] own personal task, as a means of achieving [their] own integrity. [They see] the external manifestations of this internal achievement as beginning with caring for individual persons, in ways that require dedication and skill and that help them grow and become healthier, stronger, and more autonomous [Greenleaf, 1970, p. 37].

As Pike admitted to them upon his arrival (basic leadership skill: *communication*), "If I were you, I'd have doubts about me, as well" (Sullivan et al., 2019). Indeed, Greenleaf (1970) cautioned that servant leadership is often not popular, but it absolutely can be effective. In the episode, the fate of the Federation might be hanging on their concerted actions as a crew. Pike acted in a manner that demonstrated his integrity and his abilities, but in a manner that made clear he took no one for granted (basic leadership skill: *patience*). Trust in leadership must be earned; anxiety due to change is all but guaranteed. By striking the right balance of reason and compassion (basic leadership skill: *relationship*), Pike was able to navigate a seemingly insurmountable situation.

New

"Strange New Worlds" (*Star Trek: Strange New Worlds* S01E01; Goldsman et al., 2022) is easily one of the strongest premiers of any

Chapter 4. Pike: Reluctant Warrior

series in the *Star Trek* franchise as it introduces us to a captain at once familiar and new. The episode also provides much fodder for consideration through the lens of leadership. It begins with Pike having taken some time off from his command duties aboard *Enterprise*. Months ago, while assisting the crew of *Discovery* to save the Galaxy, Pike learned the specifics of his death, or as he put it, of the death of the individual he thought knew himself to be. We then observe how Pike attempts to address his own mortality through the thoughtfully crafted B-story of the episode. The irony is that leaders rarely are provided with such insight to the future. Instead of knowing exactly what will happen going forward, leadership is instead typified by the challenges of uncertainty.

As Ursin and Eriksen (2004) observed, "predictability, a sense of control, and feedback all permit the organism to reduce it [*sic*] levels of arousal" (p. 581). In other words, knowing an event is going to be quite likely or quite unlikely tends to provide a sense of comfort in planning. A leader can proceed with some degree of confidence in what to expect. Of course, in the episode, Pike was overcome by the dread certainty of how he would be met by his mortality. He was also struck by the irony of the situation. As he related to his chief of security, he had often observed not fear, but surprise, on the faces of those about to meet their end. Considered through the lens of leadership, we often tend to imagine reality as far more certain than it really is. This is a defense mechanism, an automatic attempt to ward against the anxiety of the unknown. In the short term, the resultant yet illusory sense of comfort can help us to cope with the apprehension of what lies ahead. In the long term, however, such an emotional shield risks preventing us from responding dynamically to the needs of those we serve.

At the end of the episode, we get a hint of Pike's growth in grappling with the certainty of his otherwise uncertain future. When asked as to their mission, he reiterates the importance of exploration, of seeking out new problems to be solved. He did so in a manner that indicated his comfort at facing uncertainty (basic leadership skill: *communication*). Pike did not offer specifics or mandates, but instead created an emotional space for his bridge crew to process their charge (basic leadership skill: *patience*). Perhaps as importantly as any of it, he addressed his crew with a tone that welcomed their participation in the adventures of leadership facing them in the viewscreen (basic leadership skill: *relationship*). As Pike expressed toward the end of the episode (Goldsman et al., 2022), "our ability to work together, that's our greatest strength." How much more so this is true in the face of uncertainty.

Children

Leadership is an exercise in the practice of navigating obstacles. Some obstacles are structural, such as presented by time-consuming chains of approval or the antiquated requirement of signatures on digital forms. These roadblocks are often external to the problem to be solved and are clearly identifiable along the way. Other obstacles are social or political, manifest by the beliefs if not outright agendas of those with whom one must work during the making of decisions. These obstructions to progress are typically much less obvious and sometimes more potent in derailing the work of a leader. In our experience, it is the latter category of obstacles that tends to be the more pernicious and thus require the leader to remain vigilant regarding the ground-truth of the situation.

In "Children of the Comet" (*Star Trek: Strange New Worlds* S01E02; Myers et al., 2022), Pike and his crew faced a similar conundrum when they sought to assist the pre-warp civilization of Persephone III from what appeared to be an inevitable extinction-level event. They consequently got to work on formulating methods that might safely redirect the rapidly approaching comet past the planet. Although the challenge appeared significant, Pike recognized the physical parameters of the situation and responded accordingly. He was thus surprised when their initial attempt at intervention met with the comet raising shields. What was going on here? It was soon revealed that there was more than met the eye about the situation. The comet possessed a secret. We might even say it revealed an agenda. This is often the reality of leadership. Problems that appear to have relatively clear-cut solutions sometimes manifest complications that require a shift in understanding.

Yin et al. (2019) found a notable difference in the failure dynamics (use that one in polite conversation when you get the chance) of more and less successful teams. Whereas some teams responded to failure with greater time spent in review, those teams who subse-

Chapter 4. Pike: Reluctant Warrior

quently found success appeared to be more likely to "fail forward" by making more rapid leaps in problem-solving. Indeed, Wuchty et al. (2007) found that essentially all fields of inquiry have undergone a shift from the lone researcher to a team-based approach toward inquiry. Pike demonstrated such findings through his decision-making in the Persephone system. When his initial response to the manifest obstacles of the situation resulted in failure, he sought alternative perspectives and quickly retooled. Key to this process was a reliance on his bridge crew (go Team Enterprise!) to help identify those obstacles not yet obvious.

In this way, Pike demonstrated his ability to leverage the best of his crew through the patient recognition of their individual skill sets (basic leadership skill: *communication*). Even amidst the urgency of the episode, he paused when necessary to conceptually regroup and search for new solutions (basic leadership skill: *patience*). Pike also recognized the value in sometimes addressing the absurdity of a situation. As he said, "sometimes things go so badly you just have to laugh" (Myers et al., 2022). In doing so, he rallied the confidence of his crew (basic leadership skill: *relationship*) while never giving up.

Ghosts

During World War II, "loose lips sink ships" became a common trope heard on the streets and among the media. It was a time of war and anxieties in the United States ran high regarding the potential of seemingly harmless information to be leveraged in service of military aggression. It was also coincident with this time that the practice of leadership took on an overt focus on transaction-based management. Leadership was said to work best within hierarchical schemes typified by the rationing of information and closely held trade secrets. In "Ghosts of Illyria" (*Star Trek: Strange New Worlds* S01E03; Cooper et al., 2022), perhaps the franchise's best incarnation so far of the "shipwide contamination" plot device, the first officer of *Enterprise* finds herself between a proverbial rock and a hard place when an unknown infection spreads among the crew. As Commander Chin-Riley observed, "people are always hiding things" (Cooper et al., 2022). Our own experiences have taught us that this often remains true in leadership. Whether in the far future or just the other day, keeping secrets regularly seems par for the course.

With the advantage of historical retrospect, we would suggest the obverse. It is a bad idea to keep secrets in leadership. There are, of course, situations that require a great deal of tact. Other items necessitate by law the keeping of strict confidentiality. Yet, such issues typically represent a mere fraction of cases for most leaders. Secrets are more likely the result of anxiety and a wish to defend one's interests than they are justifiable means to be an effective leader. Think about this idea for a moment. Why do you keep secrets in your personal life? Is it to protect someone? Or is it to protect yourself from the anxieties inherent to the truth you seek to prevent others from seeing? Now, consider the broader implications of keeping secrets within an organization and the message it might send to those one serves. As O'Toole and Bennis (2009) observed,

> No organization can be honest with the public if it's not honest with itself. But being honest inside an organization is more difficult than it sounds. People hoard information, engage in groupthink, tell their boss only what they think he wants to hear, and ignore facts that are staring them in the face.... To counter these natural tendencies, leaders need to make a conscious decision to support transparency and create a culture of candor.

Pike revealed this natural tendency when he was trapped on the surface of Hetemit IX and admitted that "I don't like feeling helpless" (Cooper et al., 2022). None of us do.

Nonetheless, we each have the option to not keep secrets unnecessarily in our leadership while modeling a culture of trust among those we serve by how we respond to their own secrets. When presented with such a situation at the end of the episode and the possibility of losing a good officer, Pike responded with enlightened empathy instead of derision. He listened intently to his officer without introducing his own preconceived notions into the discussion (basic leadership skill: *communication*). Pike also recognized the gravitas of the conversation and allowed it to unfold (basic leadership skill: *patience*). When asked how he might address the secret, Pike quietly responded that he would welcome the discussion (basic leadership skill: *relationship*). Organizations are not ships to be sunk. Secrets are not tools to be wielded for effective leadership.

Chapter 4. Pike: Reluctant Warrior

Momento

Leadership can be akin to exploration in that both endeavors often result in encountering the unknown. Moreover, as Pike observed in "Memento Mori" (*Star Trek: Strange New Worlds* S01E04; Perez et al., 2022), "when we seek out the unknown, we will find things that challenge us." This is part of the joy as well as difficulty of assuming the mantle of leadership. Although one might possess a great deal of experience, and no little passion for the cause, it is impossible to foresee all of the circumstances and their nuances on the proverbial horizon. In the episode, Pike was required to consider unconventional solutions to what appeared to be an intractable problem, one that grew in extremity over the course of the episode. Pike and his crew had encountered the Gorn Hegemony, a society both unfamiliar and different to Federation norms. As might be expected of anyone, he initially responded by relying on his previous experience and a set of seemingly tried-and-true assumptions. When this reasonable response to the situation at hand proved unsuccessful, Pike advised his crew to "Be vigilant. Get creative…. We survive this by working together" (Perez et al., 2022).

Leadership is fundamentally about problem-solving. Sometimes, the problems set before us are sufficiently novel to require a rethinking of one's options for response. As Reiter-Palmon and Illies (2004) wrote, the work of leadership is often beset by poorly defined problems that require novel solutions. Leaders cannot merely rely on their people to navigate those problems but must lend the requisite support to ensure their generation (Reiter-Palmon & Illies, 2004). Mumford and Todd (2020) similarly stressed the importance of creativity, "the capacity to produce original, high-quality, and elegant" (p. 4) solutions as the hallmark of innovative decision-making in leadership. While we think that the expectation of elegance in one's solutions might be more than necessary on a daily basis, their point remains valid. Novel situations periodically necessitate new response sets.

In the episode, Pike recognized the importance of changing his tactics in order to survive the encounter with the Gorn Hegemony. He understood that leadership is not about winning, but succeeding in solving the problems that lay before us. Along the way, Pike demonstrated his ability to cognitively pivot by actively responding to suggestions from his officers (basic leadership skill: *communication*) and taking the

Leadership in *Star Trek*

time for the problem to more fully manifest itself (basic leadership skill: *patience*). Pike also took the time to ensure his crew that things would be all right even in the darkest hour (basic leadership skill: *relationship*). Put simply, leadership calls us to be both creative and humble.

Hit It

How can we take these lessons and apply them to our own leadership? It is one thing to respect a giant of leadership like Pike but another to implement his lessons into our daily choices. Let's take each of the examples above and see how they might fit with our own needs.

Human behavior is complex, especially when you put a bunch of people (human or otherwise) together within an organizational environment. "The Cage" (*Star Trek: The Original Series* S00E01; Roddenberry & Butler, 1988) reminds us that our first perceptions will always be biased due to personal preconceptions and incomplete information. Although Pike initially accepted his interaction with the Talosians on face value, he and his crew came to recognize that there were inconsistencies. They were clearly missing the bigger picture. The key was to ask questions. How could Vina have lived for so long as a young human on Talos IV. Why couldn't a mounted phaser of unusual size melt through the entrance to the cave? In leadership, it is important to assume that we never have all of the information and that our own perceptions of a problem are necessarily limited. Thinning rationally is key. After all, we are not Q.

In addition to ensuring that we consider problems from multiple perspectives, leadership also requires that we recognize that change often breeds anxiety. We are called on to lead with compassion, with a recognition of the emotional needs of others. In "Brother" (*Star Trek: Discovery* S02E01; Sullivan et al., 2019), Pike stepped unannounced into the command chair of *Discovery* during a time of crisis. Acting Captain Saru was already respected by the crew and they knew how he managed challenging situations. Now, there was a new captain in town without warning. A lesser individual would have bristled at having his hooves stepped on in such a manner. Similarly, it would have been understandable for the bridge crew to question such a transition. Everyone did what they needed to do, and did so with integrity, in order to meet the crisis

Chapter 4. Pike: Reluctant Warrior

of the moment because they were Starfleet, the best of the best (except for that scientist who modified the Tribbles) and that's what they do. Alas, we do not (yet) live in the Federation and we cannot assume that those we lead will respond with such quickness of understanding. Pike recognized that he had to relate with the bridge crew and not merely lead them.

Remembering to connect with those one serves can prove especially challenging when faced with uncertain situations. Anxiety is a natural response to the unknown. In "Strange New Worlds" (*Star Trek: Strange New Worlds* S01E01; Goldsman et al., 2022), Pike was called back to duty at a time in his life when the future before him seemed quite unsettling. He even questioned whether he had the right to lead. Although every leader can be expected to encounter a unique set of larger or smaller challenges, the reality is that everyone of us will be faced with unclear options if we choose to lead. This is simply a common feature of leadership. Will we muster the ability to move forward or find ourselves stuck in the concerns of the moment? Most of us are not going to have the benefit (or curse) of finding a time crystal along the way. Instead, we can choose to lead through uncertainty by relying on our skills, looking toward our responsibilities, and remembering that we need not lead alone.

Obstacles are a constant in leadership. Regardless of the arena in which one leads, something unexpected is guaranteed to arise (just ask Badgey). This is as true in education as it is in business. Of course, space presents its own set of problems to be solved. In "Children of the Comet" (*Star Trek: Strange New Worlds* S01E02; Myers et al., 2022), we saw how beliefs can pose as much of a challenge as can astronomical bodies. Yet, Pike was able to leverage teamwork as part of the solution to the difficulties that faced the crew of *Enterprise*. So, too, in our own leadership have we found collaborating with others to be one of the most useful approaches toward effective leadership. Pike did not lead in isolation, nor did he hesitate to leverage the capacity of his officers to augment his own. Failing forward can result in success, but it is important to remember that one need not fail or succeed alone.

We obviously do not like secrets. With the exception that a good spoiler can ruin an episode or film, it is better to keep information on instead of below the proverbial table. This was made abundantly clear in "Ghosts of Illyria" (*Star Trek: Strange New Worlds* S01E03; Cooper et al., 2022), a beautiful episode that reminds us that secrets in leadership can hurt people. Such a practice is orthogonal to effective leadership as it can promote groupthink and its inherent polarization of thought. Yes, there are those select matters where ethics or law require a leader to protect the privacy of another individual. Such instances, however, do not come up with frequency in most leadership roles (unless you work in human resources). One need only to read or watch the news to see demonstrations of seemingly intelligent people who are completely polarized in their perceptions of the world. We question how such a limited ability to make decisions can meaningfully contribute to the world.

Unconventional solutions, by definition, can be difficult to come by. This tends to be especially true when the problems before us promote anxiety and even fear caused by a future unknown. "Memento Mori" (*Star Trek: Strange New Worlds* S01E04; Perez et al., 2022) demonstrated the importance of remaining grounded in the present when considering the future. In the episode, Pike and his crew were faced with seemingly impossible odds. Instead of sending a bunch of red shirts in to handle the situation, Pike sought options from some of his crew and relied on others to fulfill their roles even in a time of crisis. Such leadership requires both experience and trust. It also can benefit, as Pike observed, from a belief in one's ability as a team to solve the presenting problem. There might not be many quick fixes in leadership, but there is no shortage of opportunities to think creatively, collaborate closely, and execute with intention.

Jason once served as an interim dean at a previous college during a time when there was a fair bit of anxiety among the faculty regarding course enrollment. Shortly after accepting the role, he called a division meeting and asked all of the faculty he served, tenure-stream and adjunct alike, to join him for an opportunity to chat. Having never before served in administration, he spent significant time preparing a detailed handout that plotted the enrollment numbers over time of every one of the relevant departments. When the meeting came to order, he distributed the handout to the 70-plus faculty in attendance and began to dive into the data. Instead, the graph was dead on arrival. The faculty wanted to talk, to ask questions, to know what they could expect from their new interim dean. So, on the spot, he pivoted in response to the needs of those he served. He still made sure to address

Chapter 4. Pike: Reluctant Warrior

the points he wanted to cover. But he did so in a way that demonstrated a willingness to relate as professionals with common goals in mind. The result was that the faculty were willing to hear him out and work with him.

Aaron also can appreciate what it is like to sit in the proverbial captain's chair when it has been recently vacated, particularly when it is previously occupied by someone who was very well liked. He encountered this situation when he took a directorship at a university. The incumbent had left the position but stayed on at the university to assume a similar role in a different division. It was clear that his staff held their former supervisor in high regard. He thus made it a point to sit down with his new faculty and staff and acknowledge the great work of his predecessor. He even sought their advice at times. However, he was also careful to navigate each situation with his own approach. This allowed him over time to develop a rapport with his colleagues in a manner that facilitated an enjoyable work environment for all involved.

It is worth mentioning that Pike was one of the most decorated officers in the history of Starfleet. These accolades came from his actions during times of military conflict. Yet, Pike recognized the value of a little bit of humor to defuse even the most dire of situations. By doing so, he created space in which those he led could feel more comfortable to suggest solutions. Pike understood that almost any situation is better served when one remains flexible on the way to meeting their obligations. We might take a page from his lesson book and remember that a little bit of humor can help us to better serve the people we are expected to lead.

GUIDANCE FROM GUINAN

Imagine yourself sitting at a small table under the arching windows of Ten Forward, the frontmost point and social hub of the U.S.S. *Enterprise*. The view out the windows is one of stark blackness punctuated by countless points of light, stars of every imaginable color. Sitting across the table is Guinan, the unofficial sage of the starship. Wise beyond measure, Guinan has served for centuries as a guide to innumerable leaders. Now she is fully present in the moment with you.

"What's on your mind?" Guinan asks you with that knowingly subtle smile. "You mentioned you were thinking about Captain Pike. What about him stands out to you as a leader to model?"

Leadership in *Star Trek*

Guinan continues to look at you expectantly. There is no hint of impatience, just that twinkle in her eye. "Think of Pike's approach to leadership," she suggests. "How does your behavior as a leader compare with his?"

Guinan looks out the windows to the stars for a moment, and then turns back to you. "How do you *communicate* with others in a manner that is intentional and transparent?"

After giving you a moment to think and respond, Guinan asks you, "How do you exercise *patience* by listening to what others have to say?"

Guinan listens to your response, momentarily closes her eyes and nods with a smile, and then poses one more question to you. "How do you develop a relationship with others so that they feel seen and heard?"

After you respond, you and Guinan chat a bit longer before she has to return to her customers. You look back out at the stars, toward the seemingly endless potential of leadership, and think about how to lead more like Pike.

CHAPTER 5

Kirk: Charismatic Cowboy

The meeting, and it had been a long one, was finally nearing its end. You feel it in the way the timbre of the room begins to change, note it by the barren table once laden with cookies and now covered in crumbs and coffee stains. There are many looks of approval around the table, a few looks of disagreement, and at least one colleague looking down at their lap (get off your PADD, Jennifer!). People are beginning to arrange their sundries slowly as if not to draw attention to themselves. You put away your own tablet as plans are agreed upon for the next meeting.

Your thoughts drift to a review of your own performance during the meeting. The report had gone about as well as could be expected. You knew that some of your colleagues would raise challenges, but you remained confident in your conclusions based on the available evidence. At the same time, you know they raised fair points and accept you might be wrong on a few of those points. As organizational psychologist Adam Grant (2021) demonstrated in his research centuries ago, it is important to think again and again about one's strongly held positions.

The meeting over, you watch with bemusement as a number of your colleagues meander back to the carbs table in search of scraps before departing. As you stand from your chair and stretch, the muscles of your back quietly protest their ergonomic subjugation of the past hours. It would be a while until you had to catch your flight. Knowing this, you take your time milling around the conference room, making certain to connect with a number of your colleagues. It seems there is never enough time in the standard year to catch up with one another. Chatting via viewscreen just isn't the same thing as kibitzing in person.

Eventually, you remove yourself from the dwindling group and head toward the door. As it swooshes apart to allow your passage you notice the long shadows cast across the lobby floor. There is a stop you would like to

Leadership in *Star Trek*

make before the sun sets, a place of quietude that will allow you time to reflect on the happenings of the day.

After a turbolift ride down to street level, you find yourself once again amidst the beauty of San Francisco. The golden light at the end of the day is everywhere, reflecting off the shining towers and spilling along the streets between the shadows. The hovercar traffic seems exceptionally heavy overhead this evening. Although largely silent, it only adds to the vibrancy of this place.

You stretch once more, welcoming the cracks you hear and feel, and hail an automated cab. You settle into the comfortable seat (finally...) and take out your tablet to compose a series of communications in follow-up to the meeting. As you prepare to dictate your first message, you stop for a moment to consider the importance of crafting messages in a manner that will generate useful dialogue instead of defensiveness. Captain Kirk comes to mind, likely triggered by the docuvid you watched last week. When not attempting to score a date, how might he have expressed himself in such a moment? You exhale, allowing your thoughts to settle, and begin dictating your message with honesty (basic leadership skill: **communication***) and the intent to clarify a number of points for consideration (basic leadership skill:* **patience***). You explain the logic of your thinking and close the message with a request for feedback (basic leadership skill:* **relationship***).*

Captain's Log

There is likely no captain more eminent in the annals of *Star Trek* canon than James Tiberius Kirk (played by William Shatner). Numerous series and films have introduced multiple generations to canon, with James T. Kirk ostensibly the most recognized character in all of Trekdom due to both his status and his behavior. Born in 2233 on the plains of Iowa, Earth, and later raised on Tarsus IV, Kirk distinguished himself as an exceptionally talented cadet while studying at Starfleet Academy. Although better known for his gregarious personality, Kirk was in fact exceptionally intelligent. This admixture of abilities manifested itself prominently during his studies and later throughout his exceptional career. Kirk's character development also demonstrated how mainstream perspectives on gender in the real world evolved from the 1960s to the 2000s.

One of the most notable examples of Kirk's approach toward

Chapter 5. Kirk: Charismatic Cowboy

problem-solving was his response to the *Kobayashi Maru*, a scenario infamous within *Star Trek* and designed to assess the ability of future officers to navigate impossible situations and thereby test their mettle (Memory Alpha, n.d. f). It is interesting to note that the notion of leaders being tested by way of their training is a recurrent theme in *Star Trek*. Certainly, all leaders are tested by the situations in which they lead. However, in canon we are privy to intentional attempts to discover the limits of a leader's self-awareness of their weaknesses. The *Kobayashi Maru* scenario offers the example of a situation in which testing is designed to reveal how issues such as personal pride and fear of loss can interfere with successful leadership in high-stress situations. Years later, we similarly witness Welsy Crusher being challenged during the "psych test" portion of the Starfleet entrance examinations (*Star Trek: The Next Generation* S01E19; Fries & Vejar, 1988).

What makes the *Kobayashi Maru* unique both within *Star Trek* lore and for our purposes of leadership training is that it offers an example of an unwinnable test. The scenario also offers a prime demonstration of Kirk's unique style of leadership. He was able to beat the test by reprogramming it before taking it for a third time. Indeed, Kirk repeatedly demonstrated a willingness to take chances when he thought there to be a likelihood of success. This perspective was coupled to a belief that he could escape negative consequences. Indeed, although Kirk was initially accused of cheating on the test (an accusation he vigorously denied), he was ultimately awarded a commendation for original thinking. Later in life, when questioned about the event, Kirk observed that "I don't believe in the no-win scenario" (*Star Trek II: The Wrath of Khan*; Bennett et al, 1982). This attitude toward seeing all problems as having solutions would typify his future leadership.

Kirk demonstrated myriad examples of such spirited leadership throughout his career, beginning with assignments to the U.S.S. *Farragut* and the U.S.S. *Republic*, and eventually followed by a career-spanning captaincy of the U.S.S. *Enterprise*. It was during his initial five-year mission as captain aboard *Enterprise* (no bloody A, B, C, or D) that we can observe how a breadth of experience can prompt maturity from being a brash captain (just watch "The Man Trap"; *Star Trek: The Original Series* S01E05; Johnson & Daniels, 1966) to an individual who would one day serve as an admiral. Yet, the joie de vivre that Kirk demonstrated in his youth never left him. Even at the end of his days, Kirk summed up his life as having been "fun" (*Star Trek: Generations*; Berman et al., 1994). He was dedicated to seeking solutions until the very end.

Kirk was a character larger than life whose certainty regarding his own abilities was regularly supported by the evidence of his successes. Especially instructive for us is that Kirk did so without losing his ability to reason regardless of the direness of the situation. He experienced loss and challenge (Khan!!!!) again and again, yet remained passionate about his work and derived meaning from the crises that challenged him and his crew on a seemingly weekly basis. It is this final point that merits special attention for experienced as well as aspiring leaders. Kirk demonstrated a recognition of purpose in his work. He treated obstacles not as threats but as intriguing problems to be solved. As Kirk stated to his bridge crew during his early tenure as captain, "The face of the unknown, I think I owe you a look at it" (Sohl & Sargent, 1966). As a *charismatic cowboy*, it was with this unabashed boldness that he carried into every facet of his career and life.

Canon Fodder

Kirk manifested a seemingly illimitable spirit that affected the lives of many. He was a highly rational individual, yet also a passionate one. As the most infamous of the captains, Kirk set a model for countless other characters to emulate by portraying a complex individual able to leverage the basic leadership skills of *communication, patience*, and *relationship*. Kirk was never one to back down from a fight. Nonetheless, he knew it was better to find solutions than to engage when outgunned. Kirk was thus an adherent to Boyd's (Wikipedia, n.d. c) OODA principles (observe, orient, decide, and act) during times of crisis. In spite of his tendency toward quick thinking, he regularly weighed his odds before acting.

Through it all, Kirk provides an example of a passionate leader guided by the ideals of Enlightenment thinking. He recognized that rational thought molded by compassion for the needs of others was the ideal basis for solving problems. Indeed, *Star Trek: The Original Series* was noted from its first episodes for its forward thinking perspective on social matters. An example of such progressiveness was the kiss between Kirk and Lieutenant Uhura (Dolinsky & Alexander, 1968). Although it

Chapter 5. Kirk: Charismatic Cowboy

demonstrated exceptionally poor decision-making in leadership (Kirk was Risa long before Commander Riker bought a hor'ghan), it was also one of the first black-white kisses on television. Kirk offers us an example of an all too human leader who put his trust in rational thought and went out of his way to recognize the worth of others.

Indeed, the reality is that while Kirk portrayed a deeply ethical leader, he was not an exceptionally actualized individual. However, he learned. It has been said that growing up is hard to do. Nowhere is this more true than in the practice of leadership. Kirk demonstrated that even the most self-assured individual has the potential to evolve if they are willing to look honestly at themselves and their leadership skills. His character truly grew over the course of the franchise.

Paradise

It has been said that when things seem too good to be true, they probably are. One example of such a situation is the phenomenon of groupthink. A term coined by Whyte (1952), groupthink can occur when the social pressure to conform to group norms results in impoverished decision-making. "This Side of Paradise" (*Star Trek: The Original Series* S01E25; Butler et al., 1967) presents us with an example of how leaders can become caught up in groupthink. In the episode, Kirk and crew were ordered to catalog the remains of a former human colony on the poetically named Omicron Ceti III. They instead discovered upon arrival that the colony remained very much inhabited. Kirk was thus ordered to evacuate the colonists for their own good due to recognized environmental challenges on the planet. At this point, we can surmise that the remainder of the episode is going to feature conflict. Whenever there is a forced evacuation in *Star Trek*, there is going to be conflict.

However, the real challenge of the situation manifested when the officers of *Enterprise* discovered something more to be amiss. It seemed that the colonists were inordinately of one mind on all matters of importance. More concerning, the longer Kirk's crew remained on the surface of the planet, the more congenial they were toward the perspective of the colonists. Officers and crew alike became increasingly enamored

Leadership in *Star Trek*

with the perspective of the colonists. Even the stoic Commander Spock seemed to fall in love with a botanist he had met six years prior. The result was a wholesale conversion, save Kirk, to groupthink.

What is important for our purposes is that Kirk was initially able to resist the lure of groupthink. True to his keen intellect and dedication to mission, he continually challenged the status quo among his officers as they intellectually defected to a more limited perspective. Kirk did so in a manner that was questioning but not confrontative. Contrary to those caught up in the groupthink (Janis, 1971), Kirk continued to express doubts about the decisions his crew were making. In this way, the episode offers us an example of just how difficult it can be for a leader to remain steadfast amidst rapidly changing norms in an organizational setting. Kirk was somewhere out in the Alpha Quadrant and isolated from his support systems as he sought to maintain his independence of thought. We are each mired in technologically mediated social networks that would have been unfathomable to the episode writers of the 1960s. Modern leadership, nonetheless, can be isolating in a different and perhaps more challenging sense of the term. Leaders are exposed to mass communication, social memes, and a news cycle that seems able to change at a moment's notice. The result can be a sort of isolation not created by geographic distance but by social walls.

Kirk demonstrated the importance of always questioning the status quo. We, too, must remain vigilant of not becoming entangled in the latest conceptual fads before testing their predicate ideas against our previous experiences and the current ground truth. This is where the basic leadership skills can serve us well. Kirk recognized that the groupthink maintained by the colonists had spread among his crew and attempted time and again to convince them of their cognitive drift (basic leadership skill: *communication*). It would have been easy after a time for Kirk to submit to the attractiveness of the ideas being accepted on face value all around him. Instead, he remained steadfast to his own thoughts as the situation worsened at every turn (basic leadership skill: *patience*). Ultimately, it was Kirk's ability to recognize the needs of those he served that allowed him to unlock the secret to the mystery of Omicron Ceti III and bring around his most trusted bridge crew to a more reasonable point of view (basic leadership skill: *relationship*). The episode serves as a reminder that leadership benefits when we understand those we lead as whole people.

Chapter 5. Kirk: Charismatic Cowboy

Devil

For the past three months, something had been attacking miners on the planet Janus IV. With more than 50 miners dead and the cause unknown, *Enterprise* was dispatched to investigate. Thus began "The Devil in the Dark" (*Star Trek: The Original Series* S01E26; Coon & Pevney, 1967), an episode about the risk of misunderstanding in leadership (and a warning about the danger of overacting). It is an episode that demonstrates the inherent risk of a lack of awareness on the part of one or both parties. In the episode, it became apparent that the deaths were caused by some unknown creature residing in the mining tunnels. Kirk's initial response was that his officers should shoot to kill and thus prevent any more miner deaths. As he opined to a fellow officer, "there's nothing more dangerous than a wounded animal." However, with the help of his logical friend, Kirk eventually realized that the behaviors of the "creature" were not indiscriminate but instead suggested intelligence.

The episode provides an important lesson relevant for our modern (albeit twenty-first century) times. The world is populated by diverse peoples with myriad ideas, perspectives, beliefs, and backgrounds, to say nothing of their languages. This richness is one of the most wonderful things about humanity and is embodied in the ideal of *IDIC* (infinite diversity in infinite combinations). It has been known for some time that more diverse workgroups are more productive than their homogeneous counterparts (Rock & Grant, 2016). This is science, not merely *Star Trek*. Yet, with diversity comes the potential for misunderstanding. In the episode, Kirk initially was unable to understand the motives of the Horta (i.e., the "creature") who was killing the miners. It was only after his science officer helped translate that it became clear that the Horta had its own view of the conflict. In the episode, the perspective of the miners changed when they came to understand what the Horta had been attempting to communicate. It was this misperception of incompatible interests between the Horta and the miners that perpetuated conflict and bloodshed (not to mention so much paaaaain!).

Of course, leadership in real life rarely results in behavioral change that can fit into an hour-long episode. Misunderstanding is always a risk in leadership. Sometimes it arises from the desire of the various parties to defend their own interests (Mayer, 2000), but other times it is more a matter of poor awareness. This is an onus that rests on the leader. Do we recognize the many different perspectives of those who sit at the proverbial table (or live in the fictional mine)? Are we sufficiently aware of everyone's voice? Delpit (2006) found in their research with communities across the globe that social power differentials are not merely pervasive but tend to encourage misunderstanding from the top down. As she wrote, "Those with power are frequently least aware of—or least willing to acknowledge—its existence, and those with less power are often most aware of its existence" (Delpit, 1988, p. 283). Those in leadership are, by definition, in positions of power. Whether that power be formal or tacit, large or small, that power has the potential to cloud the leader's understanding of what they are seeing, hearing, and assuming.

It is thus incumbent upon us to recognize the limitations of our own assumptions, consult with others when we fear we might be misunderstanding, and actively work to bridge the divides that are all too pervasive in the modern workplace. A Horta's going to do what a Horta's going to do. It is up to those in leadership to better understand the reality of a situation before seeking to adjudicate it.

The reality was that Kirk needed help to meaningfully read the signs of the situation (basic leadership skill: *communication*). Once he became aware that there was more than met the eye, Kirk was motivated to hold off on his original orders. He recognized that they no longer adequately addressed the ground truth basic leadership skill: (*patience*). It might be an exaggeration to assert that Kirk was able to get by with a little help from his friend (Spock, not a Beatle). Yet, he was able to bridge the gap between himself and a hereto unknown species with an entirely different outlook on life (basic leadership skill: *relationship*). We probably can't assume that bridging misunderstandings with those we lead will rectify life-and-death situations. However, it is fair to surmise that reaching a joint understanding can prevent wounded feelings, poor performance, and future obstacles to organizational success.

Mercy

What is a leader to do when they are completely certain of what is right and others can't see it? How can one lead from a reasoned stance yet remain aware of the perspectives and concerns of others? In "Errand of Mercy" (*Star Trek: The Original Series* S01E27; Coon & Newland, 1967),

Chapter 5. Kirk: Charismatic Cowboy

Kirk and his crew were sent to intercede with the peaceful, agrarian society of Organians to accept Federation protection. Kirk explained to their Council of Elders upon arrival that war was imminent between the Federation and the Klingon Empire and that the location of the Organians' planet would put them at grave risk from attack. The Council thanked Kirk for the concern of the Federation and then turned down the offer of protection. They simply did not perceive a clear and present danger. The Organians remained unconcerned even when a fleet of Klingon battle cruisers appeared in orbit and began to beam down an invasion force. This presented Kirk with a dilemma. He and his crew were morally obligated to defend the apparently helpless and hapless Organians from certain catastrophe (curse that Prime Directive). What is a leader to do when they perceive a clear obligation that is not recognized by those they seek to serve?

In the episode, hostilities escalated and Kirk decided that the last hope of doing what was best for the Organians would be to attack the newly established Klingon outpost under the cover of night (because flashlights were apparently not available in the twenty-second century). Kirk (and Spock) made their way into the compound and phaser fire was met with disruptor discharge. It was thus a surprise when the Organians decided they had enough of observing what was mounting toward an all-out war and decided to intercede. The episode ended with Kirk admitting to Spock that he sometimes forgot the Federation was not the most powerful society in the Galaxy.

This observation bears repeating. A major risk of leadership is to presume that one's beliefs are representative of the entire organization. It is incumbent upon leaders to recognize that they are not the only nor most important force in an organization. Although normally cognizant of the need to constantly reevaluate the incoming ground truth during a tense situation, Kirk made the mistake of assuming that he could best solve the crisis before the Organians. Instead, it turned out that there was no crisis other than the one he inadvertently created. Leadership asks that we recognize our own values. It demands that we refrain from imposing those values on others. This ability to check our own assumptions is especially important at times when there is significant polarization in the organization or in society at large. Who are we to be arbiters of right and wrong for all those we lead?

With this caveat in mind, let's look at this situation through the lens of the basic leadership skills. As Kirk said to the Council of Elders, "I'm a soldier, not a diplomat. I can only tell you the truth" (Coon & Newland, 1967). He was clear with the Organians about his concerns for their safety (basic leadership skill: *communication*). Kirk also took the time to wrestle with his conscience before deciding to act against the Organians' wishes to push back the Klingon invasion (basic leadership skill: *patience*). Finally, Kirk relied heavily upon his trust in those with whom he served to solve the situation, although he clearly would have benefited from listening more and asserting his own (mis)understanding of the situation less (basic leadership skill: *relationship*). Perhaps the lesson is that even the most skilled leader can err regardless of the merit of their intent.

Forever

It had been something of a challenge to acclimate to Earth in the 1930s. The clothing was different. The idioms of speech were unfamiliar. Constructing a subspace receiver from radio tubes was nigh impossible. However, the greatest challenge Kirk faced was to allow his current love interest (or was it his past love interest?) to die. It was a tragedy he knew would occur and one he could have prevented. This dilemma also made the episode one of the most heralded in all of Trekdom. It would be so easy for Kirk to shirk his duty, save Edith Keeler, and irrevocably alter the future. "The City at the Edge of Forever" (*Star Trek: The Original Series* S01E28; Ellison & Pevney, 1967) thus presents us with a range of ethical conundra. However, we shall limit ourselves to the reality that sometimes a leader must act against their own wishes in order to meet their responsibilities.

Leadership is typically characterized by an alignment between a leader's values and their professional obligations. Think of the CEO of a corporation, the president of a nonprofit organization, or the principal of an elementary school. Each of these individuals is presumably invested in the goals of their organization as an extension of their own purpose. The decisions they make are aided by the congruence between their values and their responsibilities. But what about those situations in which our personal beliefs do not align with our professional duty? In the episode, Kirk was stuck between a time crystal and a hard place. On the one

Chapter 5. Kirk: Charismatic Cowboy

hand, his personal feelings for Ms. Keeler (not to mention his Federation ideals) motivated him to prevent her death. On the other hand, the evidence strongly suggested that saving Ms. Keeler would result in massive and horrific changes to the timeline. What was a captain to do?

We are guessing that most of our own daily leadership struggles do not yield such far-reaching outcomes as saving the future. Alternatively, there is little doubt that all of us have faced situations in which the objectively "better" choice was the personally distasteful one. Such circumstances call for consultation regarding how to balance reason and compassion (basic leadership skill: *communication*). Instead of summarily deciding on a course of action, Kirk verbalized his internal debate, sought feedback from a trusted colleague, and only then committed to a decision (basic leadership skill: *patience*). Boyd (Wikipedia, n.d. c) stressed that central to effective leadership is the importance of receiving continuous feedback before taking action (basic leadership skill: *relationship*). Not all of us have a Guardian of whom to ask questions. But we likely have colleagues who can challenge our thought process. If not, find some. After all, it's only logical.

Wrath

Much has been written about the relative merits of the various *Star Trek* films. It is widely believed, for example, that the even-numbered films are generally better than the odd-numbered films. However, it strikes us as indisputable that *Star Trek II: The Wrath of Khan* (Bennett et al., 1982) remains the single best film of the franchise. Period. Now, you might have been told otherwise by friends or family. They are wrong. From the plot, to the soundtrack, to the stately battle amid the swirling mists of the Mutara Nebula, *Star Trek II: The Wrath of Khan* is the greatest *Star Trek* film yet produced. End of discussion. Now, where were we?

The film begins with the explosive challenge of the *Kobayashi Maru* simulation at Starfleet Academy. However, we are more interested in the B-plot of the story. We learn that Kirk, who was now 50 years old, had accepted promotion to the rank of admiral and was no longer serving aboard a starship. Instead, he faced what psychologist Erik Erikson (1950) had labeled as the crisis of generativity versus stagnation. Kirk

Leadership in *Star Trek*

found himself questioning what a middle-aged officer could still contribute while wrestling with the developmental limitations of growing older. As Kirk bemoaned to Dr. McCoy, "Galloping around the cosmos is a game for the young" (Bennett et al., 1982). What was the once dashing and dangerously virile captain to do with his newly acquired reading glasses? How was he to make a difference in the Galaxy?

Captain Spock answered this existential question in one of the most poignant scenes in all of canon. Offering to return command of the *Enterprise* to Kirk so that they might head to Regula I on an emergency mission, Spock counseled that Kirk should never have accepted promotion. In Spock's opinion, pursuing a path that did not capitalize on one's strengths was a "waste of material" (Bennet et al., 1982). In this pithy scene, Spock addressed an issue in leadership that is core to the cause but so rarely addressed in training. A leader must adapt to changing situations not limited by previous assumptions but fueled by current realities. In other words, a leader must recognize when they fit, and especially when they do not fit, the needs of a situation. It is our observation that such recognition requires a fair amount of experience coupled with a healthy dose of humility.

By the end of the film, Kirk was able to return to the bridge, ready to galavant (albeit a bit more slowly) around the Galaxy once more. Each of us possesses an amalgam of abilities and experiences that facilitate our leadership. So too, each of us is limited by these abilities and experiences in ways that prevent a truly effective leader-situation fit. Enlightened leadership requires that one recognizes when and where they fit and mentor others with the necessary tools where and when they don't. This was what Spock did for Kirk, who then paid it forward through another five films. To paraphrase Kenny Rogers (1978), the most adept leaders know when to hold 'em, when to fold 'em, and even when to walk away.

Kirk was a highly accomplished but effectively retired leader being advised to return to his first, best destiny. People sometimes need that push to help them see that they can lead a situation effectively (basic leadership skill: *communication*). Is this not quite literally the purpose of mentoring? However, the obverse is also true. Sometimes, those in leadership need to step out of a situation so that others can better solve the problem at hand. This does not mean you should step down from leadership every time you question whether the fit is absent (basic leadership skill: *patience*). What does reason dictate would be the better response?

Chapter 5. Kirk: Charismatic Cowboy

Are there interpersonal (or personal) dynamics that might affect your decision (basic leadership skill: *relationship*)? It is important to regularly assess the needs of new situations and to recognize when your strengths lie not in addressing the challenge but in leading those with the requisite skill set to success.

Undiscovered

Breaking up is hard to do, but changing one's long-held beliefs can be an even greater challenge. Perhaps nowhere in canon is this better demonstrated than in *Star Trek VI: The Undiscovered Country* (Nimoy et al., 1991), the final film with the original cast. The events of the plot centered on the destruction of Qo'nos, the Klingon homeworld, and the potential for a lasting peace between the Federation and the Klingon Empire. However, the real story addressed Kirk's historical antipathy toward that noble society as encapsulated in his (rather racist) observation that "I've never trusted Klingons, and I never will." The scene is a powerful one because it sheds light on an admission of weakness by an exemplary leader. Over the next two hours of entertainment, Kirk wrestles with his conscience, manages to develop a short-lived love interest (beware of wolves in sheep's clothing), and goes on to once again change history. Yet, more instructive for our purposes is Kirk's early recognition that his beliefs are likely to be an impediment to his effective leadership. As he questioned of himself, "how on Earth can history get past people like me?" How, indeed?

It was not until he discovered that a Klingon captain was Sto'Vo'-Kor-bent on preventing the peace process from going forward that Kirk realized the depth of his biases. This realization snapped him into awareness of his own complicity. In leadership, one does not necessarily have the benefit of an approaching Bird-of-Prey to reorient one's attention to their inner thought process. Instead, we more typically encounter ongoing and often minor events (a comment here, a glance there) that might pique our attention but fail to rise to meaningful awareness. How can you, as a leader, recognize and mitigate your own beliefs? How will you ensure that you put your people before your assumptions?

We are each entitled to our own beliefs. These beliefs are typically the result of where we came from, how we were raised, and what experience has (or has not) taught us along the way. In the canon of *Star Trek*, bigotry is largely a sentiment of the past and many societies have gotten on with focusing on personal and social development. As Ensign Tendi observed when finding the fornication helmet of Kahless in a private collection, "Oh, that's fun. Safety first!" (Kula & Arndt, 2021). Any biases she might have possessed were quickly extinguished by a more inclusive and rational habit of mind. If only it were so simple for the rest of us. Kirk ultimately did the right thing, but not without a lot of self-convincing and consulting with trusted others. So, too, we as leaders must remain cognizant of how our beliefs can affect our judgment, and how in turn the power we have by dint of role might inadvertently provide purchase for our biases to manifest in our leadership.

Kirk spent a career galivanting around the Galaxy, saving countless lives, breaking innumerable hearts, and otherwise changing the course of history. Through it all he put his life at risk more times than we might count. Nonetheless, it is our assertion that the greatest challenge Kirk ever faced was the opportunity to change his mind about his former foes. The events of the film thrust him into a series of encounters that presented both old and new perspectives (basic leadership skill: *communication*). Instead of firmly standing by his traditional belief system, Kirk thought through his emotional roadblocks with a trusted therapist (i.e., his captain's log). In the end, his eyes were proverbially opened through interactions with Klingons who likewise struggled with change but were open to peace (basic leadership skill: *relationship*). The frustration we experience every time we have to work with that one person (you know the one we are talking about) can be very real. We have to ask ourselves how much of it is based on their behavior and how much on our beliefs about them? If post-retirement Kirk can change his mind, so can we.

Take Us Out

How can we take these lessons and apply them to our own leadership? It is one thing to respect a leader like Kirk who seemed never to waiver in his constitution; but another to demonstrate, much less experience, the same emotional stamina in our daily actions. We cannot simply go where angels fear to tread. Compassion must sometimes overrule the logic of the day. As Spock said to Commander Valeris, "Logic is the

Chapter 5. Kirk: Charismatic Cowboy

beginning of wisdom, Valeris, not the end" (*Star Trek II: The Wrath of Khan*; Bennett et al., 1982). Let's take the examples above and see how they might fit with our own practice.

There is in any organization the opportunity for groupthink to take hold. This might be as harmless as a collective belief that meetings should always have agendas and utilize rules of order. Alternatively, groupthink can shut down meaningful problem-solving within specific workgroups or across entire organizations. Much like Kirk demonstrated in "This Side of Paradise" (*Star Trek: The Original Series* S01E25; Butler et al., 1967), the challenge is to remain vigilant to our own sometimes subtle changes in thought toward the status quo.

Similarly, leadership is rife with the potential for misunderstanding. Although we might claim to listen to others and hear other voices, the reality is that we sometimes lack the skill set to do just that. "The Devil in the Dark" (S01E26; Coon & Pevney, 1967) provides an extreme example of the importance of communication and the risks of it going awry. It is true that you are unlikely to supervise any silicon-based lifeforms (although a leader can hope). However, no less challenging can be the responsibility to lead a group of individuals from walks of life vastly different than one's own. It has been our observation that power has a tendency to blind even the most genuine of intentions. Leadership demands that we extend our circle of awareness to all those we serve.

There is always the risk that leadership happens in a vacuum. Regardless of where one is in an organization, leadership by its very definition can be an isolating role. We can become used to the resultant autonomy over time and forget to check in with others about the efficacy of our decisions. "Errand of Mercy" (*Star Trek: The Original Series* S01E27; Coon & Newland, 1967) reiterates that leadership carries with it not only a heightened responsibility to others but an increased obligation to check our own assumptions. There are few things so potentially toxic in an organization as a leader who is convinced of their own righteousness.

Perhaps the most difficult decision in leadership is what to do when one must act against one's own wishes. "The City at the Edge of Forever" (*Star Trek: The Original Series* S01E28; Ellison & Pevney, 1967) presents this dilemma in the extreme. It is more likely that we will encounter it among the mundane. Have you ever supervised someone who could get the job done but not as well as you yourself could do it? Our own initial impulse would be to complete the task ourselves. However, there is a fine line between leadership and micromanagement. What might the individual assigned to the task learn by completing it on their own or with your guidance? Might there even be something learned by allowing them to fail? As leaders, it is important that we nurture the development of others in the long-term service of the organization.

It is also necessary to question one's own beliefs from time to time in order to better serve. An effective leader ought to be one who knows themself, who knows their strengths as well as their weaknesses. Indeed, let's forgo the gentility of speaking of "challenges" or "opportunities for growth." A weakness is a weakness. There need be no shame in not knowing something or not knowing how to do something. Among its various leadership lessons, *Star Trek II: The Wrath of Khan* (Bennett et al., 1982) demonstrates the importance of utilizing one's abilities and leaning on the adeptness of others to compensate for the gaps in our knowledge, skills, or awareness. John Donne cautioned five centuries ago that no one is an island. We each lead within a social milieu. It is important to recognize how we as whole individuals fit into the matrix. Take the red pill.

Such development must also be internalized by the leader, as so well demonstrated in *Star Trek VI: The Undiscovered Country* (Nimoy et al., 1991). The mark of a facile mind is the ability to change one's mind in response to new input. We live in an increasingly globalized society in which populations and ideas are crossing borders with a pace never before seen in the history of our species. Leaders must remain relevant to the times, and a key facet of such dynamism is the willingness to change their minds. As a Klingon diplomat observed to Kirk, "People can be very frightened of change" (Meyer, 1991). Nonetheless, effective leadership requires us to move beyond our biases toward a future that at times might be unrecognizable to us in the moment.

Whether in leadership or elsewhere, the more we seek to achieve, the greater the likelihood for setback. This is a durable truth of life whether the stakes are large or small. For example, during his graduate school meanderings, Jason had been studying in a doctoral program for a few years. Although his coursework was going well and he was becoming clinically competent, there had never been a good fit between student and program. The former was committed to scientific investigation, whereas the latter trained for clinical application. There were also problems afoot in other ways (politics, anyone?) and he began to realize that it

Chapter 5. Kirk: Charismatic Cowboy

was not the place for him. Talk about a no-win situation. After consulting with his most trusted advisors (thanks, Mom and Dad), he decided that his path had to change. It was one of the most difficult things he ever had to do, but the long-term result was net positive. For example, he eventually found himself in the position to co-author a book about leadership through the lens of *Star Trek*. We might not be able to alter the programming of our own *Kobayashi Maru*, but we can most certainly change how we navigate the tests. Effective leaders should be reflective practitioners.

Whether it is family, close friends, or crewmates, it is also important for a leader to utilize intuition to decode seemingly subtle messages. Aaron encountered the importance of doing this with one of his own students. While holding a brown-bag virtual lunch session (COVID-19), he noticed that one of his students seemed a bit "off." The student was not exuding the typically engaging and bubbly personality he had grown accustomed to seeing. Not wanting to draw attention to the student in a public setting, he emailed the student after class to just see if something was amiss. Sure enough, the student was experiencing a very difficult and delicate situation. He learned that his student had recently taken a new position in higher education. Although the student really enjoyed the work, they were dealing with a harassing co-worker. After listening to the student, he offered some guidance to his student, who was able to eventually find another position. Had he not used his intuition, he would have missed the signals that his student was hurting and in need of a listening ear (rounded, not pointy).

We cannot all lead larger than life and remain unfazed in the face of adversity. Kirk was full of personality to his very last day. As he disparagingly reflected on his own leadership style, "I'm a great one for rushing in where angels fear to tread" (Meyer, 1991). We might know such people who are larger than life, but we are betting that most of us would not fit the bill. Kirk has demonstrated that even when a leader forges ahead courageously, they might still struggle with their own inner demons. Leaders, even great ones, are not infallible. It is the truly exceptional leader who realizes this fact and takes it upon themselves to learn from their mistakes. We do not need to run from our mistakes. Instead, we can learn from the example. Kirk demonstrated across decades of canon how courage in leadership comes in many shapes and sizes.

Nachman of Breslov wrote that the important thing is to not be

Leadership in *Star Trek*

overly afraid. Courage is not the state of never being afraid but the ability of acting when we are afraid. We must be cognizant of our gifts as well as our limits and willing to seek feedback, and respond with humility. Kirk demonstrated an illimitable spirit not merely through an innate self-assuredness but through the trials and tribbles of successfully (and sometimes unsuccessfully) solving all sorts of problems. Just make certain not to take yourself too seriously along the way.

GUIDANCE FROM GUINAN

Imagine yourself sitting at a small table under the arching windows of Ten Forward, the frontmost point and social hub of the U.S.S. *Enterprise*. The view out the windows is one of stark blackness punctuated by countless points of light, stars of every imaginable color. Sitting across the table is Guinan, the unofficial sage of the starship. Wise beyond measure, Guinan has served for centuries as a guide to innumerable leaders. Now she is fully present in the moment with you.

"What's on your mind?" Guinan asks you with that knowingly subtle smile. "You mentioned you were thinking about Captain Kirk. What about him stands out to you as a leader to model?"

Guinan continues to look at you expectantly. There is no hint of impatience, just that twinkle in her eye. "Think of Kirk's approach to leadership," she suggests. "How does your behavior as a leader compare with his?"

Guinan looks out the windows to the stars for a moment, and then turns back to you. "How do you *communicate* with others in a manner that is intentional and transparent?"

After giving you a moment to think and respond, Guinan asks you, "How do you exercise *patience* by listening to what others have to say?"

Guinan listens to your response, momentarily closes her eyes and nods with a smile, and then poses one more question to you. "How do you develop a *relationship* with others so that they feel seen and heard?"

After you respond, you and Guinan chat a bit longer before she has to return to her customers. You look back out at the stars, toward the seemingly endless potential of leadership, and think about how to lead more like Kirk.

Chapter 6

Picard: Diplomatic Scholar

You find yourself back in the same conference room with its lack of windows, stark overhead lighting, and preponderance of carbs. Although there have been many meetings (so many meetings) over the past year since you were last in San Francisco, this annual meeting is the one time everyone convenes to share successes, failures, and plan for the next steps. You situate yourself at the table amidst a couple of your colleagues, exchanging pleasantries about the weather and the inability to find more comfortable chairs, and take out your tablet for a glance at the meeting agenda.

As the chair calls the meeting to order, one of your more pugnacious colleagues interrupts with a request to revisit an old item. "Shut up, Wesley!" runs through your head, but you trust in the chair's ability to quell such power plays at the table. Indeed, you have often pondered about their ability to remain unruffled regardless of what transpires. They really are an adept leader.

The ancient Earth philosopher Lao-Tzu is said to have written that "a good traveler makes no fixed plans and is not intent upon arriving" (Mitchell, 1994, p. 27). It seems to you that this observation could be equally true about leadership, certainly as it pertains to running a meeting. There are certain goals for any meeting. But one must likewise be open to what their colleagues will bring to the discussion.

Another colleague speaks up to address the first item on the agenda for today. You know they are nervous about speaking in front of everyone. Much as you did a year ago, that colleague is about to challenge some assumptions. You listen intently as they share their thoughts and nod from time to time to provide them some small measure of encouragement.

At some point, others at the table push back on various issues. You gently clear your throat and the eyes at the table all turn to you. Bringing to mind Captain Picard's multidecadal example of leadership (and *speeches, so many speeches), you praise the value of discussing a range of opinions (basic leadership skill:* **communication***). You thank your colleague for their willingness to offer new ideas (basic leadership skill:* **patience***). Finally, as you sit back in your (still ergonomically offensive) chair and wait for the tone of the debate to shift, you step out of the way so that your colleagues can do their jobs (basic leadership skill:* **relationship***).*

Captain's Log

Perhaps no other starship captain was personally witness to so many historic events as Jean-Luc Picard (played by Patrick Stewart). Born in La Barre, France on Earth in 2305, Picard was attracted from an early age to a life among the stars. This interest was paralleled by a keen intellect and a willingness to eschew the expectations of others. For example, instead of remaining on the family vineyard, Picard surprised his parents when he decided to apply to Starfleet Academy. Picard similarly demonstrated an unwavering tenacity to succeed. It was not until his second attempt to seek admission that he was accepted to study at Starfleet Academy. And although he would later be renowned for his skills of diplomacy, the young Picard was anything but a leader. His years at the Academy were academically and personally difficult. Picard began his studies "green as hell, and oh so cocky" (*Star Trek: The Next Generation* SS02E17; McCullough & Landau, 1989), a self-described "damn fool," one who was "selfish, ambitious, very much in need of seasoning" (*Star Trek: Nemesis*; Logan et al., 2002). By his own admission he was overly self-assured, rash in his handling of others, and less than empathic when it came to close relationships.

Nonetheless, as so many of us do, Picard was a character who matured past the foibles of his youth. He became an accomplished student and found within sports both an emotional outlet and a venue for accomplishment. Perhaps most important was that Picard found a mentor who could guide him in his personal growth. It was through his interactions with the chief groundskeeper Boothby, whom he would credit as one of the wisest individuals he ever knew (*Star Trek: The Next Generation* S04E09; Arnold-Ince & Allen, 1990), that Picard would slowly (and sometimes painfully) learn the value of humility. Similarly, although

Chapter 6. Picard: Diplomatic Scholar

Picard pursued the command track while at the Academy, he would forevermore be guided by the historical and empirical methods of his emphasis on archaeology, a cognitive toolbox that would serve him well on more than a few future occasions.

Picard spent the early years out of the Academy distinguishing himself as an exceptionally capable officer. This is not to say that his career as a junior officer was without event. There was that time in a tavern on Starbase Earhart when a dagger was driven through his back subsequent to questioning the parentage of a fellow patron (*Star Trek: The Next Generation* S06E15; Moore & Landau, 1993). Nonetheless, the reality is that Picard learned much from both his successes and his errors as a young officer.

Picard's assignment as helmsman to the U.S.S. *Stargazer* proved to be a turning point in his career. Although the already antiquated starship had seen better days, Picard felt it to be home and perceived its crew very much as family. For our purposes, his time aboard *Stargazer* offers special insight into the character's evolution as a leader as he was challenged to lead through some of the most difficult situations. On one significant occasion, the Stargazer's captain was killed and chaos ensued on the bridge during the battle. The young Picard assumed command amidst the resulting disarray and brought the ship and its crew to safety, an act of leadership that would see him promoted as one of the youngest captains in Starfleet history. Later, during his 22-year command of the vessel (Memory Alpha, n.d. g), Picard would again save his crew through an ingenious tactical decision born of urgency but tempered by experience.

What is intriguing for our purposes is that this moment represented both one of the highest and lowest points of his career. On the one hand, Picard saved his crew from certain death. On the other hand, in the process Picard abandoned his critically wounded ship. The result would be a court-martial. And although he would be acquitted of all charges, nonetheless with great success came great failure. How was Picard to respond? He remained tenacious in the face of setbacks. But Picard was now tempered by the experience of leadership. Eight years later he would step on to the bridge as captain of the Starfleet flagship.

A marvel of engineering both technical and social (shipboard kindergarten, anyone?), the U.S.S. *Enterprise* (NCC-1701-D) and its crew would go on to be present for much of Federation history. It was almost

Leadership in *Star Trek*

as if the crew of *Enterprise* were involved in quadrant-shattering events every week. Regardless, many of these events speak to the leadership qualities Picard demonstrated in the most harrowing of situations.

There were more such events than space allows and we will explore a few of those in the pages below. However, let us briefly consider Picard's interactions with the Borg. In "The Best of Both Worlds" (*Star Trek: The Next Generation* S03E26/S04E01; Piller & Bole, 1990a, 1990b), a two-part episode many consider to be one of the finest examples of *Star Trek* storytelling, Picard was captured by the Borg and turned into a drone. Across the ensuing season cliffhanger and following season premier, Locutus of Borg (né Jean-Luc) would oversee atrocity after atrocity before his faithful *Enterprise* crew risked assimilation (which is far worse than losing life and limb, although sometimes one lost limbs in the process of assimilation) to rescue him. Aside from it being excellent television, why do we care about this two-part episode? What does it tell us of Picard as a leader?

Two factors are especially relevant. Picard made it a habit to hand-pick his executive staff. He recognized his own strengths and weaknesses and sought to balance those with an exemplary leadership team who, as the need arose, could support and challenge his decision-making. A key example was Picard's selection of Commander William Riker as first officer; Picard had been impressed with Riker's willingness to stand up to a previous captain. It would be Riker who eventually led the mission to rescue Picard from the clutches of the Borg. Indeed, there might be no more important factor behind effective leadership than being able to keep counsel with knowledgeable and trusted advisors.

Picard also demonstrated the importance of tenacity balanced with humility, one he learned through years of hard experience. Although his post–Borg physical rehabilitation went smoothly, Picard unsurprisingly was left with long-term psychological scars (who wouldn't be after Wolf 359?). The reality is that people often carry with them the emotional scars left by challenge. What is important is that leaders seek to grow in the aftermath. Picard manifested the tenacity to return to service and lead his crew. Yet, he also recognized the benefit of talking to someone; it took humility for him to work with Counselor Deanna Troi. Indeed, contrary to popular belief, the experience of trauma is as likely to lead to growth as it is to stagnation (Weir, 2020).

These two leadership elements, the maintenance of tenacity

Chapter 6. Picard: Diplomatic Scholar

balanced with a humility buoyed by the support of trusted others, would demonstrate themselves as fundamental to Picard's success much later in his life. In the first episode of *Star Trek: Picard* (Kurtzman et al., 2020), we find Picard wallowing in retirement and remorse at his family chateau mourning the decisions he made that led to his retirement from Starfleet. Although surrounded by friends (who happened to be former Tal Shiar secret agents, but that's not important right now), he perceived himself very much alone and seemingly lost without the responsibilities of leadership.

Yet, before long and as seemingly happens on a weekly basis to captains retired or active in the franchise, Picard was called to action by an urgent Galactic need. Thus, 32 years after his fateful encounter with the Borg, Picard again found himself aboard a Borg cube. This time he arrived not to be assimilated but as a guest searching to rescue someone else from the clutches of servitude (*Star Trek: Picard* S01E06; Zayas & Vrvilo, 2020). He did not go it alone. Instead, the aged yet spry Picard relied heavily on a new team of colleagues to facilitate his leadership. As a *diplomatic scholar*, Picard stuck to his principles and did not back down in the service of others by leveraging the basic leadership skills of communication, patience, and relationship.

Canon Fodder

With the possible exception of James T. Kirk, there exists more canon on Picard than any other captain of *Star Trek*. The result is a palette of resources from which one can paint a portrait of leadership. However, we have limited ourselves to several specific examples we find illustrative of how Picard demonstrated the basic leadership skills of *communication*, *patience*, and *relationship* across a varied range of situations. In each case, he illustrated how a transformational leader works to promote the growth of those they lead (Bass & Avolio, 1994). Although Picard was a skilled logician, he also developed a growing sense of connection with others through his interactions with the bridge crew over the years by routinely seeking a range of options from others, weighed those options with care, and trusted others to perform up to their potential.

Picard very much encapsulates an example of an educated leader grounded in the possibilities of Enlightenment thinking. A budding archaeologist in his youth, he understood the value in thinking critically through observation and reflection before making decisions. Picard also manifested a true sense of compassion for those with whom he served. This is not to say that Picard was a warm and cuddly individual. On the contrary, we can see in the aptly titled episode "Disaster" (*Star Trek: The Next Generation* S07E25/26; Moore et al., 1991) that Picard lacked much facility interacting with children until well into midlife. Nonetheless, his character makes clear the importance of utilizing rational thought balanced with compassion in any number of episodes. An exemplar can be found in the episode "All Good Things..." (Moore et al., 1994) with Picard playing poker with his colleagues (and his friends) around a small table.

Perhaps even more notable is that Picard portrayed a leader who was not only guided by Enlightenment thinking but was, in fact, relatively actualized. Although the young Picard was a bit of a rapscallion, his character grew through education and experience. The result was the development of a leader who recognized quite clearly his abilities and limitations and sought to leverage them in service to others with little regard for his own ego needs.

Darmok

How is one to navigate an interpersonal conflict when they simply do not understand the perspective of the other? This is the dilemma Picard faced when he was nonconsensually beamed down to the surface of El-Adrel IV in "Darmok" (*Star Trek: The Next Generation* S05E02; LaZebnik, Menosky, & Kolbe, 1991). Arriving planetside, Picard made the acquaintance of Captain Dathon, a Tamarian who apparently maintained a fondness for Darmok and Jalad. Therein lies the rub. Whereas Federation citizens such as Picard were fluent in Federation Standard (i.e., English), the Tamarians spoke in a highly metaphorical language that had thwarted all attempts at processing by the universal translator. To make matters more complicated, Picard erroneously interpreted Dathon's initial attempts at communication to suggest the latter's desire to engage in combat. It turned out nothing could have been further from the truth (Kashon, his eyes not wide open).

Chapter 6. Picard: Diplomatic Scholar

Picard soon came to understand that Dathon had them both beamed down to the planet in order to face together a rather formidable creature seemingly intent on killing them. In this way, the episode harkens to the Robbers Cave experiment (Sherif, White, & Harvey, 1955), a groundbreaking social psychological study that found the only reliable way to motivate opposed groups to work together was to place them in a situation in which their cooperation was absolutely necessary to their success as individual groups. It eventually availed that Dathon took this finding to the extreme so that their two peoples might learn to meaningfully communicate with one another. Indeed, it would not be long before a Tamarian officer served on a Starfleet vessel.

"Darmok" (LaZebnik, Menosky, & Kolbe, 1991) is widely heralded for good reason as one of the best of *Star Trek: The Next Generation* (Roddenberry et al., 1987–1994). Leadership is regularly characterized by conflict, which we would argue is more often than not generated by misunderstanding. In the episode, Picard was faced with (an albeit extreme version of) a common situation. He was expected to understand the intentions of someone else's words. Have not we all been in similar situations? Professional settings can be especially rife with such challenges. One needs to think only of that recent email from their colleague or supervisor that made so little sense upon first reading. As Dathon was clearly aware, the onus of comprehension lies primarily not with the receiver but with the sender of the message. We often might think ourselves to be in conflict with the other person, whereas in reality there is actually a perceived incongruency of interests (Mayer, 2000). It is crucial that we take the initiative to clearly communicate our interests while actively listening to the interests of others.

To this end, over the course of the episode Picard demonstrated a growing awareness that it was important to take Dathon at face value. Picard had to listen to Dathon without allowing his own preconceived ideas to cloud his ability to receive the message (basic leadership skill: *communication*). Picard also had to temper his inherent response to defend himself. Think about this for a moment. Most of us are not attacked by beasts who can cloak and deal major bodily damage on a daily basis at work. However, we all maintain a taught desire (thanks, society!) to defend our egos against what we perceive as social threats. As Picard demonstrated when learning to communicate with Darmok, it often takes us humans a bit of time to process the cues implied in a lot of social interaction (basic leadership skill: *patience*). It might not be realistic to expect that your leadership will be so refined as to encourage others to die for the sake of communicating with you. However, it is nonetheless fundamental to understand, as Picard did, that effective leadership requires the ability to meaningfully interact with others (basic leadership skill: *relationship*).

Duty

Cadet Crusher had made a poor decision. Spurred on by the swagger of fellow squadron commander Nick Lacarno and fueled by the presumptuousness of youth, Crusher had engaged in a dangerous (not to mention forbidden) piloting maneuver with his fellow students that resulted in the death of one of them. Thus begins "The First Duty" (*Star Trek: The Next Generation* S05E19; Moore, Shankar, & Lynch, 1992), an episode we find particularly relevant to the practice of leadership due to its educational element and the relatability of our own mistakes over the years (admittedly, none of them proved fatal to us or others).

The key scene of interest occurs in the final act of the episode. We find ourselves in Picard's ready room aboard *Enterprise*, with Picard appearing less than pleased and Crusher standing there defiant as only the naiveté of youth or the certainty of self-righteousness could allow. Being the leader he was, Picard provided Crusher an opportunity to come forward with the truth about his involvement in the accident that killed his classmate. Instead, Crusher remained resilient to Picard's efforts and pleaded his innocence. Verbal push came to shove. Have we not all found ourselves in such a situation?

Realizing that Crusher was not going to admit his role in the affair (in order to protect the irascible Nacarno, no less) and would likely be expelled from Starfleet Academy, Picard spoke what we think is one of the strongest lines in all of Trekdom. Indeed, it encapsulates the Enlightenment thinking that underlies the very nature of *Star Trek* as a tool for leadership. Standing nose to nose with Crusher, Picard explained that

> the first duty of every Starfleet officer is to the truth, whether it's scientific truth or historical truth or personal truth. It is the guiding principle on which Starfleet is based. And if you can't find it within yourself to stand up and tell the truth about what happened, you don't deserve to wear that uniform [Moore, Shankar, & Lynch, 1992].

Chapter 6. Picard: Diplomatic Scholar

Mic drop.

He then offered Crusher a choice. He could admit his role in the accident or prepare to be outed. This interaction represented a transformational approach to leadership. Bass and Avolio (1994) defined such leaders as those who "behave in ways that result in their being role models ... [who are] admired, respected, and trusted ... [and who] can be counted on to do the right thing, demonstrating high standards of ethical and moral gain ... [and] using power only when needed" (p. 3). We see in the episode broadly and this scene specifically Picard attempting to educate the young Crusher. Picard was well aware of the genius of the cadet and his potential to do great things in the future (which he would, but not at all in the way any of us saw coming prior to the end of the series). Picard was also fond of the boy; he cared for him as something of a father figure. We can thus see why Picard attempted to set a tone for the interaction that was nonthreatening yet stern (basic leadership skill: *communication*). He further took his time in attempting to elicit the truth from Crusher without having to force the latter's hand (basic leadership skill: *patience*). Finally, Picard was left with little choice than to admit that if Crusher did not come clean then he would be forced to reveal the truth of the accident so as to protect the cadet's future (basic communication skill: *relationship*).

Contact

Among the pantheon of the films, *Star Trek: First Contact* (Berman et al., 1996) is easily one of the best, perhaps second only to *Star Trek II: The Wrath of Khan* (Bennett et al., 1982). While we will leave that debate to another time, we agree the film stands out as a demonstration of leadership in action. Indeed, *Star Trek: First Contact* is a film with which many people can easily relate.

We don't assume that you have ever had an encounter with the Borg, engaged in questionable decision-making around time travel, or become intoxicated with an empath (but we have hope for you). However, we suspect at least once you have been faced with an untenable situation that demanded something of you. No? Just give it some time; eventually the bell tolls for everyone in leadership.

In the film, Picard was brought face-to-face with his worst fear. Six

Leadership in *Star Trek*

years after his assimilation and rescue, the Borg made a second attempt to overtake the Federation. To make matters worse, Picard was ordered to refrain from engaging the Borg lest his presence potentially add "an unstable element to a critical situation" (Berman et al., 1996). To make matters even worse, before being destroyed, the Borg cube launched a Borg sphere that traveled back in time to change the course of history (yes, we know it's a time-travel story, but trust us, this one works if you don't think too hard about it). This created a major Borg problem. Things finally became interesting when Picard violated his orders and headed back to Sector 001 to defend Earth from its nemesis (no, not that one).

This decision is interesting from our perspective for a reason. It demonstrates what might be considered a failure in the character's thinking. As we explored above, Picard was served his entire life by his tenacity. But in the opening scenes of *Star Trek: First Contact*, we see a captain who allows his strength of character to override his own checks on self-importance. His leadership resultantly slipped into a more traditionally transactional style focused on management instead of cooperative teamwork (Bass & Avolio, 1994), sacrificing the potential of both reason and compassion to steer the course. Was Picard right to enter the battle? Was he right to then act in the moment to go back in time? Great Scott!

We shall leave you to make such an ethical judgment. Instead, let us return to the basic leadership skills. When Picard made the decision to violate his orders and head toward Earth (cue the minor chords in the background) he did not wish to obligate his bridge crew to such action, as any or all of them might face court-martial for the act. Having just listened to a static-filled subspace transmission from Federation ships defending Earth, Picard scanned the bridge and stated matter-of-factly that he was "about to commit a direction violation of our orders, any of you who wish to object should do so now, it will be noted in my log" (Berman et al., 1996). That seems like a bit of a Faustian bargain, but was it?

Picard was well-known to the bridge crew and knew he could rely on the tone of his message to be understood (basic leadership skill: *communication*). He admittedly did not allow much time for consideration when he leveled his ultimatum. Yet, Commander Data's affirmative response in the silence that ensued suggests that Picard did in fact provide adequate time for his people to process his order (basic leadership skill: *patience*). This was corroborated by the smiles that spread around

Chapter 6. Picard: Diplomatic Scholar

the bridge when Data responded that the orders should be ignored (basic leadership skill: *relationship*). Cue the major chords and lay in a course.

Candor

It had been 26 years since his last encounter with the Borg and much had changed in Picard's life. He had spent the past couple of decades writing books of history as opposed to commanding starships. Meanwhile, Picard had observed from the sidelines as the Federation had fallen to a cultural nadir of intolerance and bigotry in response to the synth attack on Mars. Was he the leader he once was? Was he still the indefatigable captain we know from the bridge of *Enterprise* (either of them)?

In "Absolute Candor" (*Star Trek: Picard* S01E04; Chabon & Frakes, 2020), we find the now long-retired Admiral Picard staring out a window (albeit on a holodeck) overlooking his vineyard below. With him was Commander Raffaela Musiker, his former first officer and until recently estranged friend, debating whether to proceed to Freecloud on the way to solicit the assistance of the Qowat Milat warrior nuns on Vashti (it's a long story, and it's awesome). Instead of the younger Picard of determination, the aged Picard was filled with uncertainty and remorse. It was clear both he and Musiker recognized the situation as nigh impossible.

What we find useful about this scene is that it reiterates three important factors of leadership that are contextually universal in application. First, as we have repeatedly asserted, effective leadership does not take place in a vacuum (even when in the vacuum of space). Picard recognized this reality amidst his sense of lost years and lost friends when he assembled the crew of *La Sirena*. Second, even the greatest of leaders fails. There is perhaps no greater truism in leadership. There inevitably comes a time when even the best of us falters, be it to the detriment of the organization or (merely) to our ego. In "Absolute Candor," we see the character brought low by events beyond his control but attempting to rise above his failures. Third, this episode is a reminder that the basic leadership skills are always applicable and must be guided by a situationally bound balance of reason and compassion.

It was clear that Musiker was willing to help Picard but she first had to overcome her own hesitations. What did Picard say to her? "One impossible thing at a time." In this way, he demonstrated a recognition of the enormity of the challenge and thereby supported his colleague through her apprehension (basic leadership skill: *communication*). He then used silence to allow Musiker to recall adventures past of their shared attempts to help many people when the challenge seemed equally insurmountable. In other words, Picard created space in the moment for Musiker to process her response (basic leadership skill: *patience*). Finally, but no less importantly, Picard offered his wry reminder of impossible odds with a smile (basic leadership skill: *relationship*). Small gestures of empathy can go a long way when interacting with others, facilitating their growth through modeling and guidance (Bass & Avolio, 1994). Especially when offered from a leader, brief moments of humanity can offer those we serve the implicit reassurance they require from us to meet their own needs.

Nepenthe

"Nepenthe" (*Star Trek: Picard* S01E07; Humphrey, Chabon, & Aarniokoski, 2020) uniquely begins as an episode in which we find Picard on the run. Having just transported via spatial trajector (we have no idea) from a recovered Borg cube, Picard and his newfound synth companion Soji arrived on the planet Nepenthe in an attempt to escape a couple of Romulan assassins (it's a long story). Picard chose this location as a temporary respite from pursuit not merely because he thought it a safe hideout but because he sought counsel. Nepenthe was home to his long-time friends Captain Will and Commander Deanna Troi Riker, both retired from Starfleet and both trusted advisors.

We find this episode particularly relevant to the real-world practice of leadership because it rings true with experience. Picard realized that he was in over his head. Instead of attempting to maneuver through the situation, he consulted with people he knew to be experts in their fields. Note the nuance in the episode. Captain Riker had established himself initially as a first officer aboard the U.S.S. *Enterprise* and later as captain of the U.S.S. *Titan*. He thereby could assist Picard in determining a viable plan of action. However, Picard was not traveling alone. He was instead responsible for the care of Soji, his traveling companion and

Chapter 6. Picard: Diplomatic Scholar

potential key to (yet again) saving the Federation. Picard also demonstrated his lack of expertise in working with someone so young (she was only a few years old, after all). Instead, Commander (Deanna) Riker spent her career as ship's counselor and was able to reach out to Soji in a manner that made her feel heard.

How have you felt when someone in a leadership position did not seem to hear you? Perhaps more importantly, how have you sought to demonstrate empathy to those you lead? Picard recognized the limits of his leadership skills and turned to others for assistance. What is more remarkable is that he made such a decision while literally running for his life. Instead of shutting down and falling back on his old habits, Picard understood that there were others better equipped to solve the problem.

When Captain Riker asked how badly he and Soji were in trouble, Picard merely replied that it was "bad enough." He and these two consultants maintained a friendship that went back decades. They were both able to understand that Picard's understatement was in fact an alert that the situation was dire (basic leadership skill: *communication*). Yet, Picard did not rush the situation. He instead took the time necessary to meaningfully problem-solve with the Rikers in order to arrive at a better solution. Picard also took the young Soji's advice as counsel. He understood that more data (not to mention more Data) tends to be preferable (basic leadership skill: *patience*). Crucially, and here we think is an area where leaders typically fail, Picard was able to take criticism and then incorporate it into his decision-making. When Captain Riker called out his former captain's "classic arrogance," Picard accepted the observation as legitimate feedback (basic leadership skill: *relationship*).

Ego

It had been a rough couple of days. Picard and the crew of *La Sirena* had finally arrived at Copellius, the homeworld of the synths, only to find yet another Soong involved in the family business. One thing led to another and Picard found himself under house arrest while the synth community worked to construct an intergalactic beacon that would call forth unimaginable destruction upon our Galaxy. Never one to be cowed, Picard cleverly used a series of brief speeches in an attempt to single-handedly stall an approaching armada of 218 Romulan warships.

There is much to commend the episode "Et in Arcadia Ego, Part 2" (*Star Trek: Picard* S01E10; Chabon & Goldsman, 2020), but what we find most compellingly relevant for leadership is its candid consideration of identity. Picard spent a lifetime in service to Starfleet from ensign to admiral. He was universally considered a leader across the sectors in response to his many valiant efforts to promote peace and exploration. One would be quite justified to assume that Picard had come to see himself through the lens of his roles. For example, there is a narrative thread through the entire series of *Star Trek: Picard* (Kurtzman et al., 2020) that portrays the character's struggle to no longer be galivanting among the stars. Therein resides the lesson for us as leaders. What does it mean to be a leader? We do not mean what does it take to be a leader, but pose the question regarding the potential for a leader to identify with their leadership role.

It has often been said that power corrupts and absolute power corrupts absolutely (just ask then-Commander Riker). We have similarly observed that leaders sometimes fail to reflect upon the importance of separating their person from the position. This is an understandable outcome of leadership over the long term. In many societies around the world, certainly in the United States, personal identity is often associated with one's work. How many times have you been introduced to someone who then asks what you do for a living by way of greeting? As Freud (probably) observed, work forms a cornerstone of identity in modern society by feeding the needs of the ego. Leadership has no shortage of such foodstuffs. If you don't believe us, note how those in middle management sometimes walk around as if they possessed far greater authority than warranted by their roles. A leader must be ever vigilant against taking themselves too seriously. Leadership by definition is a role of service to others and not to the self.

We are taught from our earliest days to defend our positions, to defend our egos. Leadership, meaningful and effective leadership, requires more of us. As Donald Hoffman (2016) observed, our perceptions of self and circumstance are not so much an accurate representation of reality as a functional interface for the successful navigation of the environment. What we perceive is just that. It is merely what we perceive.

Chapter 6. Picard: Diplomatic Scholar

The episode ends with a twist that challenges Picard's very notion of self. The effective leader must question themselves routinely, not in a manner that breeds discontent, but that one must pause and recognize when the proverbial line has blurred. As Picard taught from the bridge of *La Sirena*, "fear is an incompetent teacher." When it appeared all would be lost, Picard argued for the importance of thinking for oneself and welcomed Soji to share her own misgivings (basic leadership skill: *communication*). Instead of seeking to assert his own experience and accomplishments to save the day, Picard further allowed Soji an opportunity to think through her own motives instead of forcing the situation (basic leadership skill: *patience*). Picard ultimately rose above his own ego needs by recognizing the needs of others and trusting in their ability to lead (basic leadership skill: *relationship*).

Engage

How can we take these lessons and apply them to our own leadership? It is one thing to respect a giant of leadership like Picard but another to implement his lessons into our daily choices. Let's take each of the examples above and see how they might fit with our own needs.

Understanding the needs of others and clearly communicating with them is a perennial challenge of leadership. Although "Darmok" (*Star Trek: The Next Generation* S05E02; LaZebnik, Menosky, & Kolbe, 1991) presents the situation in the extreme, it is through such extremity that we can learn a valuable lesson. An organization is comprised of people with differing perspectives, competing needs, and their own anxieties. This is true whether the organization has 5 or 5000 people on staff. Lewin (1939) observed many decades ago that we each exist in our own "delusional fields." For example, whereas Jason thinks that *Star Trek: The Next Generation* represents the height of canon, Aaron remains befuddled that his co-author could be so inept at not recognizing *Star Trek: The Original Series* as that from which all Trek derives. The point is not who is correct, but who is listening. Our perceptions might overlap, but they will never do so perfectly.

"The First Duty" (*Star Trek: The Next Generation* S05E19; Moore, Shankar, & Lynch, 1992) represents the quite common experience of having to correct the decision-making of a subordinate. This need not

Leadership in *Star Trek*

be limited to a strictly managerial environment. We might consider the staff who report to us, the students we teach or advise, even the volunteers who work in our communities. Think back to your favorite boss, professor, or mentor. How did they respond when you made a mistake in your judgment? Jason remembers working on his dissertation proposal for months. He was nearly 60 pages into the project and went to meet with his advisor to receive the go/no-go to carry forth with the research. Confident that he knew what he was doing and did not need a lot of feedback, our intrepid author read and wrote, and wrote and read, pouring over the literature and agonizing over the design of the study. Finally, he was certain that his efforts would be rewarded. Upon sitting down with his advisor over lunch, the pleasantries exchanged, his advisor told him point blank that his design was not going to work.

Being able to clearly communicate intentions has been a central theme throughout this book and one of the three key skills (along with patience and relationship) that successful leaders should embody. Yet, communicating can be easier said than done, as Aaron discovered on one occasion. He had enlisted the help of a graduate student to assist with identifying some research for the leadership lab that he had created. He asked the student to find articles that addressed leadership best practices to strengthen the lab's resource library. The student returned after some time with some articles, but they were not the type that were being sought. He explained his request again, and the student went to seek out more material. The student came back with yet more articles, but it was clear they did not understand the assignment. Finally, he provided a specific example of the type of article he wanted for the lab. After some time, the student came back with many resources that fit the scope of the project. Leaders must take care to check that they are communicating clearly and effectively before closing the door and assuming all will go as planned. As importantly, leaders must rest the onus for confusion on themselves. If those one leads are not rising to the task, we must first question our own role in the problem. Are we leading effectively?

The moral of this story is that even the most well-intentioned people often drift wayward when they become increasingly focused (or routinized) in their work. It is all too easy to forget that those we lead are people with dreams and desires and needs. In "The First Duty" (*Star Trek: The Next Generation* S05E19; Moore, Shankar, & Lynch, 1992), Picard demonstrated how a leader can step into the situation before irreparable

Chapter 6. Picard: Diplomatic Scholar

harm is done. He leveraged the basic leadership skills to open a dialogue that resulted in at least the potential for growth. What might have happened to Cadet Crusher had his captain not interceded? How many times have we ourselves missed the opportunity, be it through a lack of awareness or a reluctance to overstep, to mentor and not merely manage those we lead?

Instead of the young Cadet Crusher, it was the esteemed Picard who was on the receiving end of a schooling when he encountered the Borg in *Star Trek: First Contact* (Berman et al., 1996). The film is a lesson in learning how to balance tenacity with humility. We are reminded of a classic scene between Picard and Commander Worf. *Enterprise* was about to be overrun by Borg drones and the lives of the remaining crew were at risk of assimilation when Picard asserted his prerogative to hold the line. Worf suggested instead that the ship should be evacuated to save as many lives as possible. In a rare moment of lost composure, Picard turned on Worf and called him a coward. Worf responded with a remarkable degree of respect amidst real anger, growling that "if you were any other man, I would kill you where you stand" (Berman et al., 1996).

Most dilemmas in leadership do not involve invading armies and life-and-death decisions (although some do, and we salute those who have to make such decisions). Nonetheless, have we not each found ourselves in a situation in which our ego is bruised and there seems no hope of success? Such challenges seem especially likely when it comes to the mundane reality of office politics (have you ever been to a faculty meeting?). This is where the basic leadership skills can really shine.

One of the surest ways to stay above office politics is through the use of transparent communication. Couple this with a willingness to hear people out and the potential for them to push back is likely to be diminished. The reality is that people need to be heard. They want to be acknowledged. We cannot assume that those we serve or with whom we work have made much progress toward self-actualization. But we can offer them opportunities to not feel threatened. It is incumbent upon the leader to not broadcast an air of superiority. Simply treat others as human beings.

Similarly, we see in "Absolute Candor" (*Star Trek: Picard* S01E04; Chabon & Frakes, 2020) the potential of empathy in service to effective leadership. One of the most enjoyable aspects of leadership is that it presents interesting problems to be solved. Of course, this is also one of the greatest frustrations of leadership. There are so many decisions (so many plasma fires and not enough water in the phaser). Sometimes the stakes are higher, and sometimes the stakes are lower. However, the invariant constant is that people are involved. is that people are involved. In other words, the decisions of leadership cannot help but affect others. This is where empathy becomes so relevant. When making decisions, do we remember to ask ourselves about the needs of those we serve? We suspect that too often we neglect to factor this important element into our equations for change.

It is important not to get caught up in the fiction of urgency before considering the downstream effects of our decisions. Both of us make it a point to involve students in our respective as well as shared research projects. Sure, adding a few high-performing students to the mix benefits us through their willingness to generate new ideas. However, the fact of the matter is that we teach students who tend to come to our programs naive to empirical thinking. The result is that we end up spending more time and energy including students as collaborators than we would flying solo. It is the reasonable course to set.

So, if the balance sheet might come out less in our favor for us on any given project, why do we do it? Just like we see in "Absolute Candor," the fruits of labor based on a willingness to lead with compassion (be it in the classroom, lab, or boardroom) are difficult to predict but always potentially rewarding for those we serve. Leadership can be more than "merely" running part or all of an organization. It can be a method through which we transform those we lead to become leaders in their own right (Bass & Avolio, 1994).

We also cannot overemphasize the importance of surrounding oneself with a cabinet of advisors who are able to offer counsel that is both wise and unvarnished. We see in "Nepenthe" (*Star Trek: Picard* S01E07; Humphrey, Chabon, & Aarniokoski, 2020) that Picard, indisputably one of the greatest captains in Starfleet history, could be scolded by a former subordinate. This is such a rare virtue among the leaders we personally know. The ability to admit ignorance, not to mention wrongdoing, seems to be lost on many leaders. Yet, Picard demonstrated a willingness when driven by necessity to admit his own limitations. And he did so in public. More than a few memes have made jest of the number of meetings held by Picard. But we think that such choices are exactly the type of behavior

Chapter 6. Picard: Diplomatic Scholar

becoming an effective leader. When did we ever watch a pointless meeting on *Enterprise*? Picard used the ready room to provide his executive staff, and regularly external experts, to create the space in which ideas could be offered, debated, and refined toward solving problems. Even when he was retired and aboard a freighter not his own, Picard utilized his holostudy as a social space in which his "crew" could come together. We can think of few examples so fine that remind us of the fundamental importance of relationship to leading effectively.

Finally, "Et in Arcadia Ego, Part 2" (*Star Trek: Picard* S01E10; Chabon & Goldsman, 2020) reminds us that we must take care not to confuse ourselves for our roles. To put it more bluntly, it is important for those we serve to not let our roles go to our heads. Modern society places heavy value upon the work we do and often the titles that work carries with it. Rogers (1963) cautioned that the most highly developed people are not those who stop at nothing to become more successful. Instead, he taught that the most evolved of us recognize ourselves for who we are and then seek to become better (much like Commander Data).

Shortly before turning 40, Jason had the opportunity to serve in a campus leadership role. He remembers walking the hallway to his office near the offices of his fellow campus administrators and recognizing quite clearly how power could corrupt. It would have been all too easy to have become overly infatuated with himself and his fancy new title. Fortunately for all those involved, he recognized the necessary separation between person and position. The character of Picard demonstrated the same recognition when presented with an ultimately existential crisis. He chose to lead instead of becoming caught up in issues of the ego. Be tenacious, but be so humbly.

GUIDANCE FROM GUINAN

Imagine yourself sitting at a small table under the arching windows of Ten Forward, the frontmost point and social hub of the U.S.S. *Enterprise*. The view out the windows is one of stark blackness punctuated by countless points of light, stars of every imaginable color. Sitting across the table is Guinan, the unofficial sage of the starship. Wise beyond measure, Guinan has served for centuries as a guide to innumerable leaders. Now she is fully present in the moment with you.

"What's on your mind?" Guinan asks you with that knowingly

subtle smile. "You mentioned you were thinking about Captain Picard. I have known Captain Picard for many years, and I could tell you many things. But I am more interested to hear from you. What about him stands out to you as a leader to model?"

Guinan continues to look at you expectantly. There is no hint of impatience, just that twinkle in her eye. "Think of Picard's approach to leadership," she suggests. "How does your behavior as a leader compare with his?"

Guinan looks out the windows to the stars for a moment, and then turns back to you. "How do you *communicate* with others in a manner that is intentional and transparent?"

After giving you a moment to think and respond, Guinan asks you, "How do you exercise *patience* by listening to what others have to say?"

Guinan listens to your response, momentarily closes her eyes and nods with a smile, and then poses one more question to you. "How do you develop a relationship with others so that they feel seen and heard?"

After you respond, you and Guinan chat a bit longer before she has to return to her customers. You look back out at the stars, toward the seemingly endless potential of leadership, and think about how to lead more like Picard.

Chapter 7

Sisko: Ethical Realist

The trip north across the Golden Gate was beautiful, with the views of Sausalito to the east and Mount Tamalpais to the north through the bubble of the automated cab inspiring a positive sense of expectation. Indeed, you have often thought there was some leadership lesson to be learned from time in nature as you cruise over and then down into the forest of ancient trees. What was it your university professor used to say? "Illegitimi non carborundum." No, that's not it. The thought slips away as the automated cab settles down at the edge of the forest, their tops shrouded in fog, as you exit the cab and walk to the hoverbus that will convey you the remaining distance to Muir Woods.

Your favorite place on Earth, or anywhere else for that matter, you think as you board the hoverbus. Long the refuge of the weary who sought to escape the hustle and bustle of the city, this remnant of redwood forest has been nurtured for hundreds of years to regain some of what once must have been its former glory.

You step off the hoverbus and find yourself passing under the wooden entryway and strolling along the boardwalk. The air is cool and slightly damp. The quiet is pervasive. Few visitors remain this early evening as the temperature begins to fall and their homes call for them. You hear the first chirps of crickets from amidst the trees as shadows reach across the dappled forest floor. Finding your favorite bench after a short walk, you sit down and allow your gaze to soften as you recall the words of biologist Robin Wall Kimmerer (2013). She believed that "the land knows you, even when you are lost" (p. 36). Of course, it is essentially impossible to be lost on Earth these days, but that's not what she meant.

As you close your eyes and take in the sounds and scents of the redwood forest, with the damp feel of the air and the musty scent of the soil, you are startled from your reverie by the chiming of your communicator. It's a colleague from today's meeting. They are wondering if you could spare a few minutes (of course now) to chat with them. So much for an hour of peace amidst these forest giants.

You acquiesce to the request with as much poise as you can muster and retrieve your tablet to pull up your notes. This is not going to be an easy conversation. You imagine Captain Sisko had many such interactions as a station administrator on the border between three conflicting societies. He led by being transparent in his perspective (basic leadership skill: **communication**) *and knowing how to focus his passion on finding solutions (basic leadership skill:* **patience**). *As your colleague begins to rattle off their litany of concerns, you force a smile for your own benefit and remind yourself that you are all friends here (basic leadership skill:* **relationship***).*

Captain's Log

Praised by some and vilified by others, Benjamin Sisko (played by Avery Brooks) would come to play a vital role in the defense of the Alpha Quadrant. However, he began his life more locally. Raised with his siblings by their father in the vibrant city of New Orleans, North America, Sisko grew up working in the family restaurant. When the time for college approached, Sisko applied to Starfleet Academy to study engineering. However, homesickness became a real problem during his first year of studies. This individual, who would become a fiercely independent leader, managed to use up all of his transporter credits that first year to beam home for nightly dinners with his family (*Star Trek: Deep Space Nine* S03E22; Bader & Bole, 1995). Sisko nonetheless learned, like so many others, to navigate the challenges of having left home.

Subsequent to graduation, Sisko spent his early years as an officer stationed aboard the U.S.S. *Livingston*, then the U.S.S. *Okinawa*, and later the U.S.S. *Saratoga*. Events on *Saratoga* were especially impactful for his development as a leader. In 2367, *Saratoga* was called to assist with the defense of the Federation against a Borg incursion (Memory Alpha, n.d. h). The events of the encounter, which would come to be known as the Battle of Wolf 359, would see 39 of the 40 assembled Federation ships destroyed. Amidst the tumult, Sisko's wife was killed and he was forced to abandon ship with his young son. Sisko was initially

Chapter 7. Sisko: Ethical Realist

tempted to resign from Starfleet after experiencing so much loss. Instead, as would become evident in his daily leadership, Sisko devoted himself to new professional tasks and was ultimately assigned as commander to *Deep Space Nine*.

Situated at the edge of the Federation, *Deep Space Nine* was no ordinary station. It was "one of the most historically, politically, and strategically important space stations in the Alpha Quadrant during the latter half of the 24th century" (Memory Alpha, n.d. i). Having previously been utilized to house enslaved Bajorans, the station was turned over to the Federation after the Cardassian withdrawal from the Bajor system. Less than a decade later, *Deep Space Nine* would serve as the front line in the Dominion War, a conflagration that would nearly see the fall of the Alpha and Beta Quadrants to control by the Founders.

Especially interesting relative to leadership is that Sisko was the only captain in *Star Trek* canon to portray the balancing of family responsibilities. From the very first episode of the series, we observe the affection Sisko had for his son and how that relationship was central to everything else he did. We also are privy to watch him struggle to balance the needs of his home life with those of his professional duties. This is a situation with which many of us can relate. How does one remain present as a parent, spouse, or otherwise while serving in a position of leadership? This is a question rarely addressed in leadership training, one Sisko did not necessarily answer for us. Instead, he offers us a demonstration of how leadership is a deeply human endeavor.

Sisko also stood out among the other captains of *Star Trek* in his willingness to flex the strictures of ethics. It is undeniable that Sisko held firmly to his duties as a Starfleet officer. There likewise is little question across the seven seasons of the series that he believed deeply in the compassionately enlightened ideals of the Federation. Nonetheless, Sisko eschewed the pollyannaish sentiments sometimes leveled against the *Star Trek* franchise. He portrayed a character who was deeply grounded in the realities in which he led. This habit remained consistent even when Sisko came to be seen as Emissary among the religious Bajorans (one of the most interesting story arcs in the entire canon).

Tested in the crucible of war and loss, Sisko served as a model of how one might toe the line of duty in service to that duty. It was not that he regularly pushed against the system. Change for its own sake is as ignorant as refusing to acknowledge the need to do better. Instead, as an *ethical realist*, Sisko offers a model of a leader who was willing to respond to the needs of the situation.

Canon Fodder

Sisko demonstrated as a character an ability to remain compassionately enlightened amidst major loss through both his successes and his failures. He thus affords us the chance to consider how the basic leadership skills of *communication, patience,* and *relationship* can be called upon to counter conflict and ego, two of the greatest threats to effective leadership. What is even more impressive is how Sisko navigated these two challenges amidst his attempts to change the culture, what Schein and Schein (2017) defined as the "accumulated shared learning of [its denizens] as it [solved] its problems of external adaptation and internal integration" (p. 6), of the space station *Deep Space Nine*. He consistently displayed his ability to be emotionally transparent (this was good and not so good), to channel such passion into problem-solving, and to respect the ideas of those around him.

Importantly, the premise of *Deep Space Nine* (Berman & Behr, 1993–1999) remains notably unique among the *Star Trek* series and films. Instead of focusing upon the crew of a starship, *Deep Space Nine* brought its viewers each week to a relatively stationary location in which adventure would come to the protagonists instead of the other way around. Additionally, as the first *Trek* series to be produced subsequent to the death of creator Gene Roddenberry, *Deep Space Nine* often featured a level of discord among its lead characters previously unseen in canon. Such conflict is now common amidst the more recent series, but at the time it presented new opportunities in which to tell stories and, for our purposes, demonstrate the trials and tribbles of leadership. The key example was the history of *Deep Space Nine* (aka, *Terok Nor*) itself, a space station constructed by a society in order to help subject an entire other society, liberated through what amounted to civil war, and then administered (or was it occupied?) by a seemingly benevolent external power.

Amidst such social turmoil came Sisko, assigned as commanding officer of the station. Sisko was clearly grounded in the values of Enlightenment thinking. As he reflected in "In the Pale Moonlight" (*Star Trek:*

Chapter 7. Sisko: Ethical Realist

Deep Space Nine S06E19; Fields & Lobi, 1998), "People are dying out there, every day! Entire worlds are struggling for their freedom. And here I am, still worrying about the finer points of morality." However, his was not a character simplistically imbued with Federations ideals. Sisko had experienced major loss prior to accepting command of *Deep Space Nine*. He also had a young son on station for whom to care. We thus see over the course of the series how Sisko repeatedly struggled to balance his dedication to the ideals of the Enlightenment with the very real exigencies of his various leadership roles.

How is one to remain actualized amidst such challenge? This was a point on which Maslow (1943) was quite clear. Self-actualization is as much a process as a destination. For one to reach such a lofty target of development, it is necessary for more basic needs to remain satiated along the way. Yet, the reality is that, during times of strife, it is common for individuals to lose traction and slide down the developmental ladder for a period of time. Alternatively, actualized individuals (who perhaps are rare, perhaps are not as rare as was once thought) are able to maintain a hold on their psychological development. Though they might struggle, they hold fast to their healthy identities and look for ways to return to growth when it again becomes possible.

We observe some of this in the behavior of Sisko. Although by no means the most actualized of *Star Trek* captains, he nonetheless demonstrated an ongoing effort to grow as an individual through and beyond his leadership. One of Sisko's hallmarks was his ability to regularly question his own motives even while carrying forth with decisions. Change might have come slowly at times, but who among us can say otherwise? Sisko was regularly caught between a wormhole and a hard place (just let us have that one), yet he never backed down from reflecting on his own actions.

Emissary

Some of us pursue leadership roles of our own accord while others are called upon to serve. Regardless of how one arrives in a position of leadership, humility is one of the most important characteristics one can manifest as an effective leader. As Lao-Tzu counseled (Mitchell, 1994, p. 61), "All streams flow to the sea/because it is lower than they are. Humility gives it its power." Of course, the reality is that humility is a skill many of us need to learn while constantly defending against the trappings of leadership. This can be made all the more difficult in times of discord when one is prompted to put problems before people. We see just such a challenge in "Emissary" (*Star Trek: Deep Space Nine* S01E01/2; Piller et al., 1993), the first episode of *Deep Space Nine* (Berman & Behr, 1993–1999), when Sisko introduced himself to his new Starfleet and Bajoran crew as the incoming commander (eventually captain) of the station.

Humility is certainly not the first feature that comes to mind when one is prompted to think of the great leaders of history. Whether in business, education, or the military, leaders who make the textbooks are often noted for their lack of humility. The "reality distortion field" of Steve Jobs comes to mind. According to Andy Hertzfeld (1981),

> The reality distortion field was a confounding melange of a charismatic rhetorical style, an indomitable will, and an eagerness to bend any fact to fit the purpose at hand. If one line of argument failed to persuade, he would deftly switch to another. Sometimes, he would throw you off balance by suddenly adopting your position as his own, without acknowledging that he ever thought differently.

In other words, leaders such as Jobs might be brilliant, but they often lead with a focus on the bottom line or their own goals and with little thought for the needs of others in the organization. Apple has proved to be a remarkably adept company that has released some revolutionary products. However, at what cost has come such fiscal mobility? Burnout among such organizations is notorious, and while many former employees have been highly complimentary of Jobs' abilities as an executive, we note a decided lack of acknowledgment regarding his ability to have leveraged the basic leadership skills.

In contrast, Sisko repeatedly demonstrated an ability to act humbly while remaining strong. The key scene of the first episode of the series occurs when the spiritual leader of the Bajoran people tells Sisko that he is to be the Emissary of the Prophets, the non-corporeal beings who created the nearby wormhole that would cause so much fuss. How many people, upon being told they held great power, would refrain from exercising that power? Yet, this is exactly what Sisko did. He held steadfast to the recognition that he was no better than anyone else with whom he served.

Chapter 7. Sisko: Ethical Realist

Such humility amidst tension can be observed throughout the episode. For example, prior to Sisko's arrival on *Deep Space Nine*, Major Kira Nerys had been tasked by the Bajoran government with running the station. However, she was demoted to second-in-command when Bajor and the Federation negotiated an agreement for shared administration of the facility resulting in the placement of a liaison from Starfleet as its executive officer. Sisko made it a point to express his recognition that it was a difficult situation (basic leadership skill: *communication*). As Sisko said to Major Kira upon arriving at the station and receiving a less than enthusiastic greeting, "I thought I'd say hello first, and then take the office, but we can do this in any order you'd like" (Piller et al., 1993). Sisko also engaged in numerous walkabouts on station to better learn the social lay of the land before exerting his own will (basic leadership skill: *patience*). He also established in his first days an open-door policy so that others might approach the new station commander with questions and concerns (basic leadership skill: *relationship*).

Cause

Sisko found himself in a catch-22. It appeared that Kasidy Yates, captain of a private freighter that frequented *Deep Space Nine*, was smuggling goods to the Maquis. Problematic was that the Maquis were recognized by the Federation as a terrorist group. Even more problematic was that Yates was Sisko's significant other. "For the Cause" (*Star Trek: Deep Space Nine* S04E22; Moore et al., 1996) presents a situation not uncommon to leadership. We don't mean to suggest that your friend with benefits might be running supplies to resistance fighters (although that sounds pretty cool on paper). However, it is reasonable to expect that many leaders can find themselves pulled between the competing obligations of home and office. Leadership does not occur in a relational vacuum.

Much current writing on leadership (which is not, let's face it, page-turning material) conveys the implicit message that truly effective leaders must always show up and thereby subordinate everything else to their chief responsibility to the organization. We would be disingenuous as authors if we did not admit to having shared that ideal at some point in our own respective careers. However, leadership is not merely about taking care of one's professional responsibilities. We must also tend to our self-care. This task can be complicated when a leader must balance their personal obligations against their professional obligations. Sometimes, these needs are simply at odds. What is a leader to do?

Sisko struggled to walk this proverbial line between his duty as captain of the station and his dedication to his partner. In the episode, we see a beautifully acted and quite realistic evolution in his thought process. Sisko initially rejected as absurd the very notion that Yates might be engaged in any nefarious activity. Yet, in the face of mounting evidence, he slowly came around toward recognizing that his professional responsibilities did not absolve him from considering the situation with a less impassioned eye. We are sometimes called from different directions and have no clear path toward satisfying both sets of obligations.

Let's reframe the discussion to make clear the relevance of the episode to daily leadership. More likely than learning one's significant other is running contraband is to find oneself as a leader struggling with "work-life" balance. It is interesting that this colloquial term pairs work against the remainder of life and not as part of it. Perhaps it would serve us better to conceptualize the issue as "work-home" balance. Indeed, we have both found ourselves on more than a few occasions torn between such competing needs for our attention. A common example is when a leader must stay late at the office to complete a report by its deadline but their child has a school performance that same evening. Alternatively, perhaps a leader's aging parent requires assistance to get to an appointment on the same day they are scheduled for an important meeting. The permutations of these situations are seemingly endless.

Sisko demonstrated that there is often no easy remedy to doing the right thing in leadership when the situation presents equally valid expectations for action. He nonetheless worked to keep his emotions in check so that he could better understand the competing needs of the situation (basic leadership skill: *communication*). Indeed, Sisko often made it a point not to rush to conclusions as to how to proceed, at least not once he backed off from his initial reluctance to consider the evidence (basic leadership skill: *patience*). Finally, although he struggled with this last point, Sisko attended to the importance of remaining engaged with individuals on both sides of the dilemma (basic leadership skill: *relationship*).

Chapter 7. Sisko: Ethical Realist

Death

"To the Death" (*Star Trek: Deep Space Nine* S04E23; Behr et al., 1996) began with Sisko and crew aboard the U.S.S. *Defiant* returning to *Deep Space Nine* after having driven away a band of Breen privateers from their assault on a Bajoran colony (which is the story we *really* would have liked to hear). Upon reaching visual sensor range with the station, it became apparent that one of its upper pylons had been destroyed. Seriously, can't a captain leave for a few hours without everything going to the fire caves? It was soon revealed that a rogue group of Jem'Hadar warriors had attacked the station in order to pursue a potentially nefarious goal. Before long, Sisko and his crew agreed to collaborate with the Jem'Hadar under the orders of Weyoun in order to foil the plans of the renegades. The episode offers many themes worthy of consideration. For example, we learn that even as a woman, Dax can still act chauvinistically.

However, we think that "To the Death" (Behr et al., 1996) most strongly demonstrates the risk of relying on positional power in leadership. French and Raven (1962) defined positional power as that authority granted to an individual by their role and recognized by others as legitimate. In the episode, Sisko manifested significant positional power due to the agreement between him, the Jem'Hadar, and their Vorta commander. This power was most evident not in Sisko's leadership during the ensuing battle but in his repeated opportunities to break up fights between the two opposed when collaborating sides (oh, Worf). Time and again, Sisko literally put himself between fisticuffs to successfully break up fights through the use of his voice and the leveraging of his authority aboard ship.

We would suggest that such a reliance on positional power tends not to come without cost. Respect might be given by dint of title, but it can only be maintained over the long term by demonstration of leadership. A comparison of the two leadership styles evinced in the episode is instructive for the purpose. Weyoun led strictly through the authoritarian power of his role and without apparent care for his warriors. Similarly, the Jem'Hadar leader under Weyoun led not merely through his role as First but via his ability to best his subordinates in combat. Sisko's approach to leadership was obviously different and informed by the values of Starfleet. As he observed during a rather heated discussion, he could not expect his officers to follow him into battle if they did not already trust him.

One might question the ethics of the route taken if one is able to successfully maintain positional power in an organization. We think it matters quite a lot. Authority, by its very nature, is tenuous. Power granted today can be taken away tomorrow. To lead with a reliance on one's positional power risks modeling for others a transactional perspective that provides little incentive for respect or support. Instead, leading with authority, but without leaning on that authority as a crutch, can demonstrate to those we serve that we see ourselves as one of them and not apart from them. It might be noble for the captain to go down with their ship. However, how much better it can be when the crew stays at their posts to help solve the problem together as a team.

The episode offers an example of how leadership, even in the most untenable of situations, needs not degenerate into a raw assertion of power on the part of the leader. Sisko's very willingness to listen to Weyoun's outlandish proposal to collaborate demonstrated an impressive display of restraint (basic leadership skill: *communication*). Equally laudable was his repeated attempt to give the joint project a chance to succeed (basic leadership skill: *patience*). Of course, it was anything but easy to interact with a group of warriors who kept verbally reiterating their plans to kill Sisko and his crew once the mission was over. Nevertheless, Sisko sought to build an albeit temporary bridge between their two sides for the sake of mutual success (basic leadership skill: *relationship*), an effort that proved no easy task. Perhaps for some victory truly is life. The leader nonetheless must question: For whom?

Moonlight

The war with the Dominion had gone poorly. The Federation and its allies had taken heavy losses in the sustained onslaught from the Gamma Quadrant. If only the Romulan Star Empire, who shared a nonaggression pact with the Dominion, could be brought into the war. Thus began "In the Pale Moonlight" (*Star Trek: Deep Space Nine* S06E19; Fields & Lobi, 1998), one of the most ethically provocative episodes in all of *Star Trek* canon. The episode depicts the moral challenges often inherent to conflict and poses the ultimate utilitarian question: Does the end justify the means?

Chapter 7. Sisko: Ethical Realist

A leader is often called upon to make difficult choices, to find the proper balance in the moment between a reasoned and compassionate approach. Sometimes, these decisions are matters of designating resources or approving (or disapproving) of ideas that can be addressed with forethought. Other times, the stakes are much higher, and the potential for conflict can be quite real. With conflict often comes the temptation to get things over with. The temptation is an understandable one. Some problems present solutions that might be functionally successful. The question remains whether they are right. Now, we are not going to assert here our own moral leanings and claim them to be true. We instead would encourage you to question your own philosophy of leadership. It is important for each of us to recognize the limits of our morality, not to mention how it has been affected by our acculturation into an organization (Schein & Schein, 2017), and to do so before we are pushed up against those limits. In other words, as a leader, where is your proverbial line in the sand?

Sisko found himself staring at a number of lines drawn in some very problematic sand at the height of the Dominion war. Most significant was his role attempting to draw the Romulan Star Empire into an alliance by sacrificing some of the Federation values he had dedicated his life to uphold (talk about a *Kobayashi Maru* moment). We think a specific scene of the episode might be the most powerful in all of *Star Trek*. Sitting alone in his quarters that evening, holding a glass of synthohol that would not be touched, Sisko confessed to his captain's log:

> So, I lied. I cheated. I bribed men to cover the crimes of other men. I am an accessory to murder. But the most damning thing of all, I think I can live with it. And if I had to do it all over again, I would. Garak was right about one thing. A guilty conscience is a small price to pay for the safety of the Alpha Quadrant. So, I will learn to live with it. Because I can live with it. I can live with it. Computer, erase that entire personal log [Fields & Lobi, 1998].

Leadership that matters is almost always tested by the ethics of its situation. In the episode, Sisko was very careful with the information he shared with others given the stakes (basic leadership skill: *communication*). He also took his time to see his plan through to completion, recognizing his own limits (basic leadership skill: *patience*). Of course, in the end, Sisko came to question those very actions and their effects on others (basic leadership skill: *relationship*)? We leave it to you to determine the merit of those actions and instead end with a question. If you cannot stand by your own decisions, then who will?

Holosuite

It was the bottom of the ninth, and Sisko and his team had not scored a single run. Recognizing the gravity of the situation, Sisko was unwilling to allow his less adept players to approach the mound. How could he act so callously toward the people he served? "Take Me Out to the Holosuite" (*Star Trek: Deep Space Nine* S07E14; Moore & Chalmers, 1998) is an amusing episode that subtly addresses a formidable challenge of leadership.

It is true that conflict is inherent to leadership. Different stakeholders will often maintain potentially incongruent interests, and navigating such situations requires deftness with the basic leadership skills. Logic alone is rarely sufficient to solve major arguments (unless you happen to be sitting in a Vulcan bar). It is never easy to push against the shared assumptions and beliefs within an organization or among a team (Schein & Schein, 2017). However, it is even more likely that leaders will be challenged by their own needs than by those of the people they serve. Conflict might be difficult, but the ego is recalcitrant.

In the episode, Sisko was invited by the captain of another starship to play a game of the ancient sport of baseball (look it up, it was quite popular back in the day). The catch was that the captain in question and his entire crew were Vulcan, thereby possessing greater speed, stamina, and dexterity than the majority of players on Sisko's crew. This is not to mention that the captain of the opposing team had an emotional bone to pick with Sisko. It was highly illogical. Further adding to the difficulty of the situation was that no one on *Deep Space Nine* besides Sisko and his son knew how to play baseball. The prudent choice as a leader would have been for Sisko to acknowledge the "invitation" and then politely dismiss it. Instead, Sisko allowed his ego to get the better of him and leveraged his authority to require his entire bridge crew to learn the game. This was not the best show of compassionate decision-making.

The lesson here is not that Sisko made a poor decision. He did. The reality is that we are only human (or Vulcan, Andorian, Tellarite, etc.) and consequently fail at times in our problem-solving when bested by our own defensiveness. We all do it. What sets apart the effective leader is their ability to recognize the error of their actions and reconsider their next steps. We observe just such a behavioral arc over the course of the episode. Initially, Sisko was monomaniacal in his efforts to prepare his team to win the baseball game. He insulted many and disaffected others of his own crew along the way. People look toward leaders as models of what it means to hold responsibility and work on behalf of others. This was no way for a leader to behave.

It was not until the end of the episode that Sisko recognized the deleterious impact his need to assuage his own bruised ego had on others (basic leadership skill: *communication*). The result was that Sisko reformed his ways at the bottom of the ninth (basic leadership skill: *patience*). It was no longer about winning the game, but about supporting his people (basic leadership skill: *relationship*). It is important that we each remain mindful of our own ego needs lest they interfere with the needs of those we lead. When we do so, people tend not to remember what we decided so much as that we treated them with respect and clearly recognized their dignity.

Behind

"What You Leave Behind" (*Star Trek: Deep Space Nine* S07E25/26; Behr et al., 1999), the final episode of the series, sets the stage for the end of the war between the Federation Alliance and the Dominion. Perhaps even more powerfully, it brings to a close (or does it?) the tale of Sisko as Emissary in the Bajoran religion. It is on this side of the story we wish to focus our attention. For seven years, Sisko successfully led the crew of *Deep Space Nine* through crisis, war, and eventual peace. Even the greatest of leaders, however, must step down from their posts whether due to decision or attrition. This begs a question often unanswered in the training of leadership. How can a leader effectively step down from their role? At least a few issues are important regarding exit strategies in leadership.

We think it better for leaders to transition by choice rather than by force. Whether chairing a committee, running a division, or serving as CEO, there inevitably comes a time when one has reached the zenith of their success in the role. One must then ask how much more good they can offer in that position. It is also important to recognize that choosing

Leadership in *Star Trek*

to step down from a position of leadership can be affected by any number of factors. Sometimes, the winds of office politics are capricious. Other times, the work of leadership that once stimulated us no longer holds the same sway. Perhaps the decision might be prompted by honestly recognizing upon reflection that we have given our best to the role.

This is not to say that leaders must be sent out to pasture. On the contrary, it is important for leaders planning their exit strategy to consider how they will assist with the transition of their replacement into the role. We realize it might be easier to proverbial wash one's hands of the situation and head for the exit. However, an effective leader understands that their responsibilities can extend beyond the rubric of their former formal role. Have you ever stepped down from a leadership position only to find yourself more called upon to help solve problems? We think this is not an uncommon situation. Leadership does not necessarily cease with the relinquishment of a title.

Importantly, both of these issues (choice and transition) are influenced to no small degree by the role of the ego. As Freud (1960) observed, people constantly work in conscious and especially less than conscious ways to protect our own sense of self. We suspect you have noticed this tendency, if not among your own actions, then amidst leaders effective and not so effective. People have a tendency to repress, to actively stuff away from conscious awareness, thoughts and emotions that bother them. Is it reasonable to assume that some leaders might be uncomfortable with the thought of stepping down from their roles and responsibilities with the titles and perquisites thereof.

Stepping down from a leadership role can be challenging to the ego. Many leaders worked hard to get where they are and the notion of giving it up can seem uncomfortable at best. Nonetheless, we have the choice to facilitate a transition that can leave us in a positive light while, more importantly, ensuring the success of a successor. In our opinion, it is better to leave a position of leadership when one is on top than when one's best days are in the shuttle pod's rearview sensor.

Sisko demonstrated just such decision-making in "What You Leave Behind" (Behr et al., 1999). Entering the final battle of the protracted Federation-Dominion War, Sisko said with a tone of certainty to the crew aboard *Defiant*, "All right, people, what do you say we end this war?" (basic leadership skill: *communication*). Afterward, he took the time to socialize with his comrades in arms (basic leadership skill: *patience*).

Chapter 7. Sisko: Ethical Realist

Even more powerfully, Sisko made certain to reach out to his loved ones to ensure their well-being (basic leadership skill: *relationship*).

We're Explorers

How can we take these lessons and apply them to our leadership? It is one thing to respect a leader like Sisko who seemed never to waiver in his constitution, but another to demonstrate (not to mention experience) the same emotional stamina as we navigate conflict and calm the ego in our own daily decisions. Let's take the examples above and see how they might fit with our own practice.

Humility is one of the most valuable yet all too rare characteristics in leadership. In "Emissary" (*Star Trek: Deep Space Nine* S01E01/2; Piller et al., 1993), Sisko demonstrated the importance of not taking himself too seriously while remaining completely dedicated to his leadership roles (station commander and Emissary to the Bajoran people). Reflect for a moment upon those leaders who really made a direct impression on you. We are not talking about the ones who had the grandest titles, the highest pay, or the offices with the windows. On the contrary, we suspect that many of us think back most fondly to those individuals who treated others with respect that was absent of condescension. Even the most powerful of leaders has the choice to be humble. The people they serve notice.

"For the Cause" (*Star Trek: Deep Space Nine* S04E22; Moore et al., 1996) reminds us of the reality that leadership sometimes involves navigating competing interpersonal spheres. Being human (and presumably Klingon, Trill, even Founder…) means having obligations to others beyond the confines of leadership. Work-home balance can be difficult to achieve. An example of such a challenge is the journey that Aaron took while completing his doctorate. Anyone who has undertaken this academic journey knows the amount of time, tears, and determination necessary to achieve such a goal. Often, those that embark upon such a journey must make difficult decisions, particularly when it comes to spending time (or not) with family. His sons were young when he studied toward his degree, and he made the choice to not want to miss out on time with them. As a result, he worked during the day, spent time with his wife and boys in the evening, and studied when everyone went to bed.

He lost a few hours of sleep each night, but the relationship with his family was what truly drove him.

The careful leveraging of positional power can serve as a potent tool in leadership so long as one does not abuse that power. In "To the Death" (*Star Trek: Deep Space Nine* S04E23; Behr et al., 1996), Sisko found himself in the unenviable role of having to use his social capital to get things done. The tradeoff was that he had to rely on the most transactional of approaches. It is our observation that such problem-solving tends to be successful at best in the short term. Over time, people tend to become weary of being told what to do. It then becomes that much more difficult for a leader to demonstrate anything approaching enlightened or compassionate leadership. We are not suggesting that there are never times when it is appropriate (and even necessary) to assert positional power. However, we do recommend one does so with great intention and as much foresight as one can muster.

"In the Pale Moonlight" (*Star Trek: Deep Space Nine* S06E19; Fields & Lobi, 1996) reiterates that conflict is inherent to leadership. As long as there are different people there will be differing ideas. Typically, a diversity of perspectives makes for better problem-solving. However, dissimilar beliefs can also yield argumentation and the potential for interpersonal conflict. Perhaps war is an extreme example to get the point across. We are not so sure. How many times have you felt yourself at odds with others, or at least at odds with their goals? Whether it is a war of might, words, or roses, it is easy to become caught up in the minutiae and fail to recognize the bigger picture. This is when the leader must step back and consider their ethical obligations to those they serve and of the implications of their decisions. As the proverb suggests, a good name is hard to come by and very easy to lose. Since avoiding conflict is simply not an option, how we choose to engage in it will prove to be a key factor in how we lead.

Similar is the necessity in leadership of managing one's ego. Our experience, and certainly our observations of others over the years, is that ego tends to prove the harder nut to crack than does "mere" conflict. We each have needs, be they more basic (can I get a good Wi-Fi signal here?) or more complex (will they recognize the amount of work I have put into this plan?), and these needs often drive our daily behaviors. Think of those leaders you most respect. Better yet, think of the people in your life you have most sought to emulate. Were they highly successful? Perhaps. Were they pompous quadrupeds? We suspect not.

Chapter 7. Sisko: Ethical Realist

Sisko was a leader of exceptional intestinal fortitude. He was thrust into the crucible of conflict from the moment he took command of *Deep Space Nine*. Nonetheless, we more typically observe him to struggle more with the challenges within him than with those around him. "Take Me Out to the Holosuite" (*Star Trek: Deep Space Nine* S07E04; Moore & Chalmers, 1998) is an amusing but relatable example of how it is often the little things that most tweak our egos. People want to be heard. They want to be acknowledged and respected. It is our job as leaders to provide social spaces, not to mention relevant work, in which their dignity can flourish.

So, let us return for a moment to the question we posed above. Who have you sought to model in your own leadership? When Jason began teaching, he often thought back to the professors who had most influenced him. Both the good and bad often came to mind. How had they treated their college students? There was one professor who had an especially potent impact on his professional development as an eventual professor. Doc, as many of his students knew him, was an intelligent and warm individual who always had a moment to spare outside of class for his students. Although it was not his major department, he had the good fortune to work for Doc as a departmental assistant. What most stood out was not Doc's intellect, nor his charming smile and laugh, but the way he treated every student with a deep sense of respect. One always felt seen and appreciated when interacting with him. How many of us have been so equitable in our dealings with those "below" us?

Perhaps one of the most personally challenging of decisions to be made is recognizing when it is time to step down. In "What You Leave Behind" (*Star Trek: Deep Space Nine* S07E26/26; Behr et al., 1999), Sisko's actions provide a fanciful but relevant case in which we see a leader at the top of their game willingly remit the authority of their formal role. This point is important. We would suggest that one's responsibility to the organization or the people one led necessarily cease upon exit from a leadership role. Indeed, you might find your voice even more sought after once people can come to you with "unofficial" requests for advising.

More than 2000 years ago, Lao-tzu wrote that "The Master doesn't talk, he acts. When his work is done, the people say, 'Amazing: we did it, all by ourselves!'" (Mitchell, 1994, p. 17). Learning to lead through conflict and to do so without your own personal baggage is central to the vocation. Every organization presents a unique cultural milieu in which some behaviors are considered appropriate and others taboo (Schein & Schein, 2017). The culture of one organization might value the power of reason, another might lean more heavily on interpersonal skills, while a third might be quite dysfunctional and ignore both. It is easy to become piqued by people questioning your motives, challenging your ideas, or working to frustrate your plans (not that either of us have ever experienced any of those things ... ever). Sisko never intended to take credit for helping to win the war. But darned if he was going to lose a baseball game to another crew. Can't we all relate?

Sisko demonstrated how one can remain independent of thought while navigating the pressures of conflict and ego during even the direst of situations. He similarly treated his crew with a basic sense of compassion for their needs, fears, and desires in uncertain times. This often required major emotional fortitude. Indeed, such independence of thought can morph into self-righteousness when one is not careful. If we have learned anything in our current twenty-first century, it is all too easy to drink the proverbial sugar water of an enticing movement or meme. The challenge before us is whether we can harness the intellectual and social courage to move ahead without leaving anyone behind.

Guidance from Guinan

Imagine yourself sitting at a small table under the arching windows of Ten Forward, the frontmost point and social hub of the U.S.S. *Enterprise*. The view out the windows is one of stark blackness punctuated by countless points of light, stars of every imaginable color. Sitting across the table is Guinan, the unofficial sage of the starship. Wise beyond measure, Guinan has served for centuries as a guide to innumerable leaders. Now she is fully present in the moment with you.

"What's on your mind?" Guinan asks you with that knowingly subtle smile. "You mentioned you were thinking about Captain Sisko. What about him stands out to you as a leader to model?"

Guinan continues to look at you expectantly. There is no hint of impatience, just that twinkle in her eye. "Think of Sisko's approach to leadership," she suggests. "How does your behavior as a leader compare with his?"

Guinan looks out the windows to the stars for a moment, and

Chapter 7. Sisko: Ethical Realist

then turns back to you. "How do you *communicate* with others in a manner that is intentional and transparent?"

After giving you a moment to think and respond, Guinan asks you, "How do you exercise *patience* by listening to what others have to say?"

Guinan listens to your response, momentarily closes her eyes and nods with a smile, and then poses one more question to you. "How do you develop a relationship with others so that they feel seen and heard?"

After you respond, you and Guinan chat a bit longer before she has to return to her customers. You look back out at the stars, toward the seemingly endless potential of leadership, and think about how to lead more like Sisko.

Chapter 8

Janeway: Tireless Thinker

As you end the call with your colleague and allow the sounds of the redwood forest to again encroach upon your awareness, it occurs to you that leadership can be a lonely voyage. That chat might have lasted no more than 20 minutes but it gave you much to ponder. Writing about the pioneers of the old Silicon Valley just 50 klicks or so to the south of your current whereabouts, Heidi Berlin (2017) observed that troublemakers often share two key traits. They tend to be persistent as well as audacious in challenging the status quo. Why was your colleague so resistant to your ideas? Was your thinking really so off the mark? You never really thought of yourself as a troublemaker. Yet, that was the label they applied to you as what may or may not have been a complement.

You look up at the giant trees. There would be time to revisit your assertions, to check your logic for errors. There would be time to hone your argument. But not now. No, you tell yourself aloud, we cannot always deliver in the moment nor predict what the future holds. And that has to be okay. Sometimes leadership must be lonely, and sometimes we are wrong. The important thing is that we move forward with a willingness to learn.

Rising from the park bench, surrounded by the song of the crickets as dusk settles, you head back toward the familiar wooden gate and out of the park. Being a troublemaker might not be a fair description, but you are nothing if not persistent.

The ride back to the city is uneventful. Indeed, you find the ride across San Francisco at night to buoy your spirits. The lights and patterns of the city at night remind you of the wonderful complexity of life and the value of the work in which you are engaged.

Upon arriving at the spaceport, you pass through security (a scan and a smile from a security agent) and walk toward your gate. It never fails to impress you how the major spaceports have such a diversity of food

Chapter 8. Janeway: Tireless Thinker

on offer from the quadrants. You grab a raktajino and briefly contemplate using the time waiting for your flight for work. But it has been a busy day, one of success and challenge, and now is the perfect time to relax and reflect upon it all. Tomorrow you will sit down to compose a considered response to your colleague, the one who interrupted your brief sojourn among the redwoods. You will keep your mind open. What did Captain Janeway demonstrate during her heroic mission of leadership when isolated? You will clarify the importance of your shared mission (basic leadership skill: **communication**), explain the balance of options before the group (basic leadership skill: **patience**), and even though they remind you a little bit of a Kazon overlord, extend a proverbial olive branch to that one colleague to ensure a continued working relationship between the two of you (basic leadership skill: **relationship**).

Captain's Log

Long before she would become the first Starfleet captain to transverse the Delta Quadrant, Kathryn Janeway (played by Kate Mulgrew) began her voyage navigating the farmland of her youth on Earth. Born in Bloomington, Indiana, in 2328 (Memory Alpha, n.d. j), Janeway was encouraged by her father from a young age to observe the world around her through the lens of a skeptic. Coupled with the apocryphal family story of an intrepid ancestor and her own scientific bent, Janeway applied to Starfleet Academy to pursue a life among the stars as a scientist (*Star Trek: Voyager* S05E23; Braga et al., 1999). However, she would end up taking a more inflected path as her time at university introduced her to the lure of command.

Reflecting back upon her studies, Janeway cited the importance of two things: coffee and mentorship. Her love of coffee (okay, it was an addiction) began at a little café not too far from the Academy grounds. The liquid motivation would help her to pull the all-nighters she relied upon to complete her coursework (*Star Trek: Voyager* S05E04; Sagan & Livingston, 1998). In addition, the chief groundskeeper Boothby served as an important mentor to Janeway. He offered wise counsel from a perspective that often differed from the professors on campus. Boothby also brought fresh roses to Janeway's quarters every morning (eww).

Leadership in *Star Trek*

Janeway's first posting subsequent to graduation was to the U.S.S. *Al-Batani*, where she soon served as chief science officer. During this time Janeway demonstrated her resolve to explore new ideas as well as an ability to blow out a series of positronic relays about the ship. Indeed, her resoluteness in the face of the unknown stood out among her peers. It is perhaps not surprising that, early in her career, Janeway switched tracks from science to command and would be assigned as commander to the U.S.S. *Billings*. It was in 2371, however, that Janeway would be given the helm as captain of the U.S.S. *Voyager*. A brand-new starship on the cutting edge of technology at the time, *Voyager* would prove to be a resilient home for Janeway and her crew.

Instructive for our purpose is how Janeway was called upon to lead a new crew amid a protracted crisis that did not allow for planning or prior team-building. In pursuit of a rebel ship (no, not those rebels), *Voyager* was caught up in a displacement wave and cast 70,000 light years to the far side of the Delta Quadrant. What is even more remarkable was Janeway's decision shortly thereafter to remain so as to protect the Ocampa, a people never before encountered by the Federation, in lieu of being able to return home to Earth. Let us be clear on this point. In a moment of epic proportion, Janeway made the decision that her duty to Starfleet principles was more important than her longing to return home. She understood that her obligation to assist others in need took precedence over all else. As Janeway so wryly summarized when questioned about her resolve, "We'll have to find another way home" (*Star Trek: Voyager* S01E01/2; Berman, et al., 1995).

Janeway's leadership during the voyage home was marked by two key features especially relevant to our discussion. First and foremost, Janeway was unwaveringly committed to the principles of Starfleet as well as to the needs of her crew. For seven years she led them homeward with tenacity in the face of seemingly insurmountable obstacles. Even during the most trying times, Janeway refused to give up in the face of the impossible. It is also true that she would ultimately violate one of the most sacred of her beloved Starfleet principles in order to rescue those bridge crew lost on the way home. All idols have clay feet.

At the same time, Janeway was the consummate explorer. Not willing to waste the opportunity to explore a quadrant of the Galaxy never before seen by the Federation, she maintained the fundamental mission

Chapter 8. *Janeway: Tireless Thinker*

to explore strange new worlds and seek out new life and new civilizations on the way home. This dedication was apparent not only in her time aboard *Voyager* but eventually as well while (sort of) aboard the U.S.S. *Protostar*. Such peregrinations would often take Janeway and her crew off course. This was a cost in time and risk that she perceived to be acceptable in return for what they might learn along the way.

Janeway was a *tireless thinker* as a captain, one characterized by duty and curiosity, both of which facilitated her ability to mobilize an often fraught crew serving aboard an often harrowed starship. These features of character allowed her, even amidst the most challenging of situations, to leverage the basic leadership skills of communication, patience, and relationship.

Canon Fodder

The character of Janeway and her efforts to bring home her beleaguered crew went down in the annals of Federation history as an example of stolid leadership in the face of insurmountable odds. She provides for us an opportunity to consider how the basic leadership skills of *communication*, *patience*, and *relationship* can be called upon in even the most dire of circumstances. Becoming stranded on the wrong side of the Galaxy was an ideal opportunity to respond with adaptive leadership style, one that balanced the intentional experimentation of new ideas within the confines of acceptable risk (Heifetz & Linsky, 2002). Not only did Janeway respond adaptively to her new situation, but she did so with an ever-changing balance of reason and compassion more dynamic than any captain before or since. Indeed, she regularly demonstrated her wonder at the mysteries of the Universe, a hesitancy to fire upon enemies who might become allies, and the importance of kinship to buoy the spirit.

Perhaps it is not surprising that, as much as any other of the captains, Janeway embodied Enlightenment thinking in her leadership across the Delta Quadrant. It would have been understandable for her to pursue the most direct route home to Federation space. Instead, in episode after episode, we saw Janeway and her crew detour for the sake of discovery. Friedman (2016) summarized such a mindset quite well:

Leadership in *Star Trek*

> In such a time, opting to pause and reflect, rather than panic or withdraw, is a necessity. It is not a luxury or a distraction—it is a way to increase the odds that you'll better understand, and engage productively with, the world around you [p. 4].

Janeway modeled for her crew the importance of learning about the world, indeed about the Galaxy, to inform problem-solving. Her desire to learn from new opportunities invariably overshadowed her anxieties about an uncertain future. How many leaders do you know who have evinced such a willingness to move forward without being concerned about what remains behind? Our own experience suggests otherwise, especially our observations of executive leaders in nonprofit sectors.

Janeway similarly demonstrated herself to be one of the more actualized captains in *Trek* canon. This can be most clearly seen in Janeway's determination to liberate and then mentor Seven of Nine. The early steps of the process were not exactly met with glee and clearly rendered the character of Janeway little in the way of good feelings, Yet, Janeway persisted because she perceived another to be in need and recognized her own ability to help coupled with a felt obligation to do so. This is a common characteristic among more actualized individuals. Maslow (1967) observed that self-actualized individuals, having already met their basic needs, become intrinsically motivated to assist others. It is worth noting that being stranded on the other side of the Galaxy likely undermined some of those basic needs. Nevertheless, Janeway persisted. She remained compassionate not merely in spite of, but perhaps because of, the challenges of her situation. She understood how to meet her own needs, and this allowed her to better address those of the individuals she led.

Alliances

Principles can be a tricky thing. For more than a year, the *Voyager* crew had navigated a path home toward the Alpha Quadrant. Along the way they encountered friends and foes, but none proved more problematic than the Kazon. A formerly enslaved people who had risen up and become a society of spacefaring warriors, the Kazon attempted (on numerous occasions) to capture or destroy *Voyager*. It thus came as a surprise to her crew in "Alliances" (*Star Trek: Voyager* S06E16; Taylor

Chapter 8. Janeway: Tireless Thinker

& Landau, 1996) when Janeway attempted to broker a peace deal with the leaders of the loosely bound Kazon Order. She did so during a time when there was growing distrust among a number of her crew. The logic of the situation warranted a strong hand. Alternatively, Janeway felt it her responsibility to care for, and not merely lead, her crew. As Heifetz and Linsky (2002) observed, "to lead is to live dangerously" (p. 65). Such problem-solving was an example of Janeway's unflinching willingness to think beyond the tridimensional containment unit. What is notably instructive for the sake of our conversation is a scene toward the end of this heralded episode.

Having failed to broker the peace agreement due to the actions of a malign third party (let's be honest, we all saw it coming), the crew of *Voyager* found themselves on the run and more vulnerable than ever. Addressing her newly combined crew of Starfleet officers and Maquis freedom fighters, Janeway stressed the importance of unity and the logic behind her attempt to broker a détente: "In a part of space where there are few rules, it's more important than ever that we hold fast to our own. In a region where shifting allegiances are commonplace, we have to have something stable to rely on" (Taylor & Landau, 1996). Think for a moment about the situation. Janeway remained committed to her principles and willing to explore new possibilities even when faced with almost certain setbacks. Can we each say the same?

How did Janeway capitalize upon the basic leadership skills to remain in control not only of the situation but of herself? She began with a willingness to seek an understanding of those who thought differently than her, and she did so by seeking consultation with others. In other words, she leaned on her team. Heifetz and Linsky (2002) wrote about such situations (albeit more locally) that

> to make real progress, sooner or later those who lead must ask themselves and the people in the organization to face a set of deeper issues—and to accept a solution that may require turning part of all of the organization upside down.... Leadership is an improvisational art [p. 66].

Janeway recognized that she needed to adapt to the reality of the Delta Quadrant.

In this case, Janeway sought counsel from Lieutenant Commander Tuvok. As an expert in tactical matters and a keen logician, what would Tuvok do to navigate the situation with the Kazon? Receiving his guidance, Janeway did what all truly adept leaders do; she made her own decision in light of multiple inputs. We consequently witness Janeway express openly to her crew the rationale to take an unpopular chance and reach out to the Kazon (basic leadership skill: *communication*) in a measured and stepwise process (basic leadership skill: *patience*). When the effort proved unsuccessful, indeed nearly catastrophic, Janeway held court with the crew and sought to unite them in solidarity of cause (basic leadership skill: *relationship*).

Year

It had been approximately three years since Janeway and her crew attempted to make peace with the Kazon. During this time, the Federation and former Maquis crews so abruptly brought together by their isolation found ways to mesh with a sense of shared purpose. Janeway's determination to adhere to Starfleet principles undoubtedly provided the guidance for such an organizational evolution. Nonetheless, threats presented themselves as *Voyager* made its way across this lawless region of space.

In "Year of Hell" (*Star Trek: Voyager* S04E08; Braga et al., 1997), *Voyager* became caught up in a space-time shock wave that rewrote history across 5000 parsecs and erased almost countless sentient lives when its chronitonic shielding protected it from attack by a Kremin temporal weapon ship (don't even try to figure it out, it's time travel, just accept it). We learn in short order that the events of the episode were driven by the desire of Krenim leader Annorax to "restore" the timeline to a point when loved ones were not lost.

We think this rather dark episode is important to leadership for at least a couple of reasons. Without doubt, the events of the temporal difficulties highlight Janeway's strength of will as captain. Facing off nose to nose with the exceptionally more powerful Kremin temporal weapon ship, she responded to the Krenim leader's ultimatum with controlled resolve by stating succinctly that "I don't respond well to threats" (Braga et al., 1997). Perhaps more importantly for our own everyday challenges (not all of us lead from the bridge of a starship), "Year of Hell" prompts us to question whether the ends justify the means. Judgment is always clouded when emotions or personal stakes are involved. Logic can falter, compassion can whither. Heifetz and Linsky (2002) cautioned that leadership can become readily clouded. As they wrote,

> we all have hungers, expressions of our normal human needs. But sometimes those hungers disrupt our capacity to act wisely or purposefully.... Everyone wants to have some measure of control over [their] life.... But in your desire for order, you mistake the means for the end [p. 71].

Attempting to adapt novelly to a situation requires that we not allow our feelings to cloud our judgment. How can a leader defend against such self-delusion?

Janeway's example teaches us that "what's important ... is that we're together, working toward a single goal..." (Braga et al., 1997). It is all too easy in moments of crisis for leaders to become convinced by their own certainty. Although to do so is human (even Vulcan), logic and the needs of those one serves dictate that we hold ourselves to a higher level of accountability. Even when she led her crew through the valley of the shadow of death, Janeway never hid herself away. She consistently solicited input from her crew present for her crew (basic leadership skill: *communication*). It is true that there were moments in the episode when Janeway was required to respond in the moment. However, most of her major decisions were predicated on consulting with others and weighing the possible outcomes (basic leadership skill: *patience*). At the end of the episode, when it seemed all was lost, Janeway spoke to the assembled crew as if they were not subordinates but family (basic leadership skill: *relationship*).

What often distinguishes an effective leader is their ability to lead collaboratively with those for whom they are responsible. Janeway demonstrated time and again that the strongest of leaders will perceive their responsibilities as those of partnership.

Collective

As Cameron and Quinn (2011) recognized, organizations have a tendency to develop their own cultures. The culture of any given organization is typified by an intermix of competing values unique to the history, work, and leadership of that organization. These factors typically take time to learn, especially given that many of their elements tend to be unwritten. The result is often that onboarding poses one of the more challenging processes for an organization to accomplish well. How effectively (and painlessly) can new hires of an organization learn the expectations of which they are now members?

"Collective" (*Star Trek: Voyager* S06E16; Taylor et al., 2000) provides an example of onboarding in the extreme. Now in their sixth year amidst the Delta Quadrant, Janeway and her officers had learned how to handle the Borg when they encountered a damaged cube ship. More remarkably, they discovered the presence of five Borg children wandering beyond the confines of their neonatal chambers. After much discussion, Janeway decided to bring the Borg children aboard *Voyager* so as to rehabilitate them so as to offer them the full lives which they were denied by assimilation.

Talk about a difficult onboarding. The Borg children experienced a sudden transition to an entirely new setting that required the relearning of their most basic assumptions. This was not merely a question of whom to contact in HR for health care paperwork. Issues of personal identity were at stake as much as expectations of communication and comportment. In other words, these young new members of the crew required not merely orientation to their new roles by integration into the cultural milieu (Byford et al., 2017). How did Janeway proceed? She worked to ensure that the Borg children received a basic orientation and guided integration to the culture aboard ship. Janeway also recognized the value of shared experience in the onboarding process and thus solicited for the children the guidance of Seven of Nine, a dedicated mentor who could help them transition from their previous roles to their new ones.

In other words, beyond merely taking in these new recruits, Janeway intentionally leveraged the human (and other) and technological resources at her disposal to facilitate the onboarding of the Borg children to *Voyager*. Instead of leaving them to the care of Seven of Nine, she made it a point to regularly interact with the children during unstructured but intentional encounters (basic leadership skill: *communication*). Given the abruptness and severity of the transition the children experienced, Janeway made certain not to rush their transition by setting unrealistic expectations of the timeline (basic leadership skill: *patience*). Notably, although she was the captain, she went out of her way to reach out to these newest and youngest members of the crew (basic leadership skill: *relationship*). How many of us can say we experienced

Chapter 8. Janeway: Tireless Thinker

the same level of thought and care when being the one onboarded to a new position?

Equinox

On an otherwise unremarkable day in the Delta Quadrant, *Voyager* received a distress signal from a ship in need of aid. To the surprise of Janeway and her bridge officers, the request for aid was being transmitted from the U.S.S. *Equinox*, a Federation vessel designed for short-range planetary research and one not expected to be roaming so far from home (Memory Alpha, n.d. k). Upon arrival at the indicated coordinates, Janeway discovered the heavily damaged *Equinox* under attack and very far from home. More revealing would be what she observed inside the ship.

Janeway had spent the past five years working to ensure a commitment among her crew to Federation ideals. *Voyager* would chart a course home to the Alpha Quadrant, but along the way they would continue to execute their mission to seek out new life and new civilizations. The captain of *Equinox*, in sharp contradistinction, identified survival as the sole mission of his crew. "Equinox" (*Star Trek: Voyager* S05E26; Berman et al., 1999) thus introduced us to a Federation starship on which order had broken down to be replaced by the trappings of urgency, loyalty, and expediency. Note that this was not a matter of polywater intoxication (*Star Trek: The Next Generation* S01E03; Black et al., 1987) but a considered decision by a leader under pressure.

Perhaps the relevance of the episode to leadership is already clear. It is important for a leader to remain disciplined in the face of adversity. We are not talking about having to follow a militaristically rigid set of expectations (although good on you if you are a military leader and must do so). Leadership requires us to self-regulate for the sake of others and the organization. Do you remember being taught the importance of the "three R's" in elementary school? We would suggest that a fourth "R" is needed from our earliest days of childhood in addition to reading, writing, and arithmetic. Self-regulation (it's an "R," trust us) ought to be taught as a basic element of educational practice. Consider how it might influence the world about us as those children so instructed become the leaders of our world.

"Equinox" (Berman et al., 1999) provides an example of what can result when leadership lacks discipline. As we can observe in the character of Captain Ransom, in its place can arise the more base elements of human anxiety. As Ransom said to Janeway, "It's easy to cling to your principles when you're standing on a vessel with its bulkheads intact, manned by a crew that's not starving." We have often opined in these pages that leadership can be difficult. It is during such times when self-regulation is especially important for effective leadership. Such discipline works in two directions. A leader must work to maintain internal discipline as a model for others. They must also remain cognizant of the responsibilities of their role to the organization. Think back to the great leaders of history. These individuals are not remembered because their lot in life was easy. Quite the opposite. It can be easy to lead when things are going swimmingly. Leaders truly demonstrate their principles when the going gets tough.

The events with *Equinox* and its crew seemed especially trying for Janeway. Yet, through it all she demonstrated the basic leadership skills with aplomb. Janeway celebrated the discovery (and rescue) of the *Equinox* crew and made clear they were now part of the *Voyager* family (basic leadership skill: *communication*). She demonstrated truly impressive restraint (i.e., self-regulation) as the realities of life and decisions aboard *Equinox* were revealed (basic leadership skill: *patience*). Even when confronting Ransom about the discovery of his ethical misdeeds, Janeway sought to broker an understanding between captains (basic leadership skill: *relationship*).

The tale of *Equinox* does not end particularly well in the subsequent episode. However, through it all, Janeway demonstrated the importance of self-regulation to an effective leader. Not every story has a happy ending. Not every leader knows only happy days. Indeed, we have yet to meet one. It is a reminder that leadership is ultimately not about the leader but those whom they serve. Serve them well.

Q Two

Unenviable tasks are often an ignored reality of leadership. We suspect it is atypical for aspiring leaders to daydream about the projects, reports, and politics they will undoubtedly have to navigate as they progress in their careers. Nonetheless, it is often the case that positions of

Chapter 8. Janeway: Tireless Thinker

leadership, especially formal positions with titles, tend to bring with them certain responsibilities expected of the roles either by organizational policy or history. "Q2" (*Star Trek: Voyager* S07E19; Doherty et al., 2001) provides us with a farcical, yet useful, example of how even the most adept leader can become mired in the unwanted responsibilities of their role.

The episode opens with Janeway being introduced to Q Junior, the son of the godlike Q. Janeway is informed by Q that his son has caused some amount of difficulty amidst the Galaxy, and that the Q Continuum (imagine the meetings...) had decided Junior and his father must make recompense. To be certain, there are no lack of problems with the episode. For example, why would a nearly omniscient and potentially omnipresent (not to mention nearly omnipotent) being capable of changing the gravitational constant of the universe be sexually attracted to human females?

Regardless, the episode can promote serious consideration of the topic under discussion. We define unenviable tasks as those responsibilities expected to be executed by a leader without it being their interest, idea, or desire. One example of such tasks might be the supervision of subordinates in the organization. Some individuals truly enjoy leading others in a shared enterprise, but others simply want to do the work of what they envisioned as a largely solo role. Another example of an unenviable task might be the direction of a program tagged to a specific role. For example, one of us (who shall remain anonymous) was required to oversee an outreach program when he served in college leadership. This responsibility had no inherent connection to the leadership role but instead had been assigned to it long ago to help distribute the proverbial weight of a number of such programs across their fellow administrators. Finally, there will always be the eternal necessity of writing reports. Enough said.

"Q2" (Doherty et al., 2001) presents to us an example of a captain doing their best to do what must be done. Instead of resenting her "assignment" from Q and lapsing into a passive-aggressive posture, Janeway sought to better understand Junior's needs (basic leadership skill: *communication*). If we give this odd episode a chance to teach us, we can see that Janeway repeatedly attempted to work with Junior regardless of his pushback because it was her responsibility (basic leadership skill: *patience*). Quite importantly for our discussion, she managed to

Leadership in *Star Trek*

maintain a noble level of civility throughout the entire adventure (basic leadership skill: *relationship*).

In the episode, Janeway tried her best to work with Junior to help him grow as an individual. She also enlisted the assistance of several of her bridge crew. Time and again their efforts met with frustration if not an interrupted bubble bath. Because this is *Star Trek*, Junior eventually begins to come around to the interventions of Janeway and her crew. However, the reality in our Prime universe is that leaders faced with unenviable tasks are just as likely to have to be the ones to adapt to those tasks. This is all part of leadership.

Con-tact

Much has been written about the value of leading with a transformational instead of transactional style. However, in "First Con-tact" (*Star Trek: Prodigy* S01E07; Pendleton-Thompson et al., 2022), Janeway (who was manifested as an emergency training hologram) demonstrates that even better is to lead through an educational lens. The episode opens with a number of revelations regarding the background of Dal, the series' main protagonist, and the U.S.S. *Protostar* on which he and his crew travel. However, the real lesson of the story revolves around the matter of first contact with the Cymari, a civilization of the Delta Quadrant never before encountered by the Federation. It is soon discovered that the Cymari are in possession of crystals of great value beyond their world. Dal and his (literally) adolescent crew dismiss hologram Janeway's admonitions about the Prime Directive and proceed planetside where they somewhat inevitably make a mess of things given their lack of training.

Instructive for our purposes is that hologram Janeway did not attempt to stop them from beaming down. Let's think about this for a moment. Although programmed to assist and not to command, hologram Janeway presumably maintained access to all sorts of ship functions. It is made pretty obvious in the series that she could exercise her will when holographic push came to shove (don't think about that one too closely). Yet, throughout the episode, hologram Janeway chose to lead by educating instead of directing. She recognized that while her crew might not be ready to take what they had chosen, they might be able to learn

Chapter 8. Janeway: Tireless Thinker

the next few steps along the way. Vygotsky (1978) wrote about such an approach decades ago (our time, not hologram Janeway's time) when he stressed that learning ideally occurs within a zone of proximal development. He argued that children learn best when they are pushed just past what they know but so far past that they become frustrated amidst too much new information. Wood et al. (1976) defined such an approach as *scaffolding*, an educational practice that "novice to solve a task or achieve a goal that would be beyond his unassisted efforts" (p. 90). This is exactly what we observe of hologram Janeway when she sought to instruct her crew without forcing them to abide by her wishes.

Scaffolding is equally valuable as a leadership skill in our organizations. More than merely seeking to transform subordinates into leaders, we each are presented countless opportunities to teach the people we lead how to better acquit themselves in their thinking, task completion, and eventual leadership. Scaffolding provides a cognitive and practical framework upon which those we lead can build their own skill sets. But it requires time and practice of our own. Imagine the possibilities of leadership when every activity is recognized as a potential moment of education.

This is how hologram Janeway led in "First Con-tact" (Pendleton-Thompson et al., 2022). She intentionally scaffolded her approach toward leading her nascent crew in the ways of Starfleet code and culture by introducing new information within their shared zone of proximal development (basic leadership skill: *communication*). Hologram Janeway recognized along the way that the process might require quite some time (basic leadership skill: *patience*). Her crew were children, after all. Interestingly, she scolded them at the end of the episode. Part of leadership is being honest even while remaining compassionate in order to provide corrective feedback (basic leadership skill: *relationship*).

Do It

How can we take these lessons and apply them to our own leadership? It is one thing to respect an implacable leader like Janeway, but another to implement her lessons into our daily choices. Let's take the examples above and see how they might fit with our own practice.

"Alliances" (*Star Trek: Voyager* S02E14; Taylor & Landau, 1996)

Leadership in *Star Trek*

reminds us that all leadership is people leadership. You might think that we are stating the obvious. We think not. How many times have we each been guilty of saying something like "that company releases really cool products every year"? Or that "this restaurant serves some of the best food in town"? Think for a moment about how often we automatically refer not to the people who make decisions within organizations but instead to the organizations themselves as sentient entities. The implicit assumption of equating organizations with the people who run them is more than a mere psychological quirk. It is a perspective literally written into American corporate law. More importantly for leadership, focusing on organizations instead of the people who comprise them means that we risk habitually losing sight of those who make the actual decisions, engage in the actual work of their organizations, and provide the actual opportunities for growth and development.

Janeway demonstrated in her dealings with the Kazon that decisions must be targeted not at organizations (or even politico-militaristic cabals, for that matter) but at the individuals within the organizations. Leadership can motivate actual people within to work with us. Intentional communication is the most direct path toward leading others. Recognizing their needs and anxieties, we can create social or structural opportunities for people to grow in their work. Both of us can think back to examples when others in power helped us by coaching professional development, challenging our assumptions, or demystifying workplace politics. These are matters of relationship.

The trials encountered by Janeway and her crew during the "Year of Hell" (*Star Trek: Voyager* S04E08; Braga, Menosky, & Kroeker, 1997) required constant vigilance in a time of crisis. Throughout the ordeal, Janeway remained resolute in her patient attention to the needs of her crew without wavering from the ideals she swore to uphold. The episode illuminates the importance of maintaining one's cool regardless of the situation, but not in isolation.

Spock once observed that nature "abhors a vacuum" (*Star Trek IV: The Voyage Home*; Nimoy, 1986). So does leadership. We have often observed a tendency, especially in the Western world, of people to worship cults of personality. Especially in the corporate arena (Silicon Valley, anyone?), it seems as often as not that organizations become identified if not actually defined by their chief executives. Think of Apple and Steve Jobs, Microsoft and Bill Gates, or SpaceX and Elon Musk (and note

Chapter 8. Janeway: Tireless Thinker

the misogyny). Without question these are examples of individuals who blazed remarkable paths. What we wish to point out is that such people exemplify the situation in which leaders and the organizations they lead are taken as synonymous. So what, one might ask: Is it not ideal to be identified with the organization one leads? We think not.

Joining a new organization can be difficult, whether it be navigating human resource paperwork, becoming acquainted with the everyday tasks of the new role, or finding the right cubicle (or regeneration chamber). Indeed, even moving positions within an organization often poses its own set of challenges. Several years ago Jason moved from his previous community college to his current university position. Both institutions were in the same state system of higher education. There even was a colleague who took it upon herself to introduce him to the workways of his new department. However, what remained fundamentally absent was an intentional onboarding process. He was left to his own devices to ask questions and navigate expectations both written and unspoken. Although this situation was nowhere as extreme as that portrayed in "Collective" (*Star Trek: Voyager* S06E16; Taylor et al., 2000), the root problem was similar. The difference was that Janeway leveraged all three of the basic leadership skills to create an onboarding process for her new crewmembers (né Borg children) to slowly but surely integrate into *Voyager's* collective.

"Equinox" (*Star Trek: Voyager* S05E26; Berman et al., 1999) serves as a reminder that self-discipline is important in leadership. One might counter that this is obvious. We agree. However, have you ever actually had training in self-regulation as a developing leader? We both teach leadership and have filled numerous opportunities large and small to lead. Yet, neither of us have ever received any formal training in discipline as leaders. Instead, we have both learned this skill set the hard way through office politics. Enough said. Actually, it is important that we say more.

We function as leaders in a beautiful and infinitely complex world. Yet, the reality is that we will be challenged by both situations and people. Once might shrug off a situation gone badly and move forward with determination. However, it is far more difficult to remain disciplined when being called out by those in your professional sphere. People often have a nasty habit of believing themselves to be right and in the right. Dunning and Kruger (Dunning et al., 2003) repeatedly found that people "tend to be blissfully unaware of their own incompetence" (p. 83). We are not suggesting that people who disagree with you are inherently incompetent. Instead, we wish to emphasize the importance of recognizing that people tend to be convinced of their own beliefs. Leadership requires us to keep our cool when dealing with them.

Indeed, leadership often brings with it certain undesirable responsibilities. Let us limit our discussion here to those tasks that are expected of a given leadership role. In "Q2" (*Star Trek: Voyager* S07E19; Doherty et al. 2001), Janeway was forced by the situation to accept responsibility for the remediation of Q Junior. The situation provided her no lack of consternation and thereby demonstrated her tenacious patience in the face of adversity. Sometimes, patience can be the most challenging of the basic leadership skills. This seems especially true in our current digital age. We are constantly being distracted not so much by pressing issues but by issues which each present themselves as pressing (Levy, 2007). A recent example we have noticed is the frequency with which we hear one of the "dings" of familiar email services during online meetings. Think for a moment about the implications. In order for us to become aware of such distractions, the individual with whom we are currently in a meeting must also have their Web browser open to their email account. In other words, like seemingly everyone these days, they are unintentionally multitasking. Unfortunately, multitasking tends not to work (American Psychological Association, 2006).

Wouldn't it be nice to have an emergency training hologram (an ETH) at our side during challenging situations? Problem solved. This is not our reality in the twenty-first century, but it was (will be?) for the crew of *Protostar*. Throughout the series and as exemplified in "Con-tact" (Pendleton-Thompson et al., 2022), hologram Janeway repeatedly presented through her actions the value of taking an educational approach to leadership. It is our contention that every leadership event provides the potential to educate those we serve (or sometimes better self-regulate ourselves). As professors of leadership, this is something with which we both engage on a regular basis. However, teaching leadership is much easier in the classroom or during a workshop than it is in the field.

Hologram Janeway made this clear when she warned her wayward crew that interfering in the lives of a pre-warp civilization was a violation of the Prime Directive. She sought to teach in a manner that allowed her crew to make mistakes. Much has been written of the importance

Chapter 8. Janeway: Tireless Thinker

of failure toward personal and organizational learning (e.g., Firestein, 2015). Think back to the adage that there are no stupid questions. As one of us teaches in his classes, that is simply untrue. The world is full of stupid questions and it is important that we ask them. There is major value in leading through the lens of education. It can prove more than transformational.

Alas, leadership can be an inherently lonely role. For example, Jason temporarily served as an interim dean at a previous college. One day he was on faculty, and the next he was sitting in an office in the administrative suite on campus. His faculty were lovely to him, which was especially important given he had left his division to lead another. Nonetheless, it was apparent that the dynamic had changed. He was no longer a colleague, he was now a supervisor among those with whom he had worked and formed relationships for years. His door was always open and his faculty were encouraging of his new role. Nonetheless, he was isolated from his former colleagues. This was neither good nor bad. It was the reality of leadership.

Your crew (and colleagues) can seem like family. This was definitely true for Aaron. In his beginnings within higher education and student affairs, he started within the field of residential life at a state comprehensive university. Anyone who has ever worked in this facet of higher education knows that one must have a special kind of trust with those on your team. Quite often, one lives in the same building with many of them. This was the case for him. When there were student emergencies, maintenance issues, or confidential information, these individuals shared it with him. The close relationship that formed between people in this area of student affairs lasted long past his time in the position. He still keeps in contact with many of those individuals. They have become like family in many ways to him, and in so doing serve as reminders of how to lead.

We can see this fictional reality in Janeway's leadership to bring her crew home. Her captaincy was characterized not merely by standing alone as the commanding officer of a starship, but leveraging her Starfleet principles and dedication to exploration. These stalwart notions allowed Janeway to persist and adapt her leadership to fit the ever changing situation of a lengthy voyage home. To paraphrase Emily Dickinson, Janeway chose to dwell in possibility. She did so by making the conscious effort to reach out to those she led (compassion) in order to make the best possible decisions (reason). This is a lesson for all of us to heed. The isolation of leadership need not be complete. There is joy in relating with those one serves in an organization. Being cognizant of boundaries, we can steer the ship in a manner that meets our own needs, too. Computer, open ETH.

Guidance from Guinan

Imagine yourself sitting at a small table under the arching windows of Ten Forward, the frontmost point and social hub of the U.S.S. *Enterprise*. The view out the windows is one of stark blackness punctuated by countless points of light, stars of every imaginable color. Sitting across the table is Guinan, the unofficial sage of the starship. Wise beyond measure, Guinan has served for centuries as a guide to innumerable leaders. Now she is fully present in the moment with you.

"What's on your mind?" Guinan asks you with that knowingly subtle smile. "You mentioned you were thinking about Captain Janeway. What about her stands out to you as a leader to model?"

Guinan continues to look at you expectantly. There is no hint of impatience, just that twinkle in her eye. "Think of Janeway's approach to leadership," she suggests. "How does your behavior as a leader compare with hers?"

Guinan looks out the windows to the stars for a moment, and then turns back to you. "How do you *communicate* with others in a manner that is intentional and transparent?"

After giving you a moment to think and respond, Guinan asks you, "How do you exercise *patience* by listening to what others have to say?"

Guinan listens to your response, momentarily closes her eyes and nods with a smile, and then poses one more question to you. "How do you develop a relationship with others so that they feel seen and heard?"

After you respond, you and Guinan chat a bit longer before she has to return to her customers. You look back out at the stars, toward the seemingly endless potential of leadership, and think about how to lead more like Janeway.

Epilogue

Times are changing. Even in this postscarcity future of the 23rd, 24th, or 32nd century (take your pick ... everyone is welcome at the dabo table), the Federation continues to wrestle with its obligation to ensure the benefits of an enlightened and compassionate society for all. Remember the Synths! And this is what gives you the greatest appreciation for being a citizen of the Federation. You live in a society that does not shy away from its challenges, be they imposed by external forces or internal events. Far removed from the identity politics of the twenty-first century (Pluckrose & Lindsay, 2020) you read about in school, individuals are encouraged to evolve toward their full potential while recognizing the inherent worth of others. It is an enlightened society in which people of all races, genders, languages, and perspectives are welcomed and supported to actualize their full potential.

Sitting in your comfortable office chair at home, jazz streaming over the subspace receiver in the background, you ponder the comments of a young Commander Michael Burnham (Goldman, Berg. & Harberts, 2018):

> *Even so, I come to ask myself the same question that young soldier asked the general all those years ago: "How do I defeat fear?" The general's answer: "The only way to defeat fear is to tell it 'No.'" No, we will not take shortcuts on the path to righteousness. No, we will not break the rules that protect us from our basest instincts. No, we will not allow desperation to destroy moral authority. I am guilty of all these things. Some say that in life, there are no second chances. Experience tells me that this is true. But we can only look forward.*

Two questions come to mind. How can you ensure that everyone has a seat at the proverbial table? How can you lead without taking yourself too seriously? Captain Saru comes to mind. He was always willing to listen to others (basic leadership skill: **communication**) and only offered his own solutions to problems with the utmost of care (basic leadership skill:

Epilogue

patience). *And just like Burnham, he always treated people with a fundamental respect (basic leadership skill:* **relationship**).

Alas, *Star Trek* is not the world in which we live. At least, not yet. As we were writing this book, humanity had been mired in a global pandemic that demonstrated the best and worst of our species. Millions of lives were lost globally to infection and its symptoms. Countless others were affected financially and most certainly psychologically as the habits of home and work were rapidly and often significantly changed. So many people suffered and often it seemed that so few were capable of taking the perspective of others. Indeed, ideological divides appear to be at an all-time high in modern history of the United States (Pew Research Center, 2014). This division in interaction with the societal stressors of the pandemic appear to be driving a range of social injustices and seemingly clouding the likelihood of an enlightened and compassionate society anytime in the future. Bigotry has always been with us as a species, but somehow it seems that there is today a growing receptivity to the expression of such biases in the public sphere. Truly, our world of the twenty-first-century faces many challenges.

Yet, there have also been reasons for hope. Instead of merely serving as brief stories in the news now and again, there has been an ongoing attention in multiple arenas focused on racial and other social injustices. Many universities, school districts, and even corporations are making earnest efforts toward mending the wrongs of the past. Similarly, instead of crumbling during the pandemic, humanity pivoted with remarkable resilience. Schools and universities moved to synchronous online instruction. Businesses discovered that meetings could remain productive albeit digital and remote (to the surprise of no one). Even social media allowed for an expansion of how we define community. In this globally challenging time, we both have found ourselves asking how leaders today can leverage the basic leadership skills of *communication*, *patience*, and *relationship* for a better world. In other words, taking a page from our own book, we sought examples in *Star Trek* of how the future can look, how it must look.

As we explored at the beginning of our journey in this book, the promise of the Federation has always been its manifestation of Enlightenment thinking grounded in a compassionate appreciation for the diversity of human lifeways that promotes self-actualization and the fulfillment of meaning (Frankl, 1966). Our argument throughout the

Epilogue

previous chapters has been that one can leverage the basic leadership skills to promote organizational growth through leadership in a manner that contributes toward the building of a brighter future for everyone. Humanity recognized this possibility almost four centuries ago, these ideas arising amidst the fallout of unimaginable suffering in a Europe that had been constantly at war. As Gleiser (2014) questioned, with all we know today about human and social functioning, how much more might we achieve through a renewed Enlightenment?

Perhaps the concept of *IDIC* can serve as our guide. Originally introduced in "Is There in Truth No Beauty?" (*Star Trek: The Original Series* S03E07; Aroeste & Senensky, 1968), IDIC is the concept that there exists "infinite diversity in infinite combinations" and that such complexity can be the source of untold good. As Dr. Miranda Jones (who looked uncannily like Dr. Katherine Pulaski) observed to Commander Spock in the episode, "the glory of creation is in its infinite diversity." To which Spock replied that "the ways of our differences combine to create meaning and beauty." How ironic that a concept initially created to provide a merchandising opportunity (seriously, look it up) became one of the most profound lessons in all of canon. It is a lesson that has not only stood the test of time but been reinvigorated with each subsequent *Star Trek* series.

Captain Saru might be the best example yet of how Star Trek can inform leadership through an IDIC-based lens. Saru was born on the planet Kaminar and from a young age questioned his place in the Universe and the ritual culling of his people (yeah, that's not good). As a young man (by Kelpien standards), Saru emigrated as a refugee from his pre-warp society to the Federation and came to serve in Starfleet as the first ever member of his species (Memory Alpha, n.d. l). He came to be known among his colleagues for his physical strength, his intellectual capacity (everyone learns 100 languages, right?), and especially his unwavering demeanor of respecting everyone with whom he interacted. Importantly, the character of Saru demonstrated not only the best of the basic leadership skills, but the utilization of those skills while the character was still developing as a leader.

When first we are introduced to Saru, we observe an exceptionally anxious individual seeking to navigate the expectations of his community with his own desire to explore whatever was beyond his small village. Yet, we also see how Saru chose his words with exceptional care (basic leadership skill: *communication*), was reluctant to rush to

Epilogue

judgment (basic leadership skill: *patience*), and actively recognized the emotional needs of those with whom he interacted (basic leadership skill: *relationship*). Eventually, as his story unfolds across the seasons of the series, Saru was promoted to acting captain of the U.S.S. *Discovery* (*Star Trek: Discovery* S02E13; Paradise et al., 2019) during an attempt to escape the grasp of the corrupted Section 31 (yes, we know that's redundant). Under Saru's leadership and having only moments ago solved the temporally recursive mystery of the Red Angel (just don't ask), *Discovery* jumped far into the future to ensure the safety of all sentient life in the Universe. In doing so, the crew was thrust into a situation very different from what they knew. Saru's perspective as the sole Kelpien aboard a starship of primarily humans proved crucial in his ability to help his crew navigate the challenges of the unknown. He proved his mettle as a captain by continuously evolving his skills born from experience and fueled by reflection to lead his crew adaptively (Heifetz & Linsky, 2002) in response to a brave new future.

Although he would occupy that chair for a brief period of time (or many centuries, depending on your reckoning), the character of Saru offers us a model of leadership in which enlightened thinking and compassionate action were immersed in a recognition that decision-making in leadership must be grounded in the potential of a worldview that recognizes the values of a multiplicity of voices over the desire for a unified one (Yogeeswaran, Adelson, & Verkuyten, 2021).

Wej

In current parlance, *IDIC* can be conceptualized as *equity*. Leadership demands that we make space for all voices at the proverbial table in the ready room. This involves more than merely being sensitive to others or aware that there are perspectives different from one's own. Equity in leadership requires us to actively educate ourselves and then act on what we have learned. This is a requirement of everyone, not only those in the majority. If *Star Trek* teaches us anything, it is that the future is dependent upon our shared willingness to engage with one another at a deeply personal level. "Wej Duj" (*Star Trek: Lower Decks* S02E09; "Three Ships"; Lyn & Suarez, 2021) present one of the finest examples in all of canon regarding the relevance of equity to effective leadership.

Epilogue

The episode follows three ensigns respectively serving aboard Starfleet, Vulcan, and Klingon starships (not to mention a couple of other culturally specific cameos). It demonstrates a fictional yet relatable set of examples of how leadership can be strongly affected by the cultural milieu. Moreover, the episode does so not merely from the perspective within each of the settings but as well through the biased perceptions of one another's societies. For example, "Wej Duj" (Lyn & Suarez, 2021) offers a number of scenes aboard the Vulcan science ship that demonstrate culturally normative expectations. The episode also offers a glimpse into the biases through which some Federation and Klingon officers might perceive the resultant behavior. Wouldn't it be nice to have such an insight reflected to us each time we sought to bridge a social gap with those we serve through our leadership?

The episode thus provides us with a humorous but relevant example of *IDIC* in action. To paraphrase the ancient scholar Hillel, it is not for us to solve the problems of the world, but neither are we free to desist from the effort. Effective leadership must be meaningfully effective for everyone we serve. Just as the "good old days" never existed for any but a few, leading through the lens of *Star Trek* necessitates helping to create good new days for all.

Kobayashi

We have attempted in this book to demonstrate the utility of the basic leadership skills to the learning and practice of effective leadership. The ability to communicate honestly and transparently will always be respected because the people you serve will know that you are a predictable commodity. In other words, they can rest assured that you will not take them by surprise in anything but the best manner. The result is that clear communication can help alleviate the anxieties people often feel during times of challenge or change. Simultaneously, it is important that a leader exercises patience in their actions. Quick decisions might appear impressive to others on the surface, but they have a tendency to produce suboptimal results. Earlier in life, decision-making tends to rely heavily on fluid intelligence, the ability to think quickly through novel information and find a solution. As we get older, there is a reliable transition in cognitive functioning toward crystallized intelligence, the ability to

Epilogue

solve problems through the identification of connections between novel and learned information. Although both aspects of intellectual processing, fluid and crystallized, can occur quite rapidly, there is a lesson to be learned from this transition. Being the first to find a solution in no way correlates with having found the best solution. It is important for leaders to take the necessary time, be it minutes or days (or potentially even longer), to mentally scout the best path forward. Finally, relationship is the pivot upon which leadership ultimately turns. We lead people, not organizations. Don't let the flashy logos and high-energy retreats convince you otherwise. At the end of the day, our ability to connect with others is fundamental to our ability to effectively lead them and thereby serve the organizations of which we are a part.

As opposed to all of the other series and films that came before it, *Star Trek: Prodigy* (Hageman et al., 2021–2022) provides something of a new twist on the canon. In the series, we observe a collection of children and adolescents form a ragtag crew aboard the (exceptionally sleek) U.S.S. *Protostar*. Notable for our purposes is Dal, the ersatz captain of the newly found *Protostar* with a sizable chip on his shoulder. The initial episodes of the series make plain that Dal has spent his young life reliant for survival upon his quick wit and cocky spirit. Alas, as he finally realizes in "Kobayashi" (*Star Trek: Prodigy* S01E06; Waltke & Wan, 2022), wit is a far more successful tool than cockiness in the captain's chair. And therein lies the entire rub of this book.

As we have explored in case studies throughout the previous chapters, leadership carries with it the risk of unnecessarily stroking the ego. Can one be successful as an arrogant leader? We are not going to argue the matter, as the evidence abounds. How many remarkably wealthy leaders are in the news these days who manifest egos the size of their bank accounts? Instead, let us ponder an adjacent question. How many of the people who work in the organizations led by such individuals feel a healthy sense of worth and well-being because of their role in the organization? Leadership through the lens of the captains of *Star Trek* reminds us that leaders must keep themselves in check. The basic leadership skills (*communication*, *patience*, and *relationship*) are pathways toward learning to lead well. However, ultimately they are but tools in the service of leading with humility, a humility that allows for Enlightenment thinking and compassionate action in service of those we lead.

Epilogue

The Captain's Chair

For better and worse, the world of the twenty-first century offers so many opportunities for leadership. Many of those opportunities we still have yet to discover. As Captain Sisko noted, "We are constantly searching, not just for answers to our questions, but for new questions" (Piller et al., 1993). The reality is that change is inherent to leadership. So is the risk of loss. Alternatively, humility is a skill that we all need to work to learn. The basic leadership skills provide a toolkit to remind us to cultivate relationships through open and patient communication. Planning is key, but so is the humility to remain flexible. As Heifetz and Linsky (2002) observed,

> Leadership is an improvisational art. You may have an overarching vision, clear, orienting values, and even a strategic plan, but what you actually do from moment to moment cannot be scripted. To be effective, you must respond to what is happening.... This takes discipline and flexibility, and it is hard to do.... Creating alternative interpretations, listening to the song beneath the words, is inherently provocative, but necessary if you are going to address the real stakes, fears, and conflicts [pp. 73–74].

We each have our own style. Allow us to share a bit more as we conclude this book.

Both of us tend to put a lot of effort into our professional communication. For example, we both tend to put a lot of thought into what we say, be it in person or via email. It is important to us both that the intent, as well as the content, of our messages are meaningfully received. We also are both fairly paced in our responses to crises. We have individually learned to take the necessary time to understand what is happening before seeking to offer solutions. Alternatively, it is on the matter of relationship that the two of us differ quite markedly. Aaron is charismatic and naturally engaging in how he interacts with others. He can easily engage others, be they individuals or a crowd of people, with his ease and warmth in social settings. Jason tends to sit back and must more intentionally engage within social situations. Although a sociable individual, small talk has never come easily to him and he must make an effort to ensure he is truly approachable. Thus, although the process for each of us tends to look a bit different, we seek to arrive at the same place so as to lead effectively.

Epilogue

Think back to Carl Rogers' (1965) three criteria. Am I communicating my intentions, questions, and concerns with others in a manner that is clear yet nonthreatening? Am I being patient with others regardless of the perceived urgency of the situation? Am I recognizing the needs of others and cultivating opportunities for them to self-actualize through our work together? Today, in our global society of diverse ideas, opinions, and peoples, am I actively creating space for all voices to be heard?

Leadership is not for the faint of heart. There are so many problems to be solved and too few solutions that have worked. We certainly don't have all of the answers. Instead, we offer some closing thoughts.

The episode "All Good Things..." (*Star Trek: The Next Generation* S07E25/26; Moore et al., 1994) remains one of the very best examples of *Star Trek*. The episode opened with Picard discovering, courtesy of Q, that he would cause the destruction of all life in the Galaxy. What followed were two hours of time-travel storytelling that (mostly) worked. However, it is toward the end of the episode that we heard a line spoken with so much relevance to leadership. There Picard was, back in the trial room we first saw in "Encounter at Farpoint" (Fontana et al., 1987) seven years prior, with Q draped in the robes of a twenty-second-century kangaroo court judge. Exasperated with the temporally twisted shenanigans of the past few days, Picard voiced his sincere desire that this would be the last time he ever saw Q. With an impish smirk upon his face, Q responded that

> The trial never ends. We wanted to see if you had the ability to expand your mind and your horizons. And for one brief moment, you did.... For that one fraction of a second, you were open to options you had never considered. That is the exploration that awaits you. Not mapping stars and studying nebulae, but charting the unknown possibilities of existence [Moore et al., 1994].

In other words and for our purposes, the trial of leadership never ends. Leaders will always be tested by the situations in which they find themselves. Sometimes, they will be called upon specifically to lead through difficult times. Much more often, leaders will simply find themselves on the receiving end of challenges. How can it be any other way?

The Enlightenment taught humanity that reason can help us rise above fear and animosity. By investigating the world in a systematic way we can better understand our place in it. Leadership requires that we

Epilogue

seek input, both perspectives and data, in order to move ourselves, our people, and our organizations forward. It necessitates an ability to maintain a degree of objectivity about the paths before us and the salience of our decisions.

At the same time, reason alone is not sufficient. People have legitimate needs and a right to have them met at home and work. Leadership offers a potential to promote self-actualization among those we lead. Leadership does not require that we put the organization before the people. Indeed, we would rather strongly argue the opposite. An organization is "nothing" more than its people and their interactions with one another relative to their work. Such a recognition urges us to put people first. To paraphrase Captain Picard's observation to Q in "Farewell" (*Star Trek: Picard* S02E10; Monfette et al., 2022), a leader need not go into the unknown alone.

In the chapters above we have offered a simple and readily mastered set of basic leadership skills (*communication*, *patience*, and *relationship*) to aid in the learning and practice of leadership. As we explained in a much earlier chapter, these skills are not intended to solve any problems. They instead are offered as a toolkit that can be kept readily at hand to help you navigate the vicissitudes of leadership.

Effective leaders can utilize the basic leadership skills to meaningful effect. Communication is critical to effectively working with others. Patience is necessary more times than one tends to realize, and most especially (and counterintuitively) during times of crisis. Relationship is the foundation upon which it all ultimately rests. And remember the value of the Boimler Effect. We need down time to process events and plan meaningful responses. Yes, even those of us who tend to always fire on all proverbial cylinders. It is better to be at the ready but with phasers set to "stun."

Leadership is an opportunity to facilitate transcendence by "harnessing all that you are in the service of realizing the best version of yourself so you can help raise the bar for the whole of humanity" (Kaufman, 2020). This is the promise of *Star Trek*, the promise of a deeply humane world characterized by knowledge and inclusion. The trial of leadership truly never ends, and we most certainly do not live in a postscarcity world absent of strife. However, it is the world we can create through our leadership. One captain, one leader, at a time.

Epilogue

Guidance from Guinan

Imagine yourself sitting at a small table under the arching windows of Ten Forward, the frontmost point and social hub of the U.S.S. *Enterprise.* The view out the windows is one of stark blackness punctuated by countless points of light, stars of every imaginable color. Sitting across the table is Guinan, the unofficial sage of the starship. Wise beyond measure, Guinan has served for centuries as a guide to innumerable leaders. Now she is fully present in the moment with you.

You look down at the now empty glass you have been holding on the little table and take a breath. As you do, Guinan offers one more thought. With that knowingly subtle smile, she begins to speak.

"I have known many captains over the years. Each one has had their strengths, and their weaknesses, too. They also had help. But at their core, they understood the value of *communication*, *patience*, and *relationship* to effectively lead for the people they served. Taken together, they demonstrate the best of whom people can become."

"Think of the captains." she continues. "Think of Archer, Burnham, Pike, Kirk, Sisko, Janeway, and Picard. Remember what you have learned from each of them. You've got this. And if you don't, you'll learn it."

Guinan slowly stands from her seat at the little table, adjusts her wide-brimmed hat, and looks you in the eye. After extending that same knowing smile in which you have come to find a certain comfort, she slips from your presence and returns to the crowds of Ten Forward just as subtly as when she first approached you. As you turn your gaze back toward the nearest observatory window and take in the countless stars gliding past, you find yourself smiling with a newfound appreciation for the intricacies of leadership.

You rise from the table and continue towards the doors that shoosh open, still with questions. However, you know there will be opportunities to seek out answers to those questions as well as new ones. With this spark ignited within, you look forward to discovering where you will go from here.

References

American Psychological Association. (2006). "Multitasking: Switching costs." https://www.apa.org/research/action/multitask.

Apter, H., Moore, R.D. (Writers), & Wiemer, R. (Director) (1991, January 7). "Data's Day" (Season 4, Episode 11) [TV series episode]. In R. Berman & M. Piller (Executive Producers) *Star Trek: The Next Generation*. Paramount Pictures.

Armstrong, K. (2005). *A Short History of Myth*. Canongate.

Armstrong, K. (2019). *The Lost Art of Scripture: Rescuing the Sacred Texts*. Knopf.

Arnold-Ince, K. (Writer), & Allen, C. (Director) (1990, November 19). Final Mission (Season 4, Episode 9) [TV series episode]. In G. Roddenberry, M. Hurley, & R. Berman (Executive Producers) *Star Trek: The Next Generation*. Paramount Pictures.

Aroeste J. L (Writer), & Senesky, R. (Director) (1968, October 18). "Is There in Truth No Beauty?" (Season 3, Episode 7) [TV series episode]. In G. Roddenberry (Executive Producer) *Star Trek*. Desilu Studios.

Aronson, E. (2010). *Not by Chance Alone*. Basic Books.

Bader, H.J. (Writer), & Bole, C. (Director) (1995, May 8). Explorers (Season 3, Episode 22) [TV series episode]. In R. Berman & I.S. Behr (Executive Producers) *Star Trek: Deep Space Nine*. Paramount Pictures.

Baird, S. (Director) (2002). *Star Trek: Nemesis* [Film]. Paramount Pictures.

Bass, B.M., & Avolio, B.J. (1994). Introduction. In B.M. Bass & B.J. Avolio (Eds.), *Improving Organizational Effectiveness Through Transformational Leadership*. SAGE.

Behr, I.S., Beimler, H. (Writers), & Kroeker, A. (Director) (1999, June 2). "What You Leave Behind" (Season 7, Episode 25/26) [TV series episode]. In R. Berman & I.S. Behr (Executive Producers) *Star Trek: Deep Space Nine*. Paramount Pictures.

Behr, I.S., Wolfe, R.H. (Writers), & Burton, L. (Director) (1996, May 13). To the Death (Season 4, Episode 23) [TV series episode]. In R. Berman & I.S. Behr (Executive Producers) *Star Trek: Deep Space Nine*. Paramount Pictures.

Bennet, H., Sowards, J.B. (Writers), & Meyer, N. (Director) (1982). *Star Trek II: The Wrath of Khan*. Paramount Pictures.

Berg, G.J., Harberts, A., Powers, K. (Writers) & Rose, L. (Director) (2017, October 15). "Choose Your Pain" (Season 1, Episode 5) [TV series episode]. In O. Osunsanmi, F. Siracusa, J. Weber, E. Roddenberry, T. Roth, H. Kadin, G.J. Berg, A. & Harberts, A. Kurtzman (Executive Producers) *Star Trek: Discovery*. CBS Television Studios; Roddenberry Entertainment; Secret Hideout.

Berlin, H. (2017). *Troublemakers: Silicon Valley's Coming of Age*. Simon & Schuster.

Berliner, D.C., & Glass, G.V. (2015). "Trust, but Verify." *Educational Leadership, 72*(5), 10–14.

Berman, R., & Behr, I.S. (1993–1999). *Star

References

Trek: Deep Space Nine. Paramount Pictures.

Berman, R., Braga, B., Coto, M. (Writers) & Kroeker, A. (Director) (2004, March 3). "Azati Prime" (Season 3, Episode 18) [TV series episode]. In R. Berman & B. Braga (Executive Producers) *Star Trek: Enterprise*. Paramount Pictures.

Berman, R., Braga, B., Decker, F. (Writers) & Dawson, R. (Director) (2001b, October 31). "The Andorian Incident" (Season 1, Episode 7) [TV series episode]. In R. Berman & B. Braga (Executive Producers) *Star Trek: Enterprise*. Paramount Pictures.

Berman, R., Braga, B., Menosky J. (Writers) & Livingston, D. (Director) (1999, May 26). "Equinox" (Season 5, Episode 26) [TV series episode]. In R. Berman & J. Taylor (Executive Producers) *Star Trek: Voyager*. Paramount Pictures.

Berman, R., Braga, B., Moore, R.D. (Writers), & Frakes, J. (Director) (1996). *Star Trek: First Contact* [Film]. Paramount Pictures.

Berman, R., Braga, B. (Writers) & Kroeker, A. (Director) (2005, May 13). "These Are the Voyages..." (Season 4, Episode 22) [TV series episode]. In R. Berman & B. Braga (Executive Producers) *Star Trek: Enterprise*. Paramount Pictures.

Berman, R., Piller, M., Taylor (Writers) & Kolbe, W. (Director) (1995, January 16). "Caretaker" (Season 1, Episode 1/2) [TV series episode]. In R. Berman, B. Braga, & J. Taylor (Executive Producers) *Star Trek: Voyager*. Paramount Pictures.

Black, J.D. F., Bingham, J.M. (Writers) & Lynch, P. (Director) (1987, October 5). "The Naked Now" (Season 1, Episode 3) [TV series episode]. In G. Roddenberry, M. Hurley, & R. Berman (Executive Producers) *Star Trek: The Next Generation*. Paramount Pictures.

Boeree, C.G. (2006a). "Abraham Maslow." https://webspace.ship.edu/cgboer/maslow.html.

Boeree, C.G. (2006b). "Carl Rogers." http://webspace.ship.edu/cgboer/rogers.html.

Bolman, L.G., & Deal, T.E. (2017). *Reframing Organizations: Artistry, Choice, and Leadership* (6th ed.). Hoboken, NJ: Jossey-Bass.

"Bow" (Season 1, Episode 1/2) [TV series episode]. In R. Berman & B. Braga (Executive Producers) *Star Trek: Enterprise*. Paramount Pictures.

Boyatzis, R.E. (1982). *Competent Manager: A Model for Effective Performance*. John Wiley & Sons.

Braga, B., Menosky J. (Writers) & Kroeker, A. (Director) (1997, November 5). "Year of Hell" (Season 4, Episode 8) [TV series episode]. In R. Berman & J. Taylor (Executive Producers) *Star Trek: Voyager*. Paramount Pictures.

Braga, B., Menosky J. (Writers) & Livingston, D. (Director) (1999, May 5). "11:59" (Season 5, Episode 23) [TV series episode]. In R. Berman & B. Braga (Executive Producers) *Star Trek: Voyager*. Paramount Pictures.

Bransford, J. (2000). *How People Learn: Brain, Mind, Experience, and School*. National Research Council.

Bristow, W. (2017). "Enlightenment." In Edward N. Zalta (Ed.), *The Stanford Encyclopedia of Philosophy* (2). Retrieved from https://plato.stanford.edu/entries/enlightenment/.

Brosschot, J.F., Gerin, W., & Thayer, J.F. (2006). "The Perseverative Cognition Hypothesis: A Review of Worry, Prolonged Stress-Related Physiological Activation, and Health." *Journal of Psychosomatic Research, 60*, 113–124.

Burton, T.H. (Writer), & Byrd, J., McGowan, J. (Directors) (2022, March 3). "Rosetta." (Season 4, Episode 11) [TV series episode]. In O. Osunsanmi, F. Siracusa, J. Weber, E. Roddenberry, T. Roth, H. Kadin, G.J. Berg, A. & Harberts, A. Kurtzman (Executive Producers) *Star Trek: Discovery*. CBS Television Studios; Roddenberry Entertainment; Secret Hideout.

Butler, N., Fontana, D.C. (Writer), & Senesky, R. (Director) (1967, March 2). "This Side of Paradise" (Season 1, Episode 25) [TV series episode]. In G.

References

Roddenberry (Executive Producer) *Star Trek*. Desilu Studios.

Byford, M., Watkins, M.D., & Triatogiannis, L. (2017, May/June). "New Leaders Need More Than Onboarding." *Harvard Business Review*. https://hbr.org/2017/05/onboarding-isnt-enough.

Cameron, K.S., & Quinn, R.E. (2011). "Diagnosing and Changing Organizational Culture" (3rd ed.). Jossey-Bass.

Carter, M.Z., Armenakis, A.A., Feild, H.S., Mossholder, K.W. (2013). "Transformational Leadership, Relationship Quality, and Employee Performance During Continuous Incremental Organization Change." *Journal of Organizational Behavioral Change, 34*, 942–958.

Chabon, M. (Writer), & Frakes, J. (Director) (2020, February 13). "Absolute Candor" (Season 1, Episode 4) [TV series episode]. In A. Kurtzman, M. Chabon, A. Goldsman, J. Duff, P. Stewart, H. Kadin, R. Roddenberry, & T. Roth (Executive Producers) *Star Trek: Picard*. CBS Television Studios; Roddenberry Entertainment; Secret Hideout.

Chabon, M. (Writer), & Goldsman, A. (Writer, Director) (2020, March 26). "Et In Arcadia Ego, Part 2" (Season 1, Episode 10) [TV series episode]. In A. Kurtzman, M. Chabon, A. Goldsman, J. Duff, P. Stewart, H. Kadin, R. Roddenberry, & T. Roth (Executive Producers) *Star Trek: Picard*. CBS Television Studios; Roddenberry Entertainment; Secret Hideout.

Cochran, J. (Writer), & Suarez, B. (Director) (2020, September 10). "Terminal Provocations" (Season 1, Episode 6). In H. Kadin, K. Krentz, A. Kurtzman, M. McMahan, R. Roddenberry, & T. Roth (Executive Producers) *Star Trek: Lower Decks* [TV series]. CBS All Access.

Comer, D.R., & Sekerka, L.E. (2014). "Taking Time for Patience in Organizations." *Journal of Management Development, 33*(1), 6–23.

Committee on Freedom of Expression. (2014). Report of the Committee on Freedom of Expression. https://provost.uchicago.edu/sites/default/files/documents/reports/FOECommitteeReport.pdf.

Coon, G.L. (Writer) & Newland, J. (Director) (1967, March 23). "Errand of Mercy" (Season 1, Episode 27) [TV series episode]. In G. Roddenberry (Executive Producer) *Star Trek*. Desilu Studios.

Coon, G.L. (Writer) & Pevney, J. (Director) (1967, March 9). "The Devil in the Dark" (Season 1, Episode 26) [TV series episode]. In G. Roddenberry (Executive Producer) *Star Trek*. Desilu Studios.

Cooper, A., Walkoff, B. (Writers) & Hope, L. (Director) (2022, May 19). "Ghosts of Illyria" (Season 1, Episode 3) [TV series episode]. In E. Roddenberry, T. North, J. Lumet, F. Siracusa, J. Weber, A. Baiers, H. Kadin, H.A. Myers, A. Goldsman, A. Kurtzman (Executive Producers) *Star Trek: Strange New Worlds*. CBS Television Studios; Roddenberry Entertainment; Secret Hideout.

Cronk, N.E. (n.d.). "About Voltaire." http://www.voltaire.ox.ac.uk/about-voltaire/.

Das, S. (2011). *Buddha Standard Time: Awakening to the Infinite Possibilities of Now*. HarperOne.

Daum, K. (2016, October 4). *21 Gene Roddenberry Quotes That Inspire a Great Future*. Inc. https://www.inc.com/kevin-daum/21-gene-roddenberry-quotes-that-inspire-a-great-future.html.

Delgado, R., & Stefancic, J. (2017). *Critical Race Theory: An Introduction* (3rd ed.). New York University Press.

Delpit, L. (1988). "The Silenced Dialogue: Power and Pedagogy in Educating Other People's Children." *Harvard Educational Review, 58*(3), 280–298.

Delpit, L. (2006). *Other People's Children: Cultural Conflict in the Classroom* (2nd ed.). The New Press.

Doherty, R., Biller, K. (Writers) & Burton. L. (Director) (2001, April 11). "Q2" (Season 7, Episode 19) [TV series episode]. In R. Berman, B. Braga, & J.

References

Taylor (Executive Producers) *Star Trek: Voyager*. Paramount Pictures.

Dolinsky, M. (Writer) & Alexander, D. (Director) (1968, November 22). "Plato's Stepchildren" (Season 3, Episode 12) [TV series episode]. In G. Roddenberry (Executive Producer) *Star Trek*. Desilu Studios.

Dunning, D., Johnson, K., Ehrlinger, J., & Kruger, J. (2003). "Why People Fail to Recognize Their Own Incompetence." *Current Directions in Psychological Science, 12*(3), 83–87.

Ellison, H. (Writer) & Pevney, J. (Director) (1967, April 6). "The City on the Edge of Forever" (Season 1, Episode 28) [TV series episode]. In G. Roddenberry (Executive Producer) *Star Trek*. Desilu Studios.

Erikson, E. (1950). *Childhood and Society*. W.W. Norton & Company.

Erjavec, K., Arsenijević, O., & Starc, J. (2018). "Satisfaction with Managers' Use of Communication Channels and Its Effect on Employee-Organisation Relationships." *Journal for Eastern European Management Studies, 23*(4), 559–578.

Fields, P.A. (Writer) & Lobi, V. (Director) (1998, April 15). "In the Pale Moonlight" (Season 6, Episode 19) [TV series episode]. In R. Berman & I.S. Behr (Executive Producers) *Star Trek: Deep Space Nine*. Paramount Pictures.

Firestein, S. (2012). *Ignorance: How It Drives Science*. Oxford University Press.

Firestein, S. (2015). *Failure: Why Science Is So Successful*. Oxford University Press.

Fisher, R., Ury, W., & Patton, B. (1991). *Getting to Yes: Negotiating Agreement Without Giving In*. Penguin Books.

Fontana, D.C., Roddenberry, G. (Writers), & Allen, C. (Director) (1987, September 28). "Encounter at Farpoint" (Season 1, Episode 1/2) [TV series episode]. In G. Roddenberry (Executive Producer) *Star Trek: The Next Generation*. Paramount Pictures.

Frankl, V.E. (1966). "Self-Transcendence as a Human Phenomenon." *Journal of Humanistic Psychology, 6*(2), 97–106.

French, J.R.P., & Raven, B. (1962). "The Bases of Social Power." In D. Cartwright (Ed.) *Group Dynamics: Research and Theory* (pp. 259–269). Harper & Row.

Freud, S. (1960). *The Ego and the Id* (J. Strachey, Ed.) (J. Riviere, Trans.). W.W. Norton & Company.

Friedman, T.L. (2016). *Thank You for Being Late: An Optimist's Guide to Thriving in the Age of Accelerations*. Farrar, Straus and Giroux.

Fries, S. (Writer), & Veja, M. (Director) (1988, March 14). "Coming of Age" (Season 1, Episode 19) [TV series episode]. In G. Roddenberry, M. Hurley, & R. Berman (Executive Producers) *Star Trek: The Next Generation*. Paramount Pictures.

Fullan, M. (2011). *Change Leader: Learning to Do What Matters Most*. Jossey-Bass.

Fuller, B. (Writer), & Kane, A. (Director) (2017, Septmber 24). "Battle at the Binary Stars" (Season 1, Episode 2) [TV series episode]. In O. Osunsanmi, F. Siracusa, J. Weber, E. Roddenberry, T. Roth, H. Kadin, G.J. Berg, A. & Harberts, A. Kurtzman (Executive Producers) *Star Trek: Discovery*. CBS Television Studios; Roddenberry Entertainment; Secret Hideout.

George, B. (2003). *Authentic Leadership: Rediscovering the Secrets to Creating Lasting Value*. Jossey-Bass.

Gerzon, M. (2006). *Leading Through Conflict: How Successful Leaders Transform Differences Into Opportunities*. Harvard Business Review Press.

Gleiser, M. (2014, July 16). *What the World Needs Now Is a New Enlightenment*. 13.7: Cosmos & Culture. https://www.npr.org/sections/13.7/2014/07/16/331974524/what-the-world-needs-now-is-a-new-enlightenment.

Goldsman, A., Berg, G,J., & Harberts, A. (Writers), & Goldsman, A. (Director) (2018, February 11). "Will You Take My Hand?" (Season 1, Episode 15). In

References

H. Kadin, K. Krentz, A. Kurtzman, M. McMahan, R. Roddenberry, & T. Roth (Executive Producers) *Star Trek: Lower Decks* [TV series]. CBS All Access.

Goldsman, A., Cochran, S. (Writers), & Frakes, J. (Director) (2019, January 24). "New Eden" (Season 2, Episode 2) [TV series episode]. In O. Osunsanmi, F. Siracusa, J. Weber, E. Roddenberry, T. Roth, H. Kadin, G.J. Berg, A. & Harberts, A. Kurtzman (Executive Producers) *Star Trek: Discovery*. CBS Television Studios; Roddenberry Entertainment; Secret Hideout.

Goldsman, A., Kurtzman, A., Lumet, J. (Writers), & Goldsman, A. (Director) (2022, May 5). "Strange New Worlds" (Season 1, Episode 1) [TV series episode]. In E. Roddenberry, T. North, J. Lumet, F. Siracusa, J. Weber, A. Baiers, H. Kadin, H.A. Myers, A. Goldsman, A. Kurtzman (Executive Producers) *Star Trek: Strange New Worlds*. CBS Television Studios; Roddenberry Entertainment; Secret Hideout.

Goleman, D. (1998). *Working with Emotional Intelligence*. Bantam.

Goleman, D. (2003). *Destructive Emotions: How Can We Overcome Them?* Bantam.

Grant, A. (2021). *Think Again: The Power of Knowing What You Don't Know*. Viking.

Greenleaf, R.K. (1970). *The Servant as Leader*. Greenleaf Publishing Center.

Gross, E., & Altman, M.A. (2016). *The Fifty-year Mission: The First 25 Years*. Thomas Dunne Books.

Hageman, K., Hageman, D., Roddenberry, Roth, T., Krentz, K., Baiers, A., Kadin, H., & Kurtzman, A. (2021–2022). *Star Trek: Prodigy*. Paramount Pictures.

Haque, M.D., Liu, L., & TitiAmayah, A. (2017). "The Role of Patience as a Decision-Making Heuristic in Leadership." *Qualitative Research in Organizations and Management: An International Journal, 12*(2), 111–129.

Heifetz, R., & Linsky, M. (2002). "A Survival Guide for Leaders." *Harvard Business Review, 80*(6), 65–74.

Heiftez, R. A., & Linksy, M. (2002). *Leadership on the Line: Staying Alive Through the Dangers of Leadership*. Harvard Business School Press.

Hertzfeld, A. (1981). "Reality Distortion Field." https://www.folklore.org/StoryView.py?story=Reality_Distortion_Field.txt.

Hoffman, D.D. (2016). "The Interface Theory of Perception." *Current Directions in Psychological Science, 25*(3), 157–161.

Humphrey, S., Chabon, M. (Writers), & Aarniokoski, D. (Director) (2020, March 5). "Nepenthe" (Season 1, Episode 7) [TV series episode]. In A. Kurtzman, M. Chabon, A. Goldsman, J. Duff, P. Stewart, H. Kadin, R. Roddenberry, & T. Roth (Executive Producers) *Star Trek: Picard*. CBS Television Studios; Roddenberry Entertainment; Secret Hideout.

Hutchinson, J.B., & Barrett, L.F. (2019). "The Power of Predictions: An Emerging Paradigm for Psychological Research." *Current Directions in Psychological Science, 28*(3), 280–291.

Ionescu, T. (2012). "Exploring the Nature of Cognitive Flexibility." *New Ideas in Psychology, 30*, 190–200. doi:10.1016/j.newideapsych.2011.11.001.

Janis, I.L. (1971). "Groupthink." *Psychology Today*. http://agcommtheory.pbworks.com/f/GroupThink.pdf.

Jarrow, K. (Writer), & Osunsanmi, O. (Director) (2022, March 10). "Species 10-C" (Season 4, Episode 12) [TV series episode]. In O. Osunsanmi, F. Siracusa, J. Weber, E. Roddenberry, T. Roth, H. Kadin, G.J. Berg, A. & Harberts, A. Kurtzman (Executive Producers) *Star Trek: Discovery*. CBS Television Studios; Roddenberry Entertainment; Secret Hideout.

Johansson, C. & Bäck, E. (2017). "Strategic Leadership Communication for Crisis Network Coordination." *International Journal of Strategic Communication, 11*(4), 324–343.

Johnson, C.A. (2012). *The Information Diet: A Case for Conscious Consumption*. O'Reilly.

References

Johnson, G.C. (Writer) & Daniels, M. (Director) (1966, September 8). "The Man Trap" (Season 1, Episode 5) [TV series episode]. In G. Roddenberry (Executive Producer) *Star Trek*. Desilu Studios.

Josef, F. (1986). *Star Fleet Technical Manual*. Ballantine Books.

Kaufman, J.A., & McNay, G.D. (2017). "At the Intersection of Technology and Nature: The Potential for a Bright Green Future." *Ecopsychology, 9*(4), 253–259.

Kaufman, J.A., & Peterson, A.M. (2021, June 16). "Leadership from the Ready Room." https://www.startrek.com/news/leadership-from-the-ready-room.

Kaufman, S.B. (2020). *Transcend: The New Science of Self-actualization*. Teacher Perigee.

Kemper, D. (Writer) & Scheerer, R. (Director) (1989, July 10). "Peak Performance" (Season 2, Episode 21) [TV series episode]. In R. Berman & M. Piller (Executive Producers) *Star Trek: The Next Generation*. Paramount Pictures.

Kim, A. (Writer), & Kelly, B.J. (Director) (2020, August 27). "Moist Vessel" (Season 1, Episode 4). In H. Kadin, K. Krentz, A. Kurtzman, M. McMahan, R. Roddenberry, & T. Roth (Executive Producers) *Star Trek: Lower Decks* [TV series]. CBS All Access.

Kim, B.Y., Lippoldt, E. (Writers), & Aarniokoski, D. (Director) (2019, April 4). "Through the Valley of Shadows" (Season 2, Episode 12) [TV series episode]. In O. Osunsanmi, F. Siracusa, J. Weber, E. Roddenberry, T. Roth, H. Kadin, G.J. Berg, A. & Harberts, A. Kurtzman (Executive Producers) *Star Trek: Discovery*. CBS Television Studios; Roddenberry Entertainment; Secret Hideout.

Kim, W.C., & Mauborgne, R. (1997). "Fair Process: Managing in the Knowledge Economy." *Harvard Business Review, 75*(4), 65–75.

Kimmerer, R.W. (2013). *Braiding Sweetgrass: Indigenous Wisdom, Scientific Knowledge and the Teachings of Plants*. Milkweed Editions.

Kirkpatrick, S.A., & Locke, E.A. (1991). "Leadership: Do Traits Matter?" *Academy of Management Perspectives, 5*(2), 48–60.

Kissinger, H. (2014). *World Order*. Penguin Press.

Kitayama, S. (2021, January/February). "Perspectives and Truth: Another Case for Diversity and Inclusion." *Observer, 34*(1), 6–10.

Kouzes, J.M., & Posner, B.Z. (2017). *The Leadership Challenge: How to Make Extraordinary Things Happen in Organizations* (6th ed.). John Wiley & Sons.

Kula, C. (Writer), & Arndt, K. (Director). (2021, August 19). "Kayshon, His Eyes Open" (Season 2, Episode 2). In H. Kadin, K. Krentz, A. Kurtzman, M. McMahan, R. Roddenberry, & T. Roth (Executive Producers) *Star Trek: Lower Decks* [TV series]. CBS All Access.

Kurtzman, A., Chabon, M., Goldsman, A., Duff, J., Stewart, P., Kadin, H., Roddenberry, R., & Roth, T. (2020). *Star Trek: Picard* [TV series]. CBS Television Studios; Roddenberry Entertainment; Secret Hideout.

Lakoff, G., & Johnson, M. (1980). *Metaphors We Live By*. The University of Chicago Press.

LaZebnik, K., Bryant, M. (Writers) & Straiton, D. (Director) (2005, January 14). "Daedelus" (Season 4, Episode 10) [TV series episode]. In R. Berman & B. Braga (Executive Producers) *Star Trek: Enterprise*. Paramount Pictures.

LaZebnik, P., Menosky, J. (Writers), & Kolbe, W. (Director) (1991, September 30). "Darmok" (Season 5, Episode 2) [TV series episode]. In G. Roddenberry, M. Hurley, & R. Berman (Executive Producers) *Star Trek: The Next Generation*. Paramount Pictures.

Levy, D.M. (2007). "No Time to Think: Reflections on Information Technology and Contemplative Scholarship." *Ethics and Information Technology*, 9, 237–249.

Lewin, K. (1939). "Field Theory and Experi-

References

ment in Social Psychology: Concepts and Methods." *American Journal of Sociology, 44*(6), 868–896.

Loeb, A. (2021). *Extraterrestrial: The First Sign of Intelligent Life Beyond Earth.* Houghton Mifflin Harcourt.

Lyn, K. (Writer), & Suarez, B. (Director) (2021, October 7). "wej Duj" (Season 2, Episode 9). In H. Kadin, K. Krentz, A. Kurtzman, M. McMahan, R. Roddenberry, & T. Roth (Executive Producers) *Star Trek: Lower Decks* [TV series]. CBS All Access.

MacInnis, J. (2012). *Deep Leadership: Essential Insights from High-risk Environments.* Knopf Canada.

Maslow, A.H. (1943). "A Theory of Human Motivation." *Psychological Review, 50*(4), 370–396.

Maslow, A.H. (1967). "A Theory of Metamotivation: The Biological Rooting of the Value-Life." *Journal of Humanistic Psychology, 7*(2), 93–127.

Maslow, A.H. (1968). *Toward a Psychology of Being* (2nd ed.). Van Nostrand Reinhold.

Mayer, B. (2000). *The Dynamics of Conflict Resolution: A Practitioner's Guide.* Jossey-Bass.

McClelland, D.C. (1987). *Human Motivation.* Cambridge University Press.

McCullough, R.L. (Writer), & Landau, L. (Director) (1989, May 15). "Samaritan Snare" (Season 2, Episode 17) [TV series episode]. In G. Roddenberry, M. Hurley, & R. Berman (Executive Producers) *Star Trek: The Next Generation.* Paramount Pictures.

McElroy, A., & Robbins, E.J. (Writers) & Ottman, J. (December 9, 2021). "All Is Possible." (Season 4, Episode 4) [TV series episode]. In O. Osunsanmi, F. Siracusa, J. Weber, E. Roddenberry, T. Roth, H. Kadin, G.J. Berg, A. & Harberts, A. Kurtzman (Executive Producers) *Star Trek: Discovery.* CBS Television Studios; Roddenberry Entertainment; Secret Hideout.

McMahan, M. (Writer), & Kelly, B.J. (Director) (2020, August 6). Second Contact (Season 1, Episode 1). In H. Kadin, K. Krentz, A. Kurtzman, M. McMahan, R. Roddenberry, & T. Roth (Executive Producers) *Star Trek: Lower Decks* [TV series]. CBS All Access.

Memory Alpha. (n.d. a). "United Federation of Planets." https://memory-alpha.fandom.com/wiki/United_Federation_of_Planets.

Memory Alpha. (n.d. b). "Jonathan Archer". https://memory-alpha.fandom.com/wiki/Jonathan_Archer.

Memory Alpha. (n.d. c). "22nd Century." https://memory-alpha.fandom.com/wiki/22nd_century.

Memory Alpha. (n.d. d). "Michael Burnham." https://memory-alpha.fandom.com/wiki/Michael_Burnham.

Memory Alpha. (n.d. e). "Christopher Pike." https://memory-alpha.fandom.com/wiki/Christopher_Pike.

Memory Alpha. (n.d. f). "Kobayashi Maru Scenario." https://memory-alpha.fandom.com/wiki/Kobayashi_Maru_scenario.

Memory Alpha. (n.d. g). "Jean-Luc Picard." https://memory-alpha.fandom.com/wiki/Jean-Luc_Picard.

Memory Alpha. (n.d. h). "Benjamin Sisko." https://memory-alpha.fandom.com/wiki/Benjamin_Sisko.

Memory Alpha. (n.d. i). "Deep Space 9." https://memory-alpha.fandom.com/wiki/Deep_Space_9.

Memory Alpha. (n.d. j). "Kathryn Janeway." https://memory-alpha.fandom.com/wiki/Kathryn_Janeway.

Memory Alpha. (n.d. k). "Equinox." https://memory-alpha.fandom.com/wiki/Equinox_(episode).

Memory Alpha. (n.d. l). "Saru." https://memory-alpha.fandom.com/wiki/Saru.

Milkman, K.L., Chugh, D., & Bazerman, M.H. (2009). "How Can Decision Making Be Improved?" *Perspectives on Psychological Science, 4*(4), 379–383.

Miller, S., Pfund, C., Pribbenow, C.M., & Handelsman, J. (2008). "Scientific Teaching in Practice." *Science, 322* (5906), 1329–1330.

Mitchell, S. (1994). *Tao Te Ching: A New English Version.* HarperCollins.

References

Mithen, S. (2003). *After the Ice: A Global Human History 20,000–5,000 BC*. Weidenfeld & Nicolson.

Monfette, C., Goldsman, A. (Writers) & Weaver, M. (Director) (2022, May 5). "Farewell." (Season 2, Episode 10) [TV series episode]. In A. Kurtzman, M. Chabon, A. Goldsman, J. Duff, P. Stewart, H. Kadin, R. Roddenberry, & T. Roth (Executive Producers) *Star Trek: Picard*. CBS Television Studios; Roddenberry Entertainment; Secret Hideout.

Moore, R.D., Braga, B. (Writers), & Kolbe, W. (Director) (1994, May 23). "All Good Things..." (Season 7, Episode 25/26) [TV series episode]. In G. Roddenberry, M. Hurley, & R. Berman (Executive Producers) *Star Trek: The Next Generation*. Paramount Pictures.

Moore, R.D., Gehred-O'Connell, M. (Writer) & Conway, J.L. (Director) (1996, May 6). "For the Cause" (Season 4, Episode 22) [TV series episode]. In R. Berman & I.S. Behr (Executive Producers) *Star Trek: Deep Space Nine*. Paramount Pictures.

Moore, R.D. (Writer) & Chalmers, C. (Director) (1998, October 21). "Take Me Out to the Holosuite" (Season 7, Episode 4) [TV series episode]. In R. Berman & I.S. Behr (Executive Producers) *Star Trek: Deep Space Nine*. Paramount Pictures.

Moore, R.D. (Writer), & Landau, L. (Director) (1993, February 15). "Tapestry" (Season 6, Episode 15) [TV series episode]. In G. Roddenberry, M. Hurley, & R. Berman (Executive Producers) *Star Trek: The Next Generation*. Paramount Pictures.

Moore, R.D., Shankar, N. (Writers), & Lynch, P. (Director) (1992, March 30). "The First Duty" (Season 5, Episode 19) [TV series episode]. In R. Berman & M. Piller (Executive Producers) *Star Trek: The Next Generation*. Paramount Pictures.

Morisette, A. (1995). *Not the Doctor* [vocal score]. Maverick/Reprise.

Mumford & M.E. Todd (Eds.) *Creativity and Innovation at Work* (pp. 1–15). Routledge.

Mumford, M.D., Marks, M.A., Connelley, M.S., Zaccaro, S.J., & Reiter-Palmon, R. (2000a). "Development of Leadership Skills: Experience and Timing." *Leadership Quarterly, 11*(1), 87–114.

Mumford, M.D., Zaccaro, S.J., Harding. F.D., Jacobs, T.O., & Fleishman, E.A. (2000b). "Leadership Skills for a Changing World: Solving Complex Social Problems." *Leadership Quarterly, 11*(1), 11–35.

Myers, H.A., Tarkoff, S. (Writers), & Vrvilo, M. (Director) (2022, May 12). "Children of the Comet" (Season 1, Episode 2) [TV series episode]. In E. Roddenberry, T. North, J. Lumet, F. Siracusa, J. Weber, A. Baiers, H. Kadin, H.A. Myers, A. Goldsman, A. Kurtzman (Executive Producers) *Star Trek: Strange New Worlds*. CBS Television Studios; Roddenberry Entertainment; Secret Hideout.

Nimoy, L., Bennett, H. (Writers), & Nimoy, L. (Director) (1986). *Star Trek IV: The Voyage Home* [Film]. Paramount Pictures.

Nimoy, L., Konner, L., Rosenthal, M. (Writers), & Meyer, N. (Director) (1991). *Star Trek VI: The Undiscovered Country*. Paramount Pictures.

Northouse, P.G. (2019). *Leadership: Theory and Practice* (8th ed.). Sage Publications, Inc.

O'Connor, J.J., & Robertson, E.F. (2014). "René Descartes." https://mathshistory.st-andrews.ac.uk/Biographies/Descartes/.

O'Toole, J., & Bennis, W. (2009, June 1). "A Culture of Candor." *Harvard Business Review*. https://hbr.org/2009/06/a-culture-of-candor.

Paradise, M., Lumet, J., Kurtzman, A. (Writers), & Osunsanmi, O. (Director) (2019, April 11). "Such Sweet Sorrow" (Season 2, Episode 13). In B. Fuller, E. Roddenberry, T. Roth, A. Goldsman, H. Kadin, G.J. Berg, A. Herberts, A. Kurtzman, O. Osunsanmi, F. Siracusa, J. Weber, J. Lumet, & M. Paradise

References

(Executive Producers) *Star Trek: Discovery* [TV series]. CBS All Access.

Paradise, M., Lumet, J., Kurtzman, A. (Writers), & Osunsanmi, O. (Director) (2020, October 15). "That Hope Is You, Part I" (Season 3, Episode 1) [TV series episode]. In O. Osunsanmi, F. Siracusa, J. Weber, E. Roddenberry, T. Roth, H. Kadin, G.J. Berg, A. & Harberts, A. Kurtzman (Executive Producers) *Star Trek: Discovery*. CBS Television Studios; Roddenberry Entertainment; Secret Hideout.

Paradise, M., Lumet, J., Kurtzman, A. (Writers), & Osunsanmi, O. (Director) (2020, October 22). "Far from Home." (Season 3, Episode 2). In B. Fuller, E. Roddenberry, T. Roth, A. Goldsman, H. Kadin, G.J. Berg, A. Herberts, A. Kurtzman, O. Osunsanmi, F. Siracusa, J. Weber, J. Lumet, & M. Paradise (Executive Producers) *Star Trek: Discovery* [TV series]. CBS All Access.

Paradise, M., Lumet, J., Kurtzman, A. (Writers), & Osunsanmi, O. (Director) (2021, November 18). "Kobayashi Maru" (Season 4, Episode 1) [TV series episode]. In O. Osunsanmi, F. Siracusa, J. Weber, E. Roddenberry, T. Roth, H. Kadin, G.J. Berg, A. & Harberts, A. Kurtzman (Executive Producers) *Star Trek: Discovery*. CBS Television Studios; Roddenberry Entertainment; Secret Hideout.

Paradise, M. (Writer) & Osunsanmi, O. (Director) (2022, March 17). "Coming Home" (Season 4, Episode 13) [TV series episode]. In O. Osunsanmi, F. Siracusa, J. Weber, E. Roddenberry, T. Roth, H. Kadin, G.J. Berg, A. & Harberts, A. Kurtzman (Executive Producers) *Star Trek: Discovery*. CBS Television Studios; Roddenberry Entertainment; Secret Hideout.

Pendleton-Thompson, D. (Writer), Ahn, S. I.C., & Shin, S. (Directors) (2022, January 13). "First Con-tact" (Season 1, Episode 7) [TV series episode]. In K. Hageman, D. Hageman, R. Roddenberry, T. Roth, K. Krentz, A. Baiers, H. Kadin, & A. Kurtzman (Executive Producers) *Star Trek: Prodigy*. Paramount Pictures.

Perez, D., DeMayo, B. (Writers) & Liu, D. (Director) (2022, May 26). "Memento Mori" (Season 1, Episode 4) [TV series episode]. In E. Roddenberry, T. North, J. Lumet, F. Siracusa, J. Weber, A. Baiers, H. Kadin, H.A. Myers, A. Goldsman, A. Kurtzman (Executive Producers) *Star Trek: Strange New Worlds*. CBS Television Studios; Roddenberry Entertainment; Secret Hideout.

Pew Research Center. (2014). *Political Polarization and the American Public*. https://www.pewresearch.org/politics/2014/06/12/political-polarization-in-the-american-public/.

Piller, M., Berman, R. (Writers) & Carson, D. (Director) (1993, January 3). "Emissary" (Season 1, Episode 1/2) [TV series episode]. In R. Berman & M. Piller (Executive Producers) *Star Trek: Deep Space Nine*. Paramount Pictures.

Piller, M. (Writer), & Bole, C. (Director) (1990a, June 18). "The Best of Both Worlds" (Season 3, Episode 26) [TV series episode]. In G. Roddenberry, M. Hurley, R. Berman, & M. Piller (Executive Producers) *Star Trek: The Next Generation*. Paramount Pictures.

Piller, M. (Writer), & Bole, C. (Director) (1990b, September 24). "The Best of Both Worlds, Part II" (Season 4, Episode 1) [TV series episode]. In G. Roddenberry, M. Hurley, R. Berman, & M. Piller (Executive Producers) *Star Trek: The Next Generation*. Paramount Pictures.

Pinker, S. (2018). *Enlightenment Now: The Case for Reason, Science, Humanism, and Progress*. Viking.

Pluckrose, H., & Lindsay, J. (2020). *Cynical Theories*. Pitchstone Publishing.

Popper, M. (2004). "Leadership and Relationship." *Journal for the Theory of Social Behaviour, 34*(2), 107–125.

Reeves-Stevens, J. Reeves-Stevens, G., Bormanis, A. (Writers) & Rush, M.V. (Director) (2005, May 13). "Terra Prime" (Season 4, Episode 21) [TV series episode]. In R. Berman & B.

References

Braga (Executive Producers) *Star Trek: Enterprise*. Paramount Pictures.

Reichheld, F.F. (2001, July/August). "Lead for Loyalty." *Harvard Business Review, 79*(7), 74–82.

Reiter-Palmon, R., & Illies, J.J. (2004). "Leadership and Creativity: Understanding Leadership from a Creative Problem-Solving Perspective." *The Leadership Quarterly, 15*, 55–77.

Rock, D., & Grant. H. (2016, November 4). "Why Diverse Teams Are Smarter." *Harvard Business Review*. https://hbr.org/2016/11/why-diverse-teams-are-smarter.

Roddenberry, G. (Executive Producer) (1966–1969). *Star Trek: The Original Series* [TV series]. Desilu Productions; Paramount Television.

Roddenberry, G., Berman, R., Hurley, M., Piller, M., Taylor, J. (1987–1994). *Star Trek: The Next Generation* [TV series]. Paramount Domestic Television.

Roddenberry, G. (Writer) & Butler, R. (Director) (1988, October 4). "The Cage" (Season 0, Episode 1) [TV series episode]. In G. Roddenberry (Executive Producer) *Star Trek*. Desilu Studios.

Rodgers, B. (Writer), & Suarez, B. (Director) (2020, October 1). "Crisis Point" (Season 1, Episode 9). In H. Kadin, K. Krentz, A. Kurtzman, M. McMahan, R. Roddenberry, & T. Roth (Executive Producers) *Star Trek: Lower Decks* [TV series]. CBS All Access.

Rogers, C.R. (1963). "The Concept of the Fully Functioning Person." *Psychotherapy: Theory, Research, and Practice, 1*(1), 17–26.

Rogers, C.R. (1965). *Client-centered Therapy*. Houghton Mifflin Company.

Rogers, C.R. (1967). Carl R. Rogers. In E.G. Boring & G. Lindzey (Eds.), *A History of Psychology in Autobiography*, Vol. 5, pp. 341–384. Appleton-Century-Crofts. https://doi.org/10.1037/11579-013.

Rogers, C.R., & Farson, R.E. (1957, 2015). *Active Listening*. Martino Publishing.

Rogers, K. (1978). "The Gambler" [Song]. On *The Gambler*. United Artists Group.

Runde, C.E., & Flanagan, T.A. (2008). *Building Conflict Competent Teams* Jossey-Bass.

Saadia, M. (2016). *Trekonomics: The Economics of Star Trek*. Pipertext Publishing Co., Inc.

Sagan, N. (Writer) & Livingston, D. (Director) (1998, November 4). "In the Flesh" (Season 5, Episode 4) [TV series episode]. In R. Berman & B. Braga (Executive Producers) *Star Trek: Voyager*. Paramount Pictures.

Schein, E.H. (1986). "What You Need to Know About Organizational Culture." *Training & Development Journal, 40*(1), 30–33.

Schein, E.H., & Schein, E. (2017). *Organizational Culture and Leadership* (5th ed.). Wiley.

Sheehy, G. (1976). *Passages: Predictable Crises of Adult Life*. Bantam Books.

Sherif, M., White, B.J., & Harvey, O.J. (1955). "Status in Experimentally Produced Groups." *American Journal of Sociology, 60*(4), 370–379.

Shiban, J., Black, C. (Writers), & Burton, L. (Director) (2003, May 14). "First Flight" (Season 2, Episode 24) [TV series episode]. In R. Berman & B. Braga (Executive Producers) *Star Trek: Enterprise*. Paramount Pictures.

Soares, J.M., Sampaio, A., Ferreira, L. M., Santos, N.C., Marques, F., Palha, J.A. Sousa, N. (2012). "Stress-Induced Changes in Human Decision-Making Are Reversible." *Translational Psychiatry, 2*(7), e131. doi:10.1038/tp.2012.59.

Sohl, J. (Writer) & Sargent, J. (Director) (1966, November 10). "The Corbomite Maneuver" (Season 1, Episode 2) [TV series episode]. In G. Roddenberry (Executive Producer) *Star Trek*. Desilu Studios.

Spencer, L.M., & Spencer, S.M. (1993). *Competence at Work: Models for Superior Performance*. John Wiley & Sons.

Steffen, A. (2009). "Bright Green, Light Green, Dark Green, Gray: The New Environmental Spectrum." Retrieved from http://csj.wikispaces.com/file/view/CSH+Environmental006.pdf.

References

Sternbach, R., & Okuda, M. (1991). *Star Trek: The Next Generation: Technical Manual*. Pocket Books.

Sullivan, T., Berg, G. J., Harberts, A. (Writers), & Kurtzman, A. (Director) (2019, January 17). "Brother" (Season 2, Episode 1) [TV series episode]. In O. Osunsanmi, F. Siracusa, J. Weber, E. Roddenberry, T. Roth, H. Kadin, G.J. Berg, A. & Harberts, A. Kurtzman (Executive Producers) *Star Trek: Discovery*. CBS Television Studios; Roddenberry Entertainment; Secret Hideout.

Sussman, M. (Writer) & Rush, M.V. (Director) (2005, April 29). "In a Mirror Darkly, Part II" (Season 4, Episode 19) [TV series episode]. In R. Berman & B. Braga (Executive Producers) *Star Trek: Enterprise*. Paramount Pictures.

Taylor, J. (Writer) and Landau, L. (Director) (1996, January 22). "Alliances" (Season 2, Episode 14) [TV series episode]. In R. Berman & B. Braga (Executive Producers) *Star Trek: Voyager*. Paramount Pictures.

Taylor, M., Price, A.S., Gaberman, M. (Writers) and Liddi, A. (Director) (2000, February 16). "Collective" (Season 6, Episode 16) [TV series episode]. In R. Berman & B. Braga (Executive Producers) *Star Trek: Voyager*. Paramount Pictures.

Tierney, P. (1999). "Work Relations as a Precursor to Psychological Climate for Change: The Role of Work Group Supervisors and Peers." *Journal of Organizational Change Management, 12*(2), 120–133.

Tuckman, B.W. (1965). "Developmental Sequence in Small Groups." *Psychological Bulletin, 63*(6), 384–399.

Ursin, H., & Eriksen, H.R. (2004). "The Cognitive Activation Theory of Stress." *Psychoneuroendocrinology, 29*, 567–592.

Vroom, V.H., & Jago, A.G. (2007). "The Role of Situation in Leadership." *American Psychologist, 62*(1), 17–24.

Vygotsky, L.S. (1978). *Mind in Society: The Development of Higher Psychological Processes*. Harvard University Press.

Waltke, A.J. (Writer), Wan, A. (Director) (2022, January 6). "Kobayashi" (Season 1, Episode 6) [TV series episode]. In K. Hageman, D. Hageman, R. Roddenberry, T. Roth, K. Krentz, A. Baiers, H. Kadin, & A. Kurtzman (Executive Producers) *Star Trek: Prodigy*. Paramount Pictures.

Weir, K. (2020, June 1). "Life After COVID-19: Making Space for Growth." *Monitor on Psychology, 51*(4). https://www.apa.org/monitor/2020/06/covid-life-after#.

Whyte, W.H. (1952). "Groupthink." *Fortune*. https://fortune.com/2012/07/22/groupthink-fortune-1952/.

Wikipedia. (n.d. a). "Thomas Jefferson." https://en.wikipedia.org/wiki/Thomas_Jefferson.

Wikipedia. (n.d. b). "Rosetta Stone." https://en.wikipedia.org/wiki/Rosetta_Stone.

Wikipedia. (n.d. c). "OODA Loop." https://en.wikipedia.org/wiki/OODA_loop.

Wise, R. (1979) (Director). *Star Trek: The Motion Picture* [Film]. Paramount Pictures.

Wood, D., Bruner, J., & Ross, G. (1976). "The Role of Tutoring in Problem Solving." *Journal of Child Psychology and Child Psychiatry, 17*, 89–100.

Wuchty, S., Jones, B.F., & Uzzi, B. (2007). "The Increasing Dominance of Teams in Production of Knowledge." *Science, 316*, 1036–1039.

Yin, Y., Wang, Y., Evans, J.A., & Wang, D. (2019). "Quantifying the Dynamics of Failure Across Science, Startups and Security." *Nature, 575*, 190–194.

Yogeeswaran, K., Adelson, L., & Verkuyten, M. (2021). "The U.S. Needs Tolerance More Than Unity." *Scientific American*. https://www.scientificamerican.com/article/the-u-s-needs-tolerance-more-than-unity/.

Zaccaro, S.J. (2007). "Trait-Based Perspectives of Leadership." *American Psychologist, 62*(1), 6–16.

Zayas, N. (Writer), & Vrvilo, M. (Director) (2020, February 27). "The Impossible Box" (Season 1, Episode 6) [TV

References

series episode]. In A. Kurtzman, M. Chabon, A. Goldsman, J. Duff, P. Stewart, H. Kadin, R. Roddenberry, & T. Roth (Executive Producers) *Star Trek: Picard*. CBS Television Studios; Roddenberry Entertainment; Secret Hideout.

Index

"Absolute Candor" 117
adaptation 100
adolescent explorer 15, 33; *see also* Bakula, Scott
"All Is Possible" 61
"Alliances" 150
"The Andorian Incident" 38
antisemitism 9
Archer, Jonathan 15, 33; *see also* Bakula, Scott
arrogance 170
assumptions 97
"Azati Prime" 41

Bakula, Scott 34; *see also* adolescent explorer; Archer, Jonathan
basic leadership skills 20
"Battle at the Binary Stars" 56
beliefs 97, 101
bigotry 9, 43
"Broken Bow" 37
Brooks, Avery 128; *see also* ethical realist; Sisko, Benjamin
"Brother" 78
Burnham, Michael 15, 52; *see also* rapid adapter; Martin-Green, Sonequa

"The Cage" 76
change 59
charismatic cowboy 16, 89; *see also* Shatner, William
"Children of the Comet" 80
"The City at the Edge of Forever" 98
collaboration 38, 153
"Collective" 154
communication 23

compassion 8
compromise 37
conflict 112, 138
culture 169

"Darmok" 112
defensiveness 139
"The Devil in the Dark" 95
dignity 30
diplomatic scholar 16, 107; *see also* Stewart, Patrick 108
discipline 156
diversity 16, 95

education 114, 158
ego 117, 119, 138, 170
"Emissary" 132
empathy 119
Enlightenment 8
"Equinox" 155
equity 168
"Errand of Mercy" 96
"Et In Arcadia Ego, Part 2" 120
ethical realist 16, 127; *see also* Brooks, Avery
ethics 137

fear 115
Federation 6
"First Con-tact" 158
"The First Duty" 114
"First Flight" 40
"For the Cause" 133
foresight 42

"Ghosts of Illyria" 81
goodness of fit 100

187

Index

groups 61
groupthink 93
Guidance from Guinan 17, 51, 71, 87, 106, 125, 144, 164, 174

home 133
honesty 24
humility 132
Hunter, Jeffrey 74; Mount, Anson 74; see also Pike, Christopher; reluctant warrior

identity 120
ignorance 64
"In the Pale Moonlight" 136
Infinite Diversity in Infinite Combinations (IDIC) 95, 168
intelligence 169
interests 25
interpersonal conflict 112

Janeway, Kathryn 16, 146; see also Mulgrew, Kate
judgment 152

Kirk, James T. 16, 89; see also Shatner, William
"Kobayashi" 169
Kobayashi Maru 59

listening 29
logic 56
loyalty 40

Martin-Green, Sonequa 53; see also Burnham, Michael; rapid adapter
Maslow, Abraham 10
"Memento Mori" 83
misogyny 9
Mount, Anson 74; see also Pike, Christopher; reluctant warrior
Mulgrew, Kate 147; see also Janeway, Kathryn; tireless thinker
multiframe perspective 77

natural philosophy 8
"Nepenthe" 118

obstacles 80
office 133
onboarding 154

patience 26
Picard, Jean-Luc 16, 107; see also Stewart, Patrick
Pike, Christopher 15, 73; see also Hunter, Jeffrey; Mount, Anson
planning 28
principles 150
power 44, 135

"Q2" 157
questions 171

racism 9
rapid adapter 15, 52; see also Martin-Green, Sonequa
reason 8
relationship 28
reluctant warrior 15; 73; see also Hunter, Jeffrey; Mount, Anson
research 63
responsibilities 98, 157
Rogers, Carl 10
Romulan ale 8
Rosetta 63

Saru 16, 70, 167
scaffolding 159
science 8
secrets 81
self-care 134
self-regulation 155
Shatner, William 90; see also charismatic cowboy; Kirk, James T.
Sisko, Benjamin 16, 127; see also Brooks, Avery
situation 137
"Species 10-C" 64
speech 27
stakes 137
Star Fleet Technical Manual 7
Star Trek: First Contact 115
Star Trek II: The Wrath of Khan 99
Star Trek VI: The Undiscovered Country 101

Index

Stewart, Patrick 108; *see also* diplomatic scholar; Picard, Jean-Luc
"Strange New Worlds" 78

"Take Me Out to the Holosuite" 138
team(s) 61
"Terra Prime" 43
"That Hope Is You, Part I" 57
"These Are the Voyages" 44
"This Side of Paradise" 93
tireless thinker 16, 146; *see also* Mulgrew, Kate
"To the Death" 135
transcendence 173

transformational approach 111
transition 139
transparency 24
trust 78

uncertainty 79
unconventional solutions 83
United Federation of Planets 6
untenable situation 115

"Wej Duj" 168
"What You Leave Behind" 139

"Year of Hell" 152

Milton Keynes UK
Ingram Content Group UK Ltd.
UKHW021450240124
436600UK00010B/75